D1527359

To Emil,
with warm regards,
Amila
19 March 03

STONE SPEAKER

MEDIEVAL TOMBS, LANDSCAPE, AND BOSNIAN IDENTITY IN THE POETRY OF MAK DIZDAR

BY *AMILA BUTUROVIĆ,*

WITH TRANSLATIONS BY FRANCIS R. JONES

palgrave

First published 2002 by PALGRAVE™
175 Fifth Avenue, New York, N.Y. 10010 and
Houndmills, Basingstoke, Hampshire, England RG21 6XS.
Companies and representatives throughout the world.

PALGRAVE is the new global publishing imprint of St. Martin's Press LLC
Scholarly and Reference Division and Palgrave Publishers Ltd. (formerly
Macmillan Press Ltd.).

ISBN 0–312–23946–7

Library of Congress Cataloging-in-Publication Data
Buturović, Amila, 1963-
Stone speaker : medieval tombstones, landscape, and Bosnian identity in
the poetry of Mak Dizdar / by Amila Buturović ; with translations by
Francis R. Jones.
        p. cm.
Includes bibliographical references and index.
ISBN 0–312–23946–7
    1. Dizdar, Mak—Criticism and interpretation.   2. Dizdar, Mak.
Kameni spavač.   3. Bosnia and Hercegovina—In literature.
4. Ethnicity in literature.   I. Title.

PG1618.D57 Z57   2002
891.8'2154—dc21

                                                                    2001056146

Design by Letra Libre, Inc.

First edition: June 2002
10 9 8 7 6 5 4 3 2 1

Printed in the United States of America.

IN MEMORY OF
MY PARENTS AND MY SISTER

Contents

ILLUSTRATIONS

ACKNOWLEDGMENTS

The writing of this book has been a truly interdisciplinary experience, occasioning numerous conversations with friends and colleagues across scholarly and cultural boundaries. Their challenging questions and helpful insights allowed this study to evolve in directions that I could not have envisioned on my own. I have been lucky to have such a diverse network of friends and colleagues, that very real—not imagined!—community of intellectual inspiration and support.

I am especially grateful to Irvin Schick whose generous, patient, and critical involvement in the shaping of this book has been most valuable. Sincere thanks also go to the following individuals whose contributions and influences will always be appreciated: Levent Hekimoğlu, Michael Beard, Francis Jones, Hélène Lipstadt, Rosalind Morris, András Riedlmayer, Mark Rogalski, Richard Sanger, Jamie Scott, Michael Sells, Marta Simidchieva, Joan Steigerwald, Victoria Stoett, and Daphne Winland.

I owe thanks to my colleagues at York University for a steadfast support in dire times of academic "multitasking." Also, I was fortunate to receive a Faculty of Arts fellowship that released me from teaching and administrative responsibilities for one year in order to concentrate on this project.

I have been lucky to be able to work with Kristi Long at Palgrave, whose editorial experience and intellectual breadth have proven to be very beneficial. I thank her and her editorial team for their efficiency and assistance.

Most importantly, I thank little Asya.

Material printed in revised form from "Reasserting Authenticity: Bosnian Identity, Religion, and Landscape in the Poetry of Mak Dizdar," in *Mapping the Sacred in Postcolonial Literatures,* ed. J. Scott and P. Simpson-Housley (Atlanta: Rodopi BV, 2001), is reprinted with permission of Editions Rodopi BV.

Bilingual poetry is reprinted from Mak Dizdar's *Kameni spavač / Stone Speaker,* translated by Francis R. Jones (DID, Sarajevo, 1999) with permission.

INTRODUCTION

A willingness to create and destroy, to sacrifice and dispossess, to give up and take away life, all in the name of "belonging," underpins the politics and poetics of nationalism. Wherever we turn, the construction of nationhood proves to be a performance of ardent aspirations and acts. In 1992, Bosnia-Herzegovina entered the world stage as a site of the most abject kinds of national assertion witnessed in Europe since World War II: genocide, destruction, forced migration, concentration camps, and systematic rape. "Ancient ethnic hatreds" became the most popular trope in the discourse surrounding the Bosnian war. By the end of the war in 1995, thousands of people had been killed, many more displaced, and most of their material possessions confiscated or turned to rubble. Even as I write, nearly six years after the Dayton agreement, the situation in Bosnia-Herzegovina remains volatile. Although the Dayton, thankfully, secured peace on the ground, it further destabilized any sense of national unity as it dissociated many people from their prewar resources and living environments. Sadly, then, national partition, rooted in religious differences and manifested in an array of symbols and actions, is a distinct reality of Dayton. The boundaries among the three groups are highlighted as each group—Muslims/Bosniacs, Serbs, and Croats—increasingly cling to their particularist pleas, memories, and interpretations of the immediate and distant past. The few pointers to the overlapping political agenda—currency, the license plate, and the flag—while operative as formal symbols of unity, are hardly relevant in any forums concerned with the democratic future of Bosnia-Herzegovina. The idea of Bosnian national groups as stable and well defined, indeed, primordial, has been paradoxically legitimized under the United Nations banner.

Historically, however, the sentiments of group belonging in Bosnia-Herzegovina have been neither rigid nor inflammatory as their current image holds. On the contrary: They have been frequently questioned, rejected, and reconfigured, and new paradigms have been invoked in the place of old ones. In fact, Bosnia-Herzegovina can serve as a fine and rare example of cultural polyvalence that has been shaped, and occasionally challenged (albeit never to the present degree), by generations of Bosnians and many different political orders. Typically, yet paradoxically from this vantage point, the cultural history of Bosnia-Herzegovina is one of resistance to exclusivism of the extreme kind. Interconfessional relations on the ground are hardly ideologically driven. Despite a seeming clarity of internal demarcation zones and the myths of origin among the constituent collectivities of post-Dayton Bosnia-Herzegovina, life in this land has always consisted of a plethora of experiences and textured spaces of intimacy among groups and individuals across confessional, social, and economic lines. Bosnian cultural fabric, including its interlacing systems of belief, is a testimony to both the power of institutionalized forms of identification and the advantages of living in an environment in which both creative and destructive energy aligns individuals and groups. A Bosnian literary critic once remarked that "nowhere as in this space can one encounter at once such a staunch defense of claims to difference and such a spontaneous, often exaggerated, openness to others."[1]

Notwithstanding the particularities of this context, however, such a tension is not necessarily unique to Bosnia-Herzegovina. As Stuart Murray observes, "Communities, and minorities in particular, excluded from the prevailing image of the nation have often found in the notion of culture a method of self-assertion. Cultural practices and habits offer sometimes 'unofficial' versions of group and individual identity."[2] Bosnia-Herzegovina is certainly a case in point, except that, with the demise of Yugoslavia, it lacks the "prevailing image of the nation." In fact, Bosnia-Herzegovina is not a nation at all, but home to three constituent nationalities identified in a compound way as Bosnian Serbs, Bosnian Croats, and Bosnian Muslims (now Bosniacs[3]). This is a peculiar outcome of modern Bosnian history: In the age of the national awakening of the South Slavs, following the collapse of Austro-Hungarian and Ottoman empires, Bosnia-Herzegovina did not undergo a linear process of nationalization comparable to that of its neighbors (Serbia and Croatia, specifically) but a process that I have elsewhere termed "internal nationalization."[4] This paradox of Bosnian identity, of being territorially Bosnian and nationally non-Bosnian, reveals an unresolved tension between cultural practices and institutional demands. By now, this tension has been accepted as a natural state of affairs, mainly due to the fact that, amidst shifting identity formations, the territorial stability of Bosnia has been uninterrupted since times medieval.[5] In other words, while the grouping of population has undergone major political and ideological changes over the past few centuries, the fundamental commitment to Bosnia as the "homeland" has been intense and continuous among its inhabitants. In fact, the attachment to land, given the relatively minor demographic shifts over the centuries, appears to be natural and constant. Even in this war, amidst the extreme nationalist plans to carve pieces of Bosnia into Greater Serbia and Greater Croatia, the cultural differences between the Serbs and Croats of Bosnia from those of Serbia and Croatia became more prominent and their regional sentiments more enhanced.[6] This dual relationship to land epitomizes what Lisa Malkki identifies as two principles of naturalism in national association with land: One unifies culture and land, the other citizenship and land.[7] In both cases, the impact on the territorial category of belonging is profound insofar as it complicates, and potentially ignites into conflict, the intra-national relations within Bosnia-Herzegovina.

Because the borders of Bosnia-Herzegovina have, up until now, been almost unchanged since the Middle Ages, the post–1992 partition of Bosnia-Herzegovina along territorial-cum-national lines is a new and alarming state of affairs. In other words, of all the different organizing categories of Bosnian identity, the territorial one has historically been the most stable and most jealously guarded (though not always without controversy and conflict). For this reason, scholarly discussions of group belonging in Bosnia-Herzegovina should, ideally, always take recourse to geography, analyzing the shifts in the perception of land and definition of homeland. The continuous narration and celebration of "homeland" in cultural and intellectual forums before 1992, despite differences in national affiliation, speak to the complexity of the Bosnian national question and the tensions between the concepts of nation and culture as they are played out in reference to spatial belonging. After the 1992 turmoil, the gap between primordialist and constructionist understandings of homeland has manifested itself more clearly than ever; this is why the cultural practices of Bosnia's inhabitants, both vis-à-vis each other and outsiders, should offer important clues to the new ways in which Bosnia is perceived and represented.

As regards the pre-1992 imaginings of Bosnia-Herzegovina, especially of the literary kind, they are manifold. In prose and poetry of both traditional and modern genres, Bosnia features as a tapestry woven out of different historical and cultural sensibilities, not divisible along ethnonational or any other lines. Rather, its demographic layering is celebrated as a function of historical hardships as well as a collective determination to go on as an indissoluble unit. Even in those works that emphasize the differences among Bosnia's constituent communities, that favor certain cultural moments over others, or that concern themselves with limited experiences, spatial exclusion of others is not a narrative feature. In this sense, whereas the political discourse of belonging significantly demarcates the inclusion and exclusion zones among the national

communities, the experiences of belonging and spatial intermingling—
recorded in culture and manifested in architecture as much as in "inter-
ethnic" families—sharpen the awareness of the territorial unity of
Bosnian cultural identity.

In an effort to focus the examination of Bosnia away from singularly
political, journalistic, and historical analyses and toward the complex interfaces between identity and land, nationhood and culture, this book
centers on one of the most eloquent invocations of the sentiments of belonging in contemporary Bosnia-Herzegovina: the work of the Bosnian
poet Mehmedalija Mak Dizdar.

Mak Dizdar (1917–1971) is commonly hailed as one of the most
prominent authors in Bosnia-Herzegovina of the twentieth century.
Notwithstanding the political implications of the term in the aftermath of
the recent war, he is considered a true "Bosnian" poet (his face is now featured on the Bosnian KM10 banknote). Dizdar's literary career actually
began before World War II and culminated in 1966 with the publication of
Kameni spavač (*Stone Sleeper*), a collection of poetry that thematizes medieval Bosnian tombstones known as stedak. Three decades before that
momentous event in Bosnian literary history, Dizdar had published, in
1936, his first book of poetry, Vidovopoljska nod (Night in St. Vitus Field).
Written with a strong socialist orientation, the poetry received mixed reviews during and after the turbulent atmosphere of wartime. Still, critics
argue that its importance lies in inaugurating Dizdar's engagement in ob-
serving the contradictions in the world, and marking what he perceived to
be the irreconcilable binaries that govern it. Throughout the collection, the
serene beauty of landscape is contrasted to the harsh social conditions that
organize it; the spiritual gift of life is challenged by the tormenting physi-
cality of experience: "The world is a pretty flower of many colors / that either smells or stinks" (Svijet je lijep cvijet u bojama / koji mirise ili smrdi).
Two decades later, in 1954, after an active involvement in the socialist rev-
olution and the partisan movement (where he adopted the pseudonym
Mak—"poppy"), Dizdar published the poem "Plivacica" (A Lady Swim-
mer). On the one hand, this delicate love poem of extraordinary stylistic
depth and emotional vitality brought Dizdar closer to the mainstream poetic trends of Bosnia-Herzegovina in the 1950s; on the other hand, it
marked his rise as a poet of rare sensitivity to form, color, and sound. In
the collections to come,8 Dizdar continued enriching his thematic and
stylistic range and strengthening his command of language. Although he
turned away from strict socialist engagement to embrace a stylistic pastiche
in which surrealistic motifs share lines with monist reflections, folk imagery, and existentialist symbolism, Dizdar never abandoned a commitment to his historical roots—or, at least, the idea thereof. Furthermore,

despite his curiosity about a wider literary scene and his involvement with it, he saw himself as a product of the immediate natural and intellectual environment, and therefore part of the overall literary and social scene of Bosnia-Herzegovina. An ongoing interest in fantastic journeys and his homeland eventually returned Dizdar to the picturesque scenery of his place of birth, Stolac. Home to some of the most fascinating stone cemeteries of medieval Bosnia, Stolac captured Dizdar's attention as a site laden with the primordial quality of home(land)—in both cosmological and cultural connotations. Here, Dizdar set out to explore the meaning of its stone deathsites in a way comparable to myth making. After extensive research on the lapidary motifs and epitaphs of the stedak, Dizdar wrote a book of poems, Stone Sleeper, which he situated in the interface of fantasy and reality, history and mythology. Published in 1966, Stone Sleeper became an instant hit and a true masterpiece of Dizdar's poetic oeuvre, the ultimate destination of his poetic journey. As the eminent literary critic of Bosnia, Enes Durakovid, succinctly put it, "Dizdar's Ulysses is at once a Sisyphus who never ceases to be aware of the absurdity of his effort, yet never gives up the dream of defying the vicious cycle of ordinary life in order to experience the imagined comfort of 'homeland.'"9

Stone Sleeper was followed by the publication of the collection *Modra rijeka* (Blue River) in the year of his death, 1971. Taking its name after a poem published a year earlier, *Blue River* confirmed Dizdar as the leading poet of Bosnia-Herzegovina. The literary awards he received for his poetic work include the 27th July Award of Bosnia-Herzegovina, the 6th April Award of Sarajevo, the Golden Wreath Award, the Zmaj Award, and the prestigious Italian literary award "Tutti gli uomini."

The present study, without limiting itself to *Stone Sleeper*, treats this collection as the focal point of Dizdar's work and analyzes it as a *poietic* meditation on the spatial and historical belonging of Bosnia and Bosnians. One of the central theses of this study is that *Stone Sleeper*'s overwhelming and persisting popularity in Bosnia-Herzegovina testifies to Dizdar's success in situating contemporary sensibilities in a spacetime that challenges the myths of national origin of the Muslims/Bosniacs, Serbs, and Croats of Bosnia-Herzegovina. Dizdar's poetry articulates an alternative national sentiment of a shared historical and spatial experience. As a widely celebrated construction of the bond between contemporary Bosnia and its medieval landscape, it is an important testimony to the unstable quality of the national taxonomy in Bosnia-Herzegovina.

Stone Sleeper re-animates the world buried under the stećak tombstones. Naturalized by the landscape, this world was rendered powerless by the forces of history that had dispossessed Bosnia of its cultural continuity. The double imperial subjugation—first Ottoman and then

Austro-Hungarian—had severed the links between the Bosnian historical imagination and the medieval dead. This loss of memory condemned the sleepers under the stone to such silence that their quiet
survival in the landscape found no resonance or meaning during the
national awakening of the people of Bosnia-Herzegovina in the early
twentieth century. While the funerary art of the stećak began receiving
attention, typically, from foreign archeologists and historians, the
imagination of most Bosnians remained uncertain about their relationship with the "lost world" to which the stećak bore quiet witness.

Gradually, the stećak became a point of curiosity for a number of artists
and literary authors in Bosnia-Herzegovina. For the most part, however,
they exoticized it, inadvertently enhancing the invisible lines of separation
between modern and medieval culture, and thus reinforcing collective
amnesia. In contrast, Mak Dizdar animated the process of "recovery" of
memory. He counteracted his silent subjects' lack of corporeality with a
poetic reality that gave them a voice to speak to modern Bosnians. Per-
suaded by conventional historical interpretation that the stećak belonged
to a dualist Christian community known as the Bogomils, Dizdar carried
out extensive research on medieval sources (published in Sarajevo in 1969
under the title *Stari bosanski tekstovi* [Old Bosnian Texts]), lapidary symbols, and archaic language. Involved in a highly intertextual enterprise, he
drew into his poetry archeological, literary, folkloric, iconographic, and
biblical exegetical findings. The historical dualism associated with medieval Bosnia-Herzegovina was thus intermeshed with Dizdar's philosophical dualism, already inaugurated in his 1936 book of poetry.

In inviting his countrymen's collective consciousness to focus on the
medieval sacred ground, then, Dizdar refashioned the common attitude
toward landscape and history. Although not original, his rendering of medieval history was the first systematic attempt to posit the medieval landscape as the cradle of what Benedict Anderson calls an "imagined
community."[10] Dizdar saturated the theory of "Bogomil heresy" with poetic power, giving it a new geographical and historical relevance. He infused the mute subjects with wisdom conveyed to the reader through
archaic diction and aphoristic eloquence. The vernacular language—a
crucial ingredient, according to Anderson, in the rise and dissemination
of national sentiments—assumed a double function: First, it promoted a
feeling of cultural authenticity and homogeneity; and second, it blurred
the lines between reported and authorial speech. With the help of these
verses, the spatial and temporal frontiers are diminished, generating a
sense of experiential immediacy. Here Dizdar removed, as it were, the
need for exegetical mediation: His representations of "stone sleepers" en-
chant us as the very acts of self-representation.

Given the complexity of its structure and message, Dizdar's *Stone Sleeper* lends itself to several theoretical considerations. First, it raises the question of the role of poetry in nation-writing. Tensions between the political discourse and literary genres—specifically poetry—in identity formation and narration point to a variety of agencies and textual possibilities through which national/cultural identity can be interpreted, performed, or subverted. Second, *Stone Sleeper* charts intersections between the historical and poetic imaginations, the geography of identity and topography of the dead, national particularism and cultural polyphony. Dizdar's Janus-faced poetic imagination that abstracts the wisdom of the past through common religious tropes of good and evil, mortality and immortality, and loss and dispensation sets a new tone for the issue of spatial and national belonging. It offers an important insight into the ethics, politics, and poetics of place. Third, in remembering the medieval dead, Dizdar reconstructs a shared cultural experience, at once securing and expanding the roots of the genealogical tree of Bosnian culture. Through his endeavors, the dialectic of remembrance and forgetting is reconfigured, in both individual and collective terms, as a dialogue between different systems of meaning: the living and the dead, past and present, sacred and profane, history and mythology. Finally, Dizdar's singular intervention in collective memory foregrounds the question of "authority" in directing the readers' role in imagining and performing nationhood. This is particularly relevant in terms of the genre in which Dizdar wrote: Not based on a linear or sustained narrative, Dizdar's poetry counts on the reader to assign meaning to each poetic fragment with partial clues offered by the author.

Though broad in their theoretical implications, these issues are addressed here within the cultural and historical context of modern Bosnia-Herzegovina. In approaching them, this study tries to draw on an interdisciplinary framework. Two main concerns drive this orientation: First, the book seeks out assistance from several scholarly methods in order to make sense of the multi-layered experience of Dizdar's text. Because *Stone Sleeper* is appreciated for its intrinsic value and originality, we must not lose sight of its literary merit when assigning larger cultural implications to specific verses and lines. However, literary analysis must go hand in hand with a broader critical perspective that problematizes the notions of (national) identity, religious language, medieval textuality, and memory. After all, Dizdar has a much broader appeal than the immediate Bosnian environment. As in the case of many internationally acclaimed poets whose works are treated as iconic of their cultural milieux, Dizdar's ability to integrate local concerns with universal themes allows him to reach out to an audience that is unlikely to forge a cultural bond with

sleepers under the stone but is likely to be moved by the subtlety of Dizdar's poetic imagination, with the help of recognizable tropes and questions about life.

Second, in terms of area studies, this study aims to contribute to the
growing scholarly interest in Balkan cultures in general, and Bosnia-
Herzegovina in particular. On the one hand, given the political circumstances surrounding Bosnia-Herzegovina in the past decade, the recent
proliferation of scholarly and journalistic writings has tried to come to
terms with the political and social forces that may have instigated the 1992
war. On the other hand, very little has been published to elucidate the role
of literary culture in shaping and sustaining collective identity in Bosnia-
Herzegovina. We do know that literature features very centrally in these
processes. Again, this is not a phenomenon unique to Bosnia-Herzegovina. The centrality of poetic figures in the psyche of many national communities can be observed from nineteenth-century European
romanticism to anticolonial movements across the world. In the case of
Bosnia, such figures are still not given prominence in international scholarship, partly due to the force with which Bosnia entered the world scene
in 1992, and partly due to a lag in academic interest in promoting Bosnian literary culture to a wider audience.

Some progress, thankfully, has been made over the past decade. A recent collection of modern Bosnian poetry edited by Chris Agee, *Scar on
the Stone* (Newcastle upon Tyne: Bloodaxe Books, 1998), offers a glimpse
into the thriving literary scene of Bosnia-Herzegovina. *Scar on the Stone*
includes some of Dizdar's poetry as well, but its intent is not to offer a
critical reading of Bosnian literature or its dynamic links to identity formation. Michael Sells's book, *The Bridge Betrayed* (Berkeley: University of
California Press, 1996), analyzes the importance of religious symbolism in
the latest war and discusses the literary elements that were influential in
the fashioning of that symbolism. Its main interest, however, lies not in
the literary production of Bosnia-Herzegovina but in the inspiration that
the instigators of the war against Bosnia-Herzegovina found, more generally, in literature and religion. Discussing at length the works of the Bosnian Ivo Andrić and the Montenegrin bishop Petar Petrović Njegoš, Sells
demonstrates how the image-making of Muslims makes them "traitors"
to the Christo-Slavic race. In the eyes of Serbian and Croatian nationalists, they are the living reminders of the "Turkish yoke" and therefore pol-
lutants of the Christo-Slavic ethnic space. Indeed, the influence of writers
such as Ivo Andrić and Petar Petrović Njegoš on the thought and action
of Serb and Croat nationalists has been recorded elsewhere as well.[11]
While Sells's critique of the Bosnian writer Ivo Andrić is important in
light of Andrić's ideological influence, Sells does not (aim to) place Andrić

within the literary trends of Bosnia at large. That issue is discussed extensively in the collection of essays edited by Wayne S. Vucinich, *Ivo Andrić Revisited* (Berkeley: University of California Press, 1995), albeit in a more sympathetic fashion than in Sells's work. Broad in scope and detailed in analysis, Vucinich's collection does not offer a revisionist critique of Andrić as the title seems to suggest, although its usefulness in discussing the larger context of his work must be acknowledged.

More directly related to my study is Andrew B. Wachtel's book, *Making a Nation, Breaking a Nation* (Stanford University Press, 1998), which centers quite ambitiously on the cultural politics of nation-building in the former Yugoslavia. While thorough in its examination of the South Slavic idea as explored in Serbian and Croatian texts, the book overlooks an entire body of relevant literature from Bosnia-Herzegovina. Although Wachtel warns that he is interested not in "particularist nationalism" but in the literary construction of Yugoslavism,[12] the peculiar status of Bosnia-Herzegovina (often referred to as "Yugoslavia in small") warrants a more involved presence of Bosnia in a study of this scope. Wachtel does dedicate several pages to authors like Ivo Andrić, Branko Ćopić, and Meša Selimović, but he does so without an in-depth analysis of the politics of ethnonational relations of Bosnia-Herzegovina. Moreover, although explicitly concerned with the cultural trends of nation-building in Yugoslavia, Wachtel's study falls short of addressing the degree to which literature was involved in shaping and keeping the idea of Bosnia-Herzegovina alive, especially in terms of its "cultural landscape."[13] Here is where a passionate statement to that effect by one of Bosnia's foremost literary critics, Risto Trifković, comes to mind:

> With its religio-national cohesiveness, its mosaic of human differences, and its array of social customs, this diverse community shares not just the same geography and history but, even more profoundly, the same destiny, the same connection with the homeland. These people have been united by language for centuries, the language of resistance against different foreign banners and armies. The bonds that unite them are much stronger than the forces that separate them. . . . There is an experiential, human quality to [Bosnia Herzegovina] that literature has managed to penetrate, that may be unidentifiable otherwise but that circulates through arts and literature of Bosnia-Herzegovina. With its unusually complex history, location, its inexplicable, non-demonstrable quality, its substance, and with its language, Bosnia-Herzegovina, though populated by the same south Slavic people that live beyond its borders, cannot be equated with anyone but itself. Its literature is not only Serbian or only Croatian, it is both Serbian and Croatian and more: it is at once Serbo-Croatian, Muslim, Bosnian, and Yugoslav.[14]

Literature, then, is central in concretizing the different trajectories of belonging in Bosnia-Herzegovina. Its engagement in reflecting the je ne sais quoi of the Bosnian experience, the unspoken, primordial quality of identity, counteracts—for many authors, critics, and readers—the vulnerability of Bosnia-Herzegovina in the Yugoslav federation, and its exclusion from the official categories of national belonging. Trifković's evocation of a common bond with the homeland, on whatever terms, is what amplifies the importance of the territorial dimension in the sentiments of belonging in Bosnia-Herzegovina. Had the territorial factor of Bosnian identity been more clearly isolated, I think Wachtel would have drawn more continuous comparative points between Selimović and Andrić in particular, the two Bosnian novelists whose depictions of Bosnia-Herzegovina reflect contrasting relationships to the cultural landscape. I also think Wachtel would have likely perceived Meša Selimović's novel *Death and the Dervish* as being concerned not with an Islamic Bosnia only,[15] but with the inappropriateness of despatializing Bosnian Islamic identity in the Yugoslav federation. After all, one cannot but be struck by the similarity of their representation of Bosnian geography, as depicted in the following brief passages that meditate on Bosnia's location between different worldviews and civilizations (which, as will be discussed later, is a common trope in modern Bosnian literature). The first passage is by Ivo Andrić:

> No one knows what it is like . . . to have two homelands and to have none, to be everywhere at home and remain forever a stranger; in short: to live as if one were crucified, as victim and torturer at the same time.[16]

And the second one by Selimović:

> We belong to no one, we are always in a twilight zone, always used as dowry for somebody else. . . . For centuries, we've been trying to find and define ourselves, and it seems that pretty soon we will not even know who we are. . . . We live in the frontiers of different worlds, at the periphery of different cultures. We are always in someone's way, always led by someone else, always guilty to someone.[17]

Finally, in considering the issue of spatial belonging and the ambivalences that entails, Wachtel would probably have been prompted to discuss, if briefly, Mak Dizdar—who, despite his centrality in re-imagining the historical legacy of Bosnia-Herzegovina amid the federal attitude to its national status, found no mention in Wachtel's study.

In an effort to problematize some of these issues through the example of Mak Dizdar's poetry, and in order to let *Stone Sleeper* speak for itself in a bilingual appendix, this book is envisioned around several layers of interdisciplinary analysis. Chapter One, "Imagining Bosnia: Of Texts and Contexts," situates Mak Dizdar's literary career within the larger concerns of identity making, the historical imagination, and national culture(s) in Bosnia-Herzegovina. The tri-national partition of Bosnia-Herzegovina is analyzed in its historical and ideological background and then discussed in terms of its effects on culture. In contrast to the advocacy of either national particularism or cultural unity as modular for the sentiments of belonging, "dichotomous identity"—one regional/cultural and the other national—is identified as the most common form of self-identification in Bosnia-Herzegovina. The sense of liminality induced by this model betrays an internal dialectic in the configuration of collective selfhood and points to a larger issue: European ambivalence toward Bosnia-Herzegovina's in-betweenness on the geopolitical and cultural map. The historical layering of the systems of belief and political order in this country is a testimony to Europe's heterogeneity and unresolved inner tensions. In consequence, Bosnia's liminality (or liminalities) is inscribed in literature as a multifaceted trope that persists in both outsiders' and insiders' representation of Bosnia. Dizdar's *Stone Sleeper* is situated within these concerns. I argue that, on the one hand, Dizdar bypasses, without denying, the official national boundaries in both descriptive and prescriptive terms. On the other, he moves through the trope of liminality to create a link with medieval Manichean cosmology that, he suggests, lies at the core of Bosnian cultural identity. The historical experience of in-betweenness intermeshes with the myth of Bogomil nonconformity inspired by the cosmological dualism of their system of belief and the structures of their life.

Because the stećak is focalized as a silent witness to Bosnia's liminality, the second chapter, "The Archeology of the Stećak: Historical and Cultural Considerations," lays out a larger historical and cultural background for the understanding of Dizdar's poetic focus—the medieval tombstone. Though presented by the poet as intrinsic, Dizdar's interest in the stećak was shaped by what had been a complex history of colonial and postcolonial interpretations of the stećak's meaning. This chapter sketches the archeology of the stećak within these interpretive frames and discusses the imprints they have left on the cultural sensibilities of contemporary Bosnians in relation to their medieval past. Emphasis is placed on the stećak's location between myth and history, remembrance and forgetting, modernity and tradition, colonialism and postcolonialism. While on the surface the chapter centers on the stećak as the subject matter of historiography, it mainly seeks to address the stećak as a motif in the collective memory of contemporary Bosnians.

In the third chapter, "The Ancestral Voices Speak: Mak Dizdar's *Stone Sleeper*," the discussion moves on to the poetic process of transforming the stećak from being a neglected ruin scattered around the landscape to becoming central for the reunification of Bosnian national communities. Dizdar's technique of disclosing the lapidary fragments is analyzed as a strategy of reader participation in the re-imagining of Bosnia. The analysis moves on to the four thematic cycles of *Stone Sleeper*. It looks at Dizdar's poetic motifs and his use of different tropes and linguistic formulae, and it investigates Dizdar's technique in resurrecting the voices of the dead. Making use of the epitaphs and lapidary motifs, Dizdar posits his poetry as a mimetic enterprise through which the dead can tell their story. The employment of religious and naturalistic tropes allows him to establish that zone as both deeply rooted in the landscape and transcendental, in that the historical experience of medieval Bosnians is distilled into a narrative of cultural survival and perseverance comparable to more universal dilemmas of humanity.

Finally, the last chapter, "Mapping the Bosnian Identity: Sacred Space, Rootedness, and Continuity in *Stone Sleeper*," examines Dizdar's grounding of national identity in the Bosnian landscape. For Dizdar, "remembering" is a *poietic* act that establishes a dialogue between binary opposites: the dead and the living, individual and universal, mortal and immortal. The dead do not lay claim to knowledge of the future, nor do they take possession of history. Rather, they pose didactic questions of continuity, genealogy, and culture. They lay claim to the land in which they are embedded. Both "retrospective" and "prospective," to borrow Erwin Panofsky's term,[18] their personal narratives are posited as cultural autobiography encoded in visual and linguistic texts of the stećak and inscribed in the stones that at once belong to nature and culture. The production of the landscape as a sacred site of Bosnian national culture lays emphasis on the territory of belonging. The land is sanctified and its identity legitimized once the dialogue with the past is initiated and the messages decoded, bit by bit, by the poetic act.

The study ends, appropriately, with selections from *Stone Sleeper*. Francis Jones, the translator of Dizdar into English, introduces the appendix with unique insights into the process of transferring Dizdar's complex diction into English, and describes challenges this has entailed. Jones's arguments reflect his own poetic élan and his academic commitment to detect and explore the linkages between languages and cultures. Like Dizdar's efforts in bringing closer the medieval and modern Bosnian readership, Jones's intertextual translations strengthen the view that the merit of a literary work lies not in its hidden, impenetrable purity, but in its ability to transcend its rudimental textual boundaries by allowing a wide readership to participate in the production of meaning. A line from *Stone Sleeper* comes to mind, doubtless applicable to this entire study:[19]

Heard by us here in the depths of this mere	Do nas stigle i kroz brenija
This word was created	Ove riječi su stvorene
Purely to be debated.	Za čista prenija.

Frontispiece 1: Radmilja Cemetery near Stolac (the birthplace of Mak Dizdar).
Photo by András Riedlmayer.

Chapter One

Imagining Bosnia

Of Texts and Contexts

Del yo al yo
la distancia es inmensa.
Cuerda sobre el vacío
Cómo reunir los extremos
compilar la infinita dispersión de una vida?
Memoria rota, luz vesperal.
Cruda materia o signo?

—*Juan Goytisolo*, Flujos momentáneos[1]

From me to my self, the distance is immense. Enticing the reader to participate in the search for the broken strings, blurred traces, and faint echoes of the self, Juan Goytisolo's poem invokes questions about identity in relation to space and time, integrity and displacement, immanence and transcendence. He sets the mood and mode for an introspective drama of suturing scattered segments of the self, whose presence vibrates through space but betrays a metaphysical absence of answers.

The choice of Goytisolo's poem as an entry into this chapter on Bosnia and Bosnian identity may appear random and anachronistic. But it is not: Included in the appendix to Goytisolo's book *El sitio de los sitios* about the 1992–1995 siege of Sarajevo, the poem punctures another hole in the European humanist notion of a unified self as it underscores its importance as the subject and object of individual exploration.[2] Goytisolo's observation and experience of the "sitio"—in the double entendre of siege and place—points to the various denominators, internal and external, that affirm but also destabilize the individual self. His literary and actual encounter with Sarajevo under siege is at once a confirmation of his selfhood but also a testimony to its shattering in the wake of a human catastrophe. The vitality of the self thus lies not only in its autonomy or anatomy, but also in interaction with—to borrow Julia Kristeva's phrase—"strangers to ourselves."[3]

In a way, this chapter addresses what the opening line of Goytisolo's poem poignantly encapsulates: a fragmented experience of the self steered by the ethics of "answerable unity." This is Mikhail Bakhtin's term, by which he means the fusion of an individually intimated *akt* (deed) and culturally determined *postupok* (answerable deed), which makes every person accountable for the integrity of being. As Bakhtin suggests, "This is the living fact of primordial act or deed which produces for the first time the answerable performed act—produces its actual heaviness, compellentness; it is the foundation of my life as a deed-performing [*postuplenie*], for to *be* in life, to be *actually,* is to *act,* is to be unindifferent toward the once-occurrent whole."[4] In the subject matter of this study, however, the quest for the "whole" is not situated so much within the philosophical standpoint of an individual as within a historical and psychological framework of a *communitas* in which the individual nurtures the bond of "a deep, horizontal comradeship."[5] The drama of individual and collective self-affirmation here takes a slippery turn toward the concept of nationhood, specifically Bosnian nationhood, highlighting the modes of its literary narration. Such a framework serves as a background to the poetry of Mak Dizdar, for whom Bosnian nationhood is primarily a cultural construct inseparable from collective memory and physical landscape. The poetics and politics of nationhood are thereby treated as ethically inclusive modes of identity construction, in space as in memory: As Bakhtin puts it, "Art and life are not one, but they must become united in myself—in the unity of my answerability."[6]

Given its uncertain condition in the aftermath of the 1992–1995 war, Bosnian nationhood has proven to be a highly contentious, often denied, but fervently defended concept in the mind of many Bosnians and many foreign sympathizers too. The attempt in this chapter is to consider some of the narrative and poetic patterns through which Bosnian nationhood has been inscribed and experienced, especially in reference to Bosnian historical culture and, subsequently, Bosnian geography. Ultimately, these inscriptions and experiences will center on Mak Dizdar's thematization of medieval Bosnian sites of death in his best-acclaimed collection of poetry, *Stone Sleeper.* Though unique in many significant ways, Dizdar's choice of poetic focus/locus is not incidental: To most Bosnians and many non-

Bosnians alike, Bosnia's location on the map holds the master key to the understanding of Bosnian culture, history, and self-definition. Notably, it is Dizdar's singular intervention in the production of that location that gave a new thrust to Bosnian nation-narration. Unlike most other literary representations of Bosnia, the national locus in the historical landscape that Dizdar charts out predates the sacred time of official national narratives. One of the starting arguments of this chapter, to be sustained throughout the book, is that Dizdar's success in transforming the space of medieval geography—specifically the stećak burial grounds—into the place of contemporary identity formation marks a turning point in Bosnian historical imagination. The mastery of bringing together these two components—geography and nationhood—transcends the issue of poetic originality and inspiration. Although their interdependence had been pondered before him, Dizdar's courage to disrupt the conventional patterns of their association and representation allowed him to refashion the myth(s) of belonging and introduce a paradigm that was ardently embraced by a wide Bosnian readership.

In that sense, the motivations and force of Dizdar's poetry can be best appreciated if one understands the scope of his challenge to the mythogenesis of Bosnian national communities. Enacting a new modality of belonging, Dizdar's poetry destabilizes the very foundations of the national question in Yugoslavia in general and Bosnia-Herzegovina in particular. In *Stone Sleeper,* the collective self is reassembled within a new mythopoeic frame. In order to assess the power of that process, which was conveyed to the reader as an act of poetic disclosure of the stećak's lapidary texts, a survey of territorial tropes of belonging and their interconnectedness with the official national categories of the former Yugoslavia is in order.

"EVERYTHING COMES ALIVE WHEN CONTRADICTIONS ACCUMULATE:"[7] BOSNIA IN THE NATIONAL IMAGINATION

First, a set of working definitions within which this study aims to be situated ought to be laid out. In light of the difficulties associated with defining the concepts of nation and nationhood in contemporary scholarship on identity, this study deploys a language that addresses the specific historical and cultural conditions of modern Bosnian categories of belonging. Whereas both modernist and medievalist trends in defining nationhood pay special attention to the theoretical implications of these categories,[8] in many ways it is the chasm between theory and practice that can be singled out as the central problem associated with the Bosnian question of nationhood. As regards vocabulary, the terms *nacija* (nation) and *narodnost* (peoplehood) are operative in the former Yugoslavia. As Tone Bringa explains, the two have had overlapping yet separate qualities: The former, stemming from the Ottoman *millet* system, identified the confessional and the ethnoreligious dimensions of identity. Hence, the grassroots mode of belonging was to the *muslimanska* (Muslim), *katolička* (Catholic), *pravoslavna* (Orthodox), and *jevrejska* (Jewish), *nacija*. In the administrative vocabulary, on the other hand, the official category was not that of "nation" but "people," whereby Bosnia consisted of three primary *narodi* (people): Serb, Croat, and Muslim.[9] While the overlap between the "people" and matrix republic in any of the other five constituent republics was much greater, Bosnia-Herzegovina was an anomaly insofar as there was no recognized Bosnian *narodnost*. Thus, the intertwining of the confessional and ethnic criteria in evoking cultural and political coherence within any given nation/people points to the historical legacy of the Ottoman period on the one hand, and the penetration of the German romantic notion of *Volk* on the other. In light of these linguistic determinants, the concept of a Bosnian nation does not exist, if by "nation" one understands a political collectivity made up of one or more ethnicities *unified* in a goal of political self-determination.[10] This absence, in turn, should logically eliminate the existence of "Bosnian nationalism" as a concept or reality. However, as the recent war has shown, "nationalism in Bosnia-Herzegovina" does exist: It is alive and kicking, and its current effects on the politics of communal relations are far too tragic to be downplayed or ignored. However, the nationalism in question is not "Bosnian" per se: It belongs to Serbs, Croats, or Muslims/Bosniacs who, in terms of the official political taxonomy of the former Yugoslavia, make up Bosnia-Herzegovina.

While it is problematic to speak of a unified Bosnian nation in the face of its political absence, it is equally erroneous to ignore the cultural praxis that represents the "unofficial" version of unified Bosnian nationhood (*narodnost*). The notion of Bosnianness, manifested in a hybrid of religious and cultural heritages and sensibilities, has been a recognizable and enduring mode of self-definition in the former Yugoslavia. To be a "Bosanac/Bosanka" has popularly been assumed to synopsize a set of discernible associations and behavioral patterns expressed through language, dress, and behavior, which, though not worked into the political language of national declaration, are nevertheless considered to lie at the heart of Bosnian regional "mentality."[11] For example, as early as 1928, the literary critic Alois Schmaus, quite typically for that day and age, spoke of "a Bosnian collective psyche." In his words, that psyche is "obsessed with things atavistic, with things which common blood and history turned into a common heritage, replete with latent passions and repressed energies. . . . It is from the depth of this collective psyche, born out of specific historical circumstances, that [Bosnian] culture draws its strength."[12] That a shared cultural heritage can give a sense of primordial coherence to Bosnians vis-à-vis other national groups of the former Yugoslavia supports the argument that, as Tom Nairn states, "the subjectivity of nationalism is an important objective fact about it; but it is a fact which, in itself, merely reposes the questions of origins."[13] In Bosnia, the ongoing interplay, and occasional tension, between political and cultural modes of collective representation highlight the fact that the national question is clearly unresolved: While on the one hand the three collectives have been historically identified and discursively framed as different, their continuous interpenetration on the other hand challenges and destabilizes the accepted boundaries. The spatial factor here is pivotal: Although treated as parochial, Bosnian-ness has nevertheless offered an anchoring sense of durability of a unified culture against the politics of national grouping. The literary critic Risto Trifković once referred to this tendency as a "cult of parochialism" that has evolved into the hallmark of Bosnian literary production.[14] Culturally, then, the absence of "Bosnian nation" as a political category does not rule out the category of unified "Bosnian nationhood" as an experiential and psychological reality for many generations of Bosnians, or its existence as a recognizable marker in outsiders' representations of Bosnia. This dichotomous paradigm—"national identities in Bosnia" and "Bosnian nationhood"—has been the emblem of identification in contemporary Bosnia-Herzegovina and a paradigm for a hybrid ethos that emerged in the throes of Bosnian history. From a theoretical angle, this condition of Bosnian identity lends itself to the bifurcation that is increasingly present in the academic study of nationalism as well—especially, one might add, in the analysis of postcolonial nation-building.

Stuart Woolf distinguishes two main trends in critical examinations of nationhood. In one, it is viewed as a ubiquitous political phenomenon of our times, consequential primarily for state formation and only secondarily, if at all, as an important cultural current. The other trend is to view it as a cultural construct that, despite its bearings on the physical reality of the state, is most specifically defined in individual and collective terms as a relational glue, and is thus likened, at least formally, to other modes of collective identification.[15] The propensity to often ignore the intersections between the two models of national identification is also persuasively addressed in Walker Connor's critique of the interutilization of the terms nation and state. In Connor's view, although nationalism draws on loyalty to the state (imagined or real), the potency of national sentiments must be understood as loyalty to consanguinity. A sense of common origins, history, and culture may or may not be politically activated, but its centrality to the process of self-definition is paramount for the understanding of the motivations propelling the political or cultural self-affirmation of any given community. In that sense, in defining a nation as "a self-aware ethnic group," Connor gives priority to the internal dynamic of belonging before examining its outward manifestations.[16] While not completely inverting Ernest Gellner's proposition that nationalism engenders nations,[17] Connor's observations convincingly remove the habitual equation between nationhood and nationalism, stressing the different trajectories, both overlapping and exclusive, along which the concept of "nation" can be charted. Thus, although the notion of consanguinity is based in psychology, it can be objectified in a number of different ways, only one of which is the concept of state.

The ambivalence between political and cultural nation-formation has been most readily observed in postcolonial societies. Homi Bhabha, most provocatively, speaks of the importance of cultural criss-crossings that necessitate a new terminology for national situation and location.[18] His arguments not only undermine the notion of singular national identity in the postcolonial world but also suggest that it is in the interaction of different forms of experience that nationhood ought to be located. Analytically, then, nations harbor both internal contradictions and coherence, which manifest themselves in a variety of political and aesthetic forms. In a similar vein but with the scholarly gaze turned to anticolonial rather than postcolonial nation-building, Partha Chatterjee identifies two domains from which nationalism reigns over collective consciousness: the material and the spiritual. The "material" refers to the outside forms of the economy and state formation, of science and technology, of Western-style progress. In contrast, the "spiritual" is the inner marker of cultural distinctiveness, appealed to as a form of self-preservation against colonial dominance. In Chatterjee's view, a fundamental feature of anticolonial nationalism in Asia and Africa is that "the greater one's success in imitating Western skills in the material domain, . . . the greater the need to preserve the distinctness of one's spiritual culture."[19]

In some ways, Chatterjee's model is comparable to the spirit of romantic nationalism in central and, especially, eastern Europe that emerged within and out of multinational empires, specifically Ottoman and Habsburg, in the second half of the nineteenth century. In response to religious differences and the changing nature of international relations within the empires, a sense of historic solidarity based on folklore, sacred tradition, language, and other "ethnic" markers appeared as effective forms of "spiritual" self-assertion.[20] In the Yugoslav context specifically, the spirit of romanticism maintained a grip over the sentiments of belonging among all cultural groups, even when "Yugoslavism" as a more multicultural synthesis gained currency among the South Slavs.[21] Whereas this dual paradigm never fully disappeared from the political and cultural building of Yugoslavia, it did bear different implications on its constituent cultures. In the case of Bosnia-Herzegovina, the duality persisted not as a utopia of the intellectual elite but as a reality that reflected the weaknesses and strengths of the Yugoslav idea in the post-Ottoman and post-Habsburg contexts. However, the Yugoslav discourse, academic and political, formed an ambivalent attitude toward Bosnia's textured identity, reiterating its national fragmentation by referring to the *millet* system of religious grouping in Ottoman times. In much of the public discourse during and after the age of national awakening, the ethnonational dissonance among the Bosnian population has been treated as a permanent scar of the *millet* system. Each *narod* (people/nation) of Bosnia-Herzegovina was instituted and treated as a primordial category, as a *nacija* whose origins are rooted in the *millet* system of Ottoman times and deeply imprinted on the ethos of the people. Culturally, then, these groups have been viewed as disparate entities coexisting in the same space. Many literary historians, for example, refer to the existence of at least three separate literary trends that were juxtaposed only physically but were otherwise fully separate by virtue of their primary alignment with the literatures of kindred religious communities elsewhere.[22] Even more decisively, some hold that "none of the three religious communities had any clue of the cultural production of any other, which is why each existed and created only for itself."[23]

The problematic nature of such exclusivist views of group sentiments can be addressed at two levels at least. As critical theory of the past three decades suggests, the quasi-Manichean bifurcation of world orders, conceived in the spirit of imperialism, fails to account for the manifestations and experiences of alterity within the seemingly homogenous orders. Bosnia is a case in point: The streaming of the Bosnian ethos into the Western or Oriental ethos masks a complex of aesthetic and linguistic polyvalence typical of Bosnian culture throughout its history, of which a few words will be said shortly. This tendency further undermines the shared culture and the ethics of inclusion, or what Mikhail Bakhtin refers to as the cultural answerability of any individual act. At a more specific historical level, sources show that *millet*-induced segregation is neither deterministic nor linear, as Yugoslav—or mainstream Orientalist—scholarship has claimed. Although the common supposition is that the *millet* system was the Ottoman administrative way of treating non-Muslim subjects as collectives, a revisionist view articulated by Benjamin Braude points out that the *millet* system was neither consistent nor premeditated, as conventional arguments propose. Instead, he shows that the *millet* system emerged as late as the seventeenth century, and that its institutionalization was accompanied by mythmaking about the uniform treatment of non-Muslim subjects throughout the imperial history despite the fact that the practice "was not an institution or even a group of institutions, but rather it was a set of arrangements, largely local, with considerable variations over time and place."[24]

In many ways, the case of Bosnia, especially as regards cultural praxis in Ottoman times, supports Braude's argument and thus challenges the one that favors the treatment of its different communities as isolated entities. Upon the establishment of Ottoman rule in 1463 and extensive conversion to Islam, Bosnia became the most important stronghold of the empire in its western regions, so much so that in 1580 it was conferred the status of *beylerbeylik,* the principal administrative unit of the empire. Although the Ottomans preserved Bosnia's territorial integrity as established by the strongest of its kings just prior to the 1463 conquest, the population underwent a new form of stratification based on religious and economic regulations of the empire, as well as a series of demographic changes.[25] Informed by the *millet* practices, the rights of all Ottoman subjects accentuated the rift in the modalities of belonging and at once generated a new framework within which the politics of intercommunal relations had to be negotiated at the local level. The religious differences often heightened the feeling of alienation from Ottoman "high" culture among local Christian communities and resentment of its system of privileging of the local Muslim converts who, in a relatively smooth and steady process, became the empowered elite of the region at large.[26] This new politics of interconfessional relations rearranged the existing categories of high and low culture, sacred and profane, and self and other. As the bulk of the non-Muslim population strengthened its ties with folkloric tradition and church teachings in an attempt to preserve a sense of collectivity, educated Bosnians of all confessional groups were streamed into the norms of the overarching structures that regulated their spiritual, intellectual, and ritual life.[27] In the case of Muslims, mainstream Ottoman culture burgeoning in and around the court offered a prestigious forum for cultural self-affirmation in the imperial context. In the case of non-Muslims, common sacred themes deriving from Jewish and Christian teachings and experiences heightened a sense of affinity with their fellow Jews and Christians within and outside the Ottoman borders.[28] Similarly, the adoption of different common languages (*koiné*) led to disparate literacy standards and a decentering of literary culture: Many Bosnian Muslim authors turned to the *diwan* literature; many Catholics to the Ragusan styles; and many Orthodox to the Peć patriarchy, whose ecclesiastical norms fostered a spirit of resistance to Islamic assimilation.

Despite such disparities, however, Bosnia's religious plurality and cultural diversity became even more enhanced as the result of the demographic changes following an increased immigration of Sephardic Jews and Orthodox Christians,[29] and the accentuation of regional cultural sensibilities. The continued interest in writing literature in the South Slavic language for the local audience is present among both Muslim and non-Muslims: the Catholic Matija Divković and Pavle Papić, the Orthodox Staka Skenderova, and the Muslim Zirai and Ahmed Karahodža, and many others, chose, albeit not exclusively, to write in the vernacular. Even among the newly formed Sephardic community, some literary works were articulated in South Slavic.[30] On the one hand, this practice allowed them to maintain a connection with regional literary sensibilities; and, on the other hand, to keep the traditions alive against the pressure of literary canons. In this sense, despite crystallization by the *millet* practices, interconfessional relations were also enriched by the new interactive space. In fact, with the *millet* system emerged a new politics and poetics of cultural polyvalence. The centripetal forces of "high" cultures, the endurance of local values in daily life, and the porous intercommunal relations in response to the political situation of the empire all point, in Muhsin Rizvić's argument, to "a democratic reflex of the cultural and confessional plurality that yet needs to be appraised."[31] Indeed, sources suggest that community life was built around two trajectories at least: At the local level, there was an enduring commitment to common resources and shared values that, regardless of an uneven distribution of power in the imperial structure, sustained the historical dynamics and preserved regional distinctiveness. At the trans-local level, a sense of belonging was also attached to the power structures that transcended regional concerns and demanded commitment to the worldviews through which identity, to put it in Herbert Mol's terms, was sacralized:[32] Catholicism, Islam, Orthodoxy, and Judaism.

Significantly, the fostering of both sets of values in Ottoman Bosnia, local and trans-local, did not necessarily claim a particular social status, language system, or sanctity of experience, nor did it imply a resistance to either the orthodoxy or orthopraxy of a particular religious system. In fact, many sources point out that Bosnian Catholic, Orthodox, or Muslim communities never systematically challenged or protected their exclusive "official" or "popular" beliefs and practices or shunned one set of values in favor of another based on social status. What sources actually offer are reports of inter-penetration between low and high culture, sacred and profane realms, and standard and vernacular languages both within and across the boundaries of any given religious culture.[33] Insofar as these criss-crossings were both spontaneous and staged, they indicate how volatile the relations of dependence between local Muslims and non-Muslims must have been. Since social behavior and creative impulse were informed by different pressures of centralization and decentralization, rather than determining the priority between the two, it seems more important to understand how that dynamics allowed the concepts of self and other to be continually negotiated, at both political and rhetorical levels. If the collective self of any given group in Bosnia was determined partly from the outside and partly from the inside, then the existence of inclusion and exclusion zones could never be decided without a multidirectional reference to all authors of that identity.

In fact, the space of interactive cultural practice was inevitably subject to multidirectional change, since it was embroiled with the imperial structure and its continuous dialogue with the peripheries. Because of its rather peculiar status in the empire, the periphery in question—Bosnia-Herzegovina—reflected the complexity of the process of self-figuration and self-preservation. As an illustration, when Tinodi, a Hungarian author of the sixteenth century, remarked that the Bosnian Muslim tradition included epic poetry based on Christian themes and that many Muslim families tended to employ Christian performers to sing at their gatherings,[34] his observation highlighted three points at least. First, that the sense of collectivity is demarcated both in reference to the *millet* system and the local cultural practices that preceded the Ottomans. Second, it points to the presence of certain inter-*millet* sensibilities that may not be characteristic of the Empire at large but of Muslim and Christian *millet* in Bosnia. Third, it hints that culture, in its inter-*millet* manifestations, was part of the larger socioeconomic transactions in the region at large. Thus, Bosnian Muslim patronage of Christian performers, while indicative of the living local tradition on the one hand, also highlights the social asymmetry in which, due to the *millet* system, Bosnian Muslims formed an economic elite aligned with the imperial center.

The historical information gained from Tinodi, however, is not an isolated incident: The practice of Bosnian Muslims' employment of Christian singers was so popular that in 1794 it led the Ottoman authorities to ban Christian singers and dancers from Muslim picnics and other gatherings.[35] Although little is known about the specifics of the practice, it is likely that such occasions engaged both the town elite and the peasantry, both Muslim and Christian. Moreover, Tinodi hints at certain overlaps in folk tradition and poetic norms that make it difficult to disentangle the "Muslim" from "non-Muslim," sacred from profane, local from imported, or general from particular. Overlapping genres, themes, and symbols became, in one instance at least, a threat to the Ottoman ruler, who took political measures against it. In this instance, the social space of separation between local Muslims and Christians diminished as the two groups staged a joint protest against the banning of the cultural practice. United in a desire to keep this practice alive, the two groups exhibited a sense of endangerment that generated a feeling of communal solidarity against the imperial power. Since the late eighteenth century was a period of ongoing foreign incursions into Ottoman border zones, as well as an increased decentralization of power to some provinces,[36] inter-*millet* cultural intimacy was obviously perceived by the central authority as yet another threat to the empire's stability.

The contingency of "loyalty" is also revealed in other forms of communal interaction: Numerous letters of correspondence between the notables of different religious communities in Bosnia illustrate different rhetorical techniques that both enforced and relaxed the power balance among different communities. Similarly, the epic poetry and ballads, both Muslim and non-Muslim, present a repository of information about such interactive tendencies, particularly in the texts originating in the Krajina (the "Margin") region of northwestern Bosnia and Croatia.[37] Here, touching love stories, heroic deeds, and neighborly ethics intercept military and religious rivalry between Muslims and Catholics. The texts are replete with anecdotes that span a wide range of relations, from acceptance of Christians as "brothers" to their rejection as "heedless infidels."[38] In a similar vein, epistolary evidence, composed in Slavic, also suggests the fluidity of intercommunal relations in which context, rather than canon, frequently determined the tone. A story is told, for example, of the seventeenth-century encounter between the envoy of Ragusa, Jacob Marušković, and the famous Bosnian vizier Mehmed Paša Sokolović, in the following way: "And so was Jacob happy about his dear brother, his brother and a great hero Sokolović Mehmed Pasha."[39] In another example, the Bosnian Catholic Andrija Kačić too mentions a correspondence between two military commanders, practically two enemies, the Muslim Mustaj Beg of Lika and the Christian Petar Smiljanić, in 1684: "I ask your excellency," writes Mustaj Beg, "to pass our regards to your hero, *harambasha* Iliya. We hear he is a great man in Krajina. God only knows how pleased we are, because he is of our blood."[40] In such cases, the appeal to consanguinity as an irrevocable signifier of common belonging bears an important rhetorical value, since, in practice, the explicitness of political affiliations created a non-negotiable decorum of separation. In that sense, introducing "blood" as a metaphor of kinship, invisible yet irrevocable, relaxes, at least momentarily, the symbols of state power—the uniform, military entourage, and diplomatic language—and questions their soundness as symbols of social and cultural disunion.

Where political context as recorded in epistles necessitated a careful navigation between internal and external markers of belonging, popular

culture was more conducive to their connection. A genre that both thrived
on and sustained inter-*millet* activities is the *sevdalinka*, a type of popular
song that is usually associated with Islamic Bosnia; however, as both historical and ethnological material indicates, its performance drew on the
participation of all *millets*. Commonly referred to as "woman's song"
and/or "town song"—the former because women have traditionally been
associated with it as both its subject matter and its performers, and the
latter because the song's origins are traced to the urban scene of Ottoman
Bosnia—the *sevdalinka* speaks of unrequited love, expressed as *dert* (from
the Turkish "melancholy" or "grief"). The word *sevdalinka* derives from
the Arabic word *sawda*, literally "black," that comes to Bosnian via its
Turkish rendition as *sevdah*. The term seeks to explain pathos in physio-
logical terms, because it is believed that love sickness generates symptoms
akin to black bile. Whereas one "feels blue" in English, in this case one
"feels black" when tormented by unrequited love. The psychodynamics of
the *sevdalinka* are similar to the troubadour poetry of medieval Provence,
but, unlike the troubadour verse, the *sevdalinka* posits women as agents of
amorous expression. Very often, however, women sing in the alienated
male "I," which allows for sexual and other forms of travesty: Not only can
a woman hide behind a male "I," but that "I" can also be poor or rich,
Muslim or non-Muslim, married or single, young or old. Indeed, among
the earliest recorded *sevdalinka* is the one about an unfulfilled love between a Muslim man named Adil and Mara, a young and pretty Catholic
woman from Split, that reportedly took place in the sixteenth century.[41]
However, this is not to say that men do not sing or recite these poems. In
fact, as yet another testimony to the crossing of cultural and social boundaries, among the earliest Bosnian records of the *sevdalinka* performance is
the 1780 travel narrative of Mula Mustafa Bašeskija that mentions bi-
weekly gatherings of young Sarajevan Muslim religious judges *(kadije)* to
sing *sevdalinkas*, even in the pilgrimage season.[42]

   The lyrics, which explore a variety of erotic relations, are commonly
situated in the Bosnian landscape. Familiar neighborhoods, cities, mountains, and valleys are the loci of many different forms of encounters; this
allows the boundaries of social relations to be expanded without trans-
gressing the boundaries of Bosnian landscape. The familiarity of the setting thus counteracts the unpredictability of experience. This contrast
between the evanescence of emotion and the certainty of place makes the
mood of the *sevdalinka* intrinsically connected with the scenic Bosnian
landscape, shared by all its inhabitants. Heinrich Renner, a journalist em-
ployed by the Austro-Hungarians, says the following in his description of
the *sevdalinka* in 1897: "As a prelude to amorous games, one can hear
sweet love songs that can be compared to the finest love songs in the West.

The people of Bosnia, in spite of their religious fragmentation, appear united in the *sevdalinka*, because these woman's songs are equally popular among the Christians as they are among Muslims."[43]

Undoubtedly, the above examples do not override important centripetal tendencies in religious cultures and the tensions that arose from the structure of the *millet* system. However, they do point to the presence of a shared cultural praxis, expressed in certain poetic conventions and styles, that allows for the flexibility and persistence of local culture against the politics of the *millet* division. Of course, the considerable difference in the conditions and forums of cultural production and consumption reflects an uneven distribution of opportunity and power among different *millets*. However, the interdependence of different *millets* rested on porous lines of separation; this exposes the questions of loyalty and belonging as contingent on internal and external conditions of the empire in different stages of its history.

Arguing in favor of precarious rather than stable sentiments of belonging in Ottoman times, Maria Todorova argues that localism was a more dominant form of loyalty throughout the region, even among Muslims who enjoyed a generally privileged status in the empire. In examining the Ottoman legacy in the Balkans, she finds that local loyalty was in sway even in Bosnia, despite the fact that Bosnian Muslims, unlike Muslims in the rest of the Balkans, occupied high positions in both administrative and cultural institutions of the empire. In other words, not only were they privileged by virtue of being Muslim, but many formed part of the ruling elite, which further elevated their ranks vis-à-vis their non-Muslim neighbors. Todorova argues that this heightened sense of status in the imperial context delayed, in post-Ottoman times, the process of de-imperialization in both psychological and political terms. Concluding that "[Bosnian Muslims] did not develop a national ideology aspiring for [to] a separate state and their fluid consciousness bore the features of the millet structure,"[44] Todorova further suggests that, although Bosnia's complex religious and ethnic structure owes much to the Ottoman framework, its contemporary political problems should not be seen as an Ottoman legacy. On the contrary: It is the post-Ottoman period that greatly disturbed the delicate balance between the Orthodox/Serb and Catholic/Croat power relations at large, which left a serious effect on Bosnia. Todorova concludes, "Bosnia was upheld as no-man's land, not because of the precarious mixture of its population, but because first Austro-Hungary was looking for an outpost in the Balkans, and later, because its quasi-independence served to prevent the upsetting of a precarious power balance between Serbs and Croats."[45]

Todorova's argument creates an important link between Bosnia-Herzegovina's ambivalent attitude to the nineteenth-century patterns of national awakening and the treatment of Bosnia, in international terms, as a no-man's land, a *tabula rasa* to be written and overwritten in and out of different imperial, national, and regional projects. Although its cultural diversity on the one hand and its imperial experience on the other led to a tardy and ambivalent awakening to the age of nationalism, the national zeal in the neighboring regions, specifically Serbia and Croatia, could not and did not circumvent Bosnia-Herzegovina. From the outset, there were at least two identifiable trends in the national awakening of Serbs and Croats as regards their attitude toward Bosnia-Herzegovina. Throughout the early twentieth century, the two trends contested the status of Bosnia-Herzegovina. One was more inclusive in character, inclined to integrate Bosnia within the Yugoslav project, albeit without giving it independent national rights. Proponents of such a solution for Bosnia formed a pro-"Yugoslav" intelligentsia in both Croatia and Serbia, which differed as regards the allocation of political power to Bosnians in general, and Muslims in particular.[46] The other direction proved to be more exclusivist and assimilationist in nature, keen on parceling Bosnia and assimilating its Muslim population. Consider, for example, the following statement of Nikola Pašić, the leader of the Serbian National Radical Party, issued in 1918, at the end of World War I. Ghastly similar to the statements made by the designers of the 1992–1995 "ethnic cleansing," it commands: "As soon as our troops cross the Drina River, we will give the 'Turks' [Bosnian Muslims] 24, perhaps 48 hours to convert to the religion of their forefathers. Those who resist we shall slay, as we have done in the past."[47] Despite their apparent difference in both form and content, both options threatened, ideologically and politically, the unity of Bosnia-Herzegovina. Paradoxically, both directions prevailed, insofar as Bosnia-Herzegovina found itself integrated in the Yugoslav project yet under the kind of nationalist push and pull that clearly nipped its potential as a unified national culture.

By the time of its liberation from the successive imperial rule of the Ottoman and Austro-Hungarian empires after World War I, then, Bosnia-Herzegovina was already deeply affected by national awakening, though neither in a linear nor a consistent way. The penetration of Serbian and Croatian agendas into the collective consciousness of the Bosnian Orthodox, Catholic, and even Muslim intelligentsia seems to have reached the point of no return, but the status of Bosnia-Herzegovina was never completely resolved. On the one hand, Bosnia-Herzegovina was never transformed into a unified nation-republic like the other five republics of the former Yugoslavia (Slovenia, Macedonia, Serbia, Croatia, and Montenegro). On the other, Bosnia-Herzegovina did succumb to the process of nationalization, which can be best characterized as "internal nationalization" along ethnoreligious lines. While its Catholic and Orthodox population embraced the national grouping as Croats and Serbs respectively, the Muslims either oscillated between the two or adopted a more explicit form of Muslim identification, as proposed by the Yugoslav Muslim Organization (JMO). Established in 1919 to defend the rights, both economic and cultural, of Bosnian Muslims, the JMO attempted to resist the government's policies toward the Muslims community, turning, ironically, into a reactive organization keen on preserving the various privileges Bosnian Muslims once enjoyed. Sakib Korkut, the JMO spokesperson at the time, articulated it as follows:

> What did the unification of Yugoslavia bring us? Fraternal forgiveness, or savage retribution? I shall not recount all the murders, robberies, and persecution of Muslims. Even children know about those. I shall only note who committed these things: Orthodox Serbs. Some object, noting that Catholic Croats were also persecuted. That is true. But that only proves that the persecution of Muslims was not a result of our non-national circumstances. We were the victims of organized religious fanaticism, and were therefore forced to group ourselves on the religious basis too.[48]

The constructedness of the national modes of self-identification as exemplified by the Muslim case in particular is visible in the fluctuations of their adoption, as many Muslims often shifted from one category to another. In fact, such fluctuations continued late into the Communist era, so much so that the political analyst Sabrina (then Pedro) Ramet remarked, as late as 1985:

> Today in Bosnia-Herzegovina, there are Muslims who consider themselves primarily "Muslim Croats," those who consider themselves "Bosnian Muslims" (i.e., in the ethnic sense), and those who, in the spirit of the "Islamic Declaration," see themselves simply as "muslims." In addition, there are those Muslims who in the 1981 census declared themselves "Yugoslavs." This already complex picture is made more so by the presence of those persons who describe themselves as "atheist Muslims," and who therefore completely divorce religion from nationality.[49]

In fact, throughout the 1960s, the issue of national identity in the republic became ideologically charged and politically controversial as the Bosnian Muslims demanded a more integrated treatment of their collective identity. While on the one hand this demand was an obvious attempt to lay claim to cultural continuity and resist assimilation by either Serbs or Croats, it was also another step in formalizing the political fragmentation of Bosnian identity. In the late 1960s, the Communist Party decided, on the urging of the Bosnian Muslim intelligentsia, to elevate Bosnian Muslims from "ethnic" to "national" status. After a resistance by some party members from Croatia and Serbia, the decision was constitutionally passed in 1971.[50] In the Yugoslav federation of six republics (Macedonia, Serbia, Slovenia, Croatia, Montenegro, and Bosnia-Herzegovina), only one—Bosnia-Herzegovina—was not a national homeland. Bosnian Muslims lost national possession of Bosnia by being elevated into a Muslim nation. Paradoxically, then, though given national rights, the Muslims of Bosnia-Herzegovina were deprived of any claim to territory, much like the Jews or the Gypsies: a community in political but not geographical space. Officially speaking, "Bosnianness" remained a regional sentiment, and "Serbness," "Croatness," and "Muslimness" national. Giving unified Bosnian nationhood a chance in the political cartography of modern Bosnia-Herzegovina seemed to have been sealed once and for all.

"WHEN WILL YOUR HOME / BE YOUR HOMELAND INSTEAD?" BELONGING IN POLITICS, NOT IN SPACE

Among different implications of this political act for the sentiments of belonging and for the treatment of Bosnia-Herzegovina by its neighbors, especially relevant here is the territorial component. Whereas the land inhabited by Serbs and Croats had been long nationalized into Serbia and Croatia, respectively, thus empowering these two communities to politicize their bond with land, Bosnia-Herzegovina, ironically, was robbed of the option of being produced and narrated as a spatial polity. Although under the pressure of both Muslim and non-Muslim intellectuals and masses the Yugoslav government responded in 1921 with a new constitution guaranteeing territorial integrity to Bosnia-Herzegovina, practically nothing was done to curb the divisionist plans of Serbia and Croatia for ideological domination over it.[51] Bosnia-Herzegovinian territory became apoliticized by virtue of being treated as a region and not as a national homeland. In fact, it became a national "ghostland": Its population, nationalized along religious-cum-ethnic lines as Serb, Croat, and Muslim nationalities, was dispossessed of a national claim to land. In creating a political framework to potentially absorb Bosnian Serbs and Croats into Serbia and Croatia—a framework put to action in the 1992–1995 attempt to carve a Greater Serbia and Greater Croatia out of Bosnian-Herzegovinian territory—the former Yugoslav policies diffused these groups' foci/loci of national belonging. Without Bosnianness as a national category, Bosnia-Herzegovina became a home to all, but a land belonging to none of its peoples. Most tragically, these policies orphaned the Muslim population by severing their political link with the land. Bosnia-Herzegovina thus became ideologically depopulated, vacated of its social content, and denied its historical experience as a political territory. Adrian Hastings summarizes this critical moment as follows:

> As Bosnia had not been permitted by the Yugoslav constitution a parallel Bosnian category of nationality but only a "Muslim" one, inherently bound to exclude its citizens of Christian background, it was placed to fall an inevitable victim through constitutional ambiguity to the nationalism of its neighbours. As Bosnia had no 'nation' of its own, its existence could be claimed as 'artificial', a consequence of the Ottoman rule and religious conversion, while Croatia and Serbia were claimed as 'natural'. The very recognition of a Muslim nation actually added to the deconstruction of legitimate identity for a specifically Muslim nation that neither had existed nor could exist. *What had existed was a territorial identity inclusive of all religious traditions, but it was an identity rendered almost invisible both by the claims of the nationalism of its neighbours and by the consequent confusion within the Yugoslav constitution.*[52]

This process of ideological deterritorialization, which led to the destruction of the very link between Bosnia's religious pluralism and territorial integrity, would prove to be perilous: The link that had historically lain at the core of Bosnia's demographic and cultural integrity was turned into the platform for its denial. Even before the national taxonomy was formalized, progressive Bosnian intelligentsia interested in maintaining Bosnian diversity through its ethnoterritorial unity articulated how dangerous was the slope onto which Bosnia-Herzegovina had been placed. Mak Dizdar himself implied it in one of his poems, incisively and succinctly:

| When will your home | Al u domu tvome |
| be your homeland instead? | Kad će domovina? |

Dizdar's observation is not unique. Although in his poetry territory acquires a new political momentum, its presence in the collective consciousness has always been prominent. Whereas in Dizdar's poetry the construction of Bosnian landscape revolves around the medieval landscape of the dead, and therefore reflects a social intervention in nature during a specific historical period, in much of Bosnian literary culture "land" is a common theme and trope. In fact, despite the political fragmentation induced by the nationalization of Bosnia-Herzegovina, a recurrent appeal to geography has been crucial in sustaining the vigor of a unified Bosnian identity. Because the very designation "Bosnian and

Herzegovinian" is territorial in character, unlike "Serbian" and "Croatian," which derive national connotations from tribal etymologies, spatiality cuts through the very core of Bosnian self-perception despite the adopted national labels.[53] In that sense, the place of Bosnia-Herzegovina on the map opens up to the question of zones, real and imaginary, and of agency, which allows these zones to be maintained, crossed, or contested. Literary expressions of cultural relationship to space have never lost currency in the collective imagination, even as the territorial component was removed from political discourse. Because of its geography, Bosnia-Herzegovina has been treated as a crossroads of imperial and communist, Eastern and Western systems of meaning. The sense of a shared destiny, thanks to the location of Bosnia-Herzegovina at a crossroads laden with contesting claims and clashes of meaning, has left a powerful impact on the Bosnian consciousness through an enhanced awareness of territorial self-identification.

Paramount to consider in examining the two modalities of belonging in Bosnia-Herzegovina, territorial and national, is that both are politically and culturally consequential; both are subject to narrative modifications despite occasional treatment of one or both as primordial; and both generate a restless set of contradictions that no theory of identity can singularly resolve. The dynamics between them has always been laden with tension, but their presence as two interdependent strands of identity signals a paradigm that has lent itself to many complex questions and few satisfactory answers. The problem with blindly applying the otherwise insightful theories of national identity to the Bosnian case is that they fail to consider this dialectic. Most often, the Bosnian case is treated either as an example of ethnic nationalism gone wild in response to ancient ethnic hatreds, or as an assault, against the will of Bosnians themselves, on the shared cultural heritage. Many recent publications on Bosnia, popular or academic, tend to fall within either camp. While there is truth to both statements, the advocacy of one stance to the exclusion of the other eclipses the experiential and psychological reality of most contemporary Bosnians and, analytically, obscures the politics and poetics of ethnic relations. How else can one explain the fact that the war itself occasioned the most touching examples of human solidarity among so many Bosnians of different nationalities, yet also the most despicable acts of violence among many others? Extending Rogers Brubaker's suggestion that nationalism is produced by political fields, not by the properties of specific collectivites,[54] one can argue that the most recent eruption of nationalist violence in Bosnia-Herzegovina came precisely as an orchestrated, not spontaneous, disturbance of balance between the two expressions of belonging. The interplay between these expressions, and the effects on them of the recent war, require much effort to understand. But neither the issues of cultural continuity and survival nor those of discontinuity and demise can be examined without a reference to their interplay throughout modern Bosnian history.

In that sense, despite national disparities in Bosnia-Herzegovina, despite the brutality of the latest clash of ideas and bodies over the sentiments of belonging, the collective sentiments have commonly been predicated on both dimensions of identity: the national and the territorial. To be a Bosnian Serb, Croat, Muslim/Bosniac, or Jew is said to embody complex intersections between several orders through which the region has been historically organized and culturally animated. The Bosnian essayist Ivan Lovrenović speaks of it in the following terms: "In determining the cultural identity of Bosnia-Herzegovina it is paramount to acknowledge its *polyvalent cohesiveness.* Diachronically speaking, the last five centuries in the culture (and literature) of Bosnia-Herzegovina have turned out to be a continuous shift of balance in the dialectic between these two components. But, the perseverance of both is a fact: Neither have the centuries of assumed mutual isolation managed to erase Bosnia's polyvalent spirit, nor has the modern period, in its emphasis on uniformity, subverted its cohesiveness."[55]

Lovrenović's statement, while not unique, encapsulates well the vertical and horizontal trajectories that continuously inform what was referred to earlier as the dichotomous reality of Bosnian identity. As Lovrenović reflects on that identity, he reinforces the argument that the interface between the two currents grants Bosnia a peculiar status in the studies and realities of nationalism. Only the two components together, in interaction, can be argued to constitute the basis for unified Bosnian nationhood. The simultaneous denial and affirmation of unified Bosnian nationhood, at times manifested as tension and at others as harmony, is a sine qua non for a full understanding of Bosnia-Herzegovina. Moreover, Lovrenović successfully places emphasis on the agential role of culture, especially literary culture, in balancing these trajectories. In fact, literary culture continuously shapes and is shaped by them. At a literary symposium held in Sarajevo in 1970 (which, it should be emphasized, took place as the Muslim national question was deliberated at the constitutional level), the literary critic Miodrag Bogićević spoke of such literary engagements in the following terms:

> The existence of several nationalities in Bosnia-Herzegovina has never been an obstacle for genuine literary authors to experience and comprehend Bosnian reality. . . . National differences are not an obstacle; they shouldn't be seen as blocks of isolation in which authors write or which

they represent. The official national categories intimate an unbroken experience of homeland and an interdependence without which Bosnia-
Herzegovina would not be possible. Therefore, despite the historical,
political, national, and confessional differences that have been promul-
gated in institutional terms, through media and sometimes in literature,
the voice of every writer has always reflected a unified, integrated, hu-
manistic Bosnia-Herzegovina, rather than a tripartite one. Only writers
lacking vision and talent have reached out to national demarcations in a
deterministic way, probably in order to mask their own literary inadequacy and an inferiority complex. . . . While most authors in Bosnia-
Herzegovina subscribe to one of the institutionally endorsed national
labels, their path is much more deeply embedded and their message more
widely disseminated than what their individual national context demands.
In fact, the creative spirit in Bosnia-Herzegovina—exemplified in the
works of Ćorović, Andrić, and Selimović—negates the barriers and stands
up to the tendencies to mystify and manipulate nationhood. This is the
nature of real art; otherwise, it would never be able to transcend mundane
concerns and fleeting emotions. This is the great heritage of the people of
Bosnia and Herzegovina, which must never be betrayed.[56]

Highlighting the role of literature in the process of collective self-definition and self-affirmation, Bogićević's somewhat evangelical tone assigns
to literature the function of preserving the tension between the two un-
dercurrents of collective identification. "Genuine" or "true" literature, he
suggests, is in service of unified culture. Authenticity thus counteracts the
divisive spirit of the national discourse and the "bad" art it produces. The
function of literature, then, is not to be "national" but meta-national, au-
thenticating, as it were, the different experiences of Bosnian identity. It
does not subvert the political agenda, but supplements it. It does not es-
sentialize the identity but interconnects with it, as both the subject and
object. Hence, Bogićević's statement reflects a proactive view of literature
to safeguard the delicate cultural balance and mediate between the public
and the private, the politically "objective" and psychologically "subjective"
spheres of life in Bosnia. This comes as no surprise: As Ramet once observed, art and music, pop in particular, were central vehicles of alternative political expression in the former Yugoslavia where the Communist
party banned alternative political views from public discourse.[57] Literature carries an ethical as well as paradigmatic value. Because of the inter-
meshing of discourses and experiences, however, "Bosnian" literature
cannot and has not been formalized as a stable category independent of
other Serbo-Croat spheres of influence. In fact, only rarely have literary
critics advocated a single definitional category for literary production in
Bosnia.[58] To that end, at the same symposium another critic, Risto

Trifković, states: "The literature of Bosnia-Herzegovina, Bosnian-Herzegovinian literature—whatever you want to call it, whatever is convenient, more practical, appropriate, it doesn't really matter since reality does not change just because of its label—does exist in reality. Its contributors come from different national groups and that is the distinctiveness and uniqueness of this literature which, until recently, was treated as merely regional, parochial. . . . Yet at its best, at its most creative, this literature proves to be anti-parochial: it is engaged and universal."[59] Here again, the modular place of literature in public culture, regardless of definitional slots and labels, suggests its centrality in facilitating the affirmation of group identity and the conceptualization of Bosnia-Herzegovina. Literature thus stands as testimonial and empirical, reflective of lived experience and paradigmatic of Bosnian cultural legacy. It is answerable, as Bakhtin would suggest, in that it is art and life at once.

Indeed, literature has, in various ways, played a prominent role in identity construction, international relations, and the formation of collective answerability toward the shared heritage in Bosnia. Whether through the paratactic style of oral heritage in the stories of Svetozar Ćorović, the lyrical rhapsody of Hamza Humo, the detailed chronicles of Ivo Andrić, or the social pathos of Aleksa Šantić's verse, literature has formed a textured framework within which Bosnian identity has been symbolically and socially constructed, and occasionally destructed. In most works, however, the interplay of modernity and tradition has been experienced as a tension between primordial national entities and their collective responsibility to modernity. That tension has been narrated from many different literary and thematic angles, but in most it is accepted as a given thanks to the texture of Bosnian ethos. However, Mak Dizdar's unique success in decreasing this tension by focusing on the historical landscape that predates the foundation myths of the national communities unfolds a more harmonious space for a collective cultural participation.

The geographical focus holds a special relevance for the different dimensions of Bosnian identity. The poetry of Aleksa Šantić, Hamza Humo, Antun Šimić; the novels of Ivo Andrić and Meša Selimović; the short stories of Ćamil Sijarić, Erih Koš, and Isak Samokovlija; the essays of Alija Isaković and many others—all reveal a complex but enduring rhetoric of land. Although the appeal to territory in Bosnian literature has often been unjustly labeled as the malaise of parochialism,[60] the theme has necessarily had political, hence hardly insular, ramifications in Yugoslavia. On the one hand, the land motif reveals a shared territorial focus that challenges the theory of the literary isolation of each of Bosnia's three national literatures. With or without irony, such literary depictions of land evolve into a dominant trope associated with Bosnia:

its in-betweenness, both geographical and cultural. The layered inter-meshing of geography and identity in the trope suggests the impor-tance of territorial belonging even in a political climate that did not foster that link. Brewed through Bosnia's different historical condi-tions—Ottoman and Austro-Hungarian subjugation, continuous eco-nomic deprivation, wars, a collective volition to carry on—the trope of liminality, geographical and other, became a commonplace in narrative and poetic reflections on Bosnia. Because this trope also features cen-trally in Dizdar's construction of Bosnian landscape, it seems useful to examine its multiple implications that have, for the last century at least, shaped local and foreign descriptions of Bosnia.

LIMITED GEOGRAPHY AND METAGEOGRAPHICAL LIMINALITY: LITERARY DEPICTIONS OF BOSNIA-HERZEGOVINA

Ivo Andrić once wrote that "no one knows what it is like to be born and live on the border between two worlds, to know and understand both of them and to be unable to do anything to help them to come closer and understand each other."[61] Quite commonly, the physical location of Bosnia on the world map has led to its representation, by many for-eigners and probably all Bosnians, as a margin of different civilizations and worldviews—and therefore as at once their meeting and dividing point. Much before Huntington's infamous dictum about the clash of civilizations,[62] the line that unites and separates the East and the West became quite frequently imagined as the territory of Bosnia-Herzegov-ina. Dizdar's own interest in the medieval landscape was clearly influ-enced by such a representation, which is what makes his quest for the meaning of medieval cemeteries all that more contextual, territorially as well as politically. The opening paragraph of his study on medieval Bosnian texts states: "By virtue of being the most remote western fron-tier overlooking the east, and the eastern overlooking the west, Bosnia has always been the crossroads of different interests and the dividing line of various influences."[63]

   In general terms, however, the representation of Bosnia as a "cross-roads" is not limited to its medieval experience, nor is it inaugurated by Dizdar. In fact, it has become the central feature of the Bosnian geo-graphical imagination. In accordance with that view, Bosnia's undeter-mined geopolitical alignments have been explained as a result of its geographical position, especially as regards different imperial occupa-tions. Connecting the central Balkan and Alpine regions on the east-west trajectory while also opening up to the sea on the north-south axis, Bosnia-Herzegovina is not perceived as anyone's destination but as an artery. Thus, the Roman Adriatic orientation prompted Bosnia to concentrate on coastal activities; the intensified trade between European and Ottoman merchants centralized its role as a transit region and a frontier zone between Ottoman and Austro-Hungarian military campaigns; and its marginalization in Austro-Hungarian times as a military outpost with no active economic role (except for the exploitation of natural resources), posited it as by and large inconsequential for the internal affairs of the Monarchy.[64] The shifts were also evident in Bosnia's religious affiliations that were determined by Eastern Orthodox, Roman Catholic, neo-Manichean, and Islamic proselytizing activities, although no religion's teaching ever gained full control over Bosnia.

Such geopolitical fluctuations, while consistent with the different imperial and confessional agendas that crisscrossed the region, led to the evolution of an ambivalent image of Bosnia in different genres of writing as a site of political rivalries and cultural marginalization, external ploys and internal imperviousness. This impetus came mainly in late- and post-Ottoman developments, that is, during the transitional period of Bosnia's "recovery" by Europe. As Bosnia became a physically accessible yet culturally exotic target for European travelers, as its political destiny was placed in external hands, and as it was washed away by waves of national awakening, the question of its situatedness on the map gained both ideological and political dimensions. The trope of in-betweenness, thus, evolved from the view that Bosnia's geographic position has occasioned a set of arduous historical and cultural conditions that have left a decisive imprint on Bosnian culture.

Of course, the interconnectedness of geography and history is a common trope in the rhetoric of place. As J. Nicholas Entrikin points out, "We understand the specificity of place from a point of view, and for this reason the student of place relies upon forms of analysis that lie between the centered and decentered view; such forms may be described as narrative-like syntheses."[65] To the extent that the process of representation involves a universalizing (or comparative) impulse in addition to the experiential relationship to the place, the "narrative-like syntheses" are common not just to the student of place but, in more general terms, to the observers of place. Useful here is the notion of metageography which, as Lewis and Wigen define it, is a "set of spatial structures through which people order their knowledge of the world: the often unconscious frameworks that organize studies of history, sociology, anthropology, economics, political science, or even natural history."[66] Posing an objection to the inadequacy of conventional geographical concepts for the age of globalism, the authors alert us to the persistence of some geographical myths—for example, of continents, the nation-state, East and West—that continue to shape our understanding of the world as instruments of ideological power.[67] The universalizing impulse of such constructs not only simplifies the usually complex set of relations that exists between two (or more) specific places but it also decontextualizes any internal structures and events of any given place, especially during its political or social transformations. In many respects, Bosnia provides an excellent example of such problematic yet persistent metageographical imaginings, especially in reference to the East-West dichotomy and the territoriality of the nation-state, the two issues central to *Stone Sleeper*'s construction of "Bosnia."

The myth of East and West, understandably, has much larger comparative implications. As suggested by the ongoing controversy galvanized by the publication of Edward Said's *Orientalism,* the two constructs have been neither fully demystified nor uniformly understood. After Said's focus on the eastern Mediterranean in his academic construction of the "Orient," other Orients surfaced as a spatial and ideological competition to Said's Levant: Japan, India, Central Asia, Russia, and so on. In response to such objections, the concept of "East" has been accepted as both broader and looser than "Orient" and "Asia," but its problems remain. To begin with, as critics point out, the concept of "East" is intimately tied with the concept of "West," so the definition of either becomes inevitably relational. As the notion of "West" has undergone changes, both geopolitically and culturally, so has the notion of "East" shrunk or expanded. [68]Accordingly, Lewis and Wigen identify at least three different metageographical constructions of East and West in modern thought: the ancient notion, associated with the equation of the West with Latin Catholicism and the East with Byzantine Orthodoxy; the Cold War notion, bifurcated by international relations along geopolitical interests of the NATO and Warsaw Pact nations; and the post-1960s notion, based on economic modes of production, which groups the West around the G7 nations—including, ironically, the Far Eastern country of Japan.[69] Undoubtedly one can add other forms of East-West groupings to this typology, in colonial, cultural, religious, economic, and other terms, each of which points to the rhetorical convenience of such metageographic binaries. Although neither "West" nor "East" has been a stable category, their habitual deployment, mutable as it is, reveals an ongoing fascination with linking space to human action. The contingency of the two categories is also visible in less global terms, as one examines regional politics and intracontinental representations. Within the European context, the East-West dichotomy has persisted as a mode of cultural and political categorization, which alludes to the lack of internal uniformity in the making of European culture.[70]

Notwithstanding the fact that voices of ambivalence were heard across Europe, it is in its border zones that the notion of cultural uniformity has been most frequently challenged, in material and nonmaterial expressions alike. This has been increasingly argued not only in the context of the age of transnational migrations and *Gastarbeiter* (immigrant laborer) communities, but in the premodern context as well. As many medievalists propose, the decentralizing impulses within Europe, and the lack of fixed perspectives and authorities, emphasize the relevance of the notion of "border" as a shifting reality of societal relations in early times.[71] Along these lines, Maria Rosa Menocal aptly emphasizes the dangers of writing "European" history without considering the implications of the many internal and external voices and influences:

> The concept of self, and ultimately of the Western self, would be strongly affected, in many cases completely dominated, by the emerging relationship between the modern and the classical worlds, a relationship viewed as ancestral. Out of this relationship there was derived, ultimately, the critical notion, which remains strong today, of the essential continuity and unity of Western civilization from the Greeks through fifteenth-century Italy, having survived the lull of the Dark Ages, and thence through the rest of Europe and European history. It is a notion of history formulated as much to deny the medieval past and its heritage as to establish a new and more worthy ancestry.[72]

Here, the Greek case is an excellent example of the problems associated with metageographical constructs, since Greece is often depicted as Western in its intellectual legacy and Eastern in its postclassical historical developments.[73] Russia is another case of such metageographic hopscotch, as is Israel.[74] Unlike these inconsistent cartographic placements, Bosnia remains represented as a location betwixt and between others, a liminality internal to and subversive of Europe's self-representation.[75] Repeatedly exposing the West's ambivalence toward itself, Bosnia has been treated as a real as well as symbolic frontier, ever detached from Europe's center yet always entrapped in its political circumference. The ongoing legacy of religious and cultural pluralism in Bosnia, enacted in history as both violence and tolerance, as well as its treatment as the East's west and the West's east, seems to have relegated Bosnia to an ongoing liminality. Yet although the concept of liminality suggests flotation and mutability, a fragility of the self as it evaluates its symbolic and social meaning, Bosnia's liminality is territorially fixed and historically continuous despite different interpretations of that history. It is born in the interface of Bosnia's geography and metageography, and it is suggestive of the displacement of others in Bosnian cultural space rather than a dispersion of Bosnia itself. The ambivalence evoked in response to Bosnia's location is perpetuated by the larger narrative representations of historical and cultural encounters between East and West. As Adrian Hastings puts it:

> It is not the fault of South Slavs that they had settled on what became the frontier dividing two increasingly different forms of Christianity, the Latin and the Greek, between which by the later Middle Ages there would be deep hostility . . . [The Ottoman conquest] meant that it became in religious terms a double frontier zone—Latin and Orthodox, and Christian and Muslim as well. For the next five hundred years all the South Slavs were either subjects of the Ottoman Empire, subjects of Vienna, or footballs kicked to and fro across the military frontier.[76]

Despite Bosnia's seeming fixedness within the fissures of worldviews and "civilizations," the trope is duplicitous. It is not linear since it rests on vested interests, and it is not even since it involves complex intersubjectivities. Just as the myth of East-West lends itself to many interpretive possibilities, so does the space that lies in between. In that sense, although liminality appears as Bosnia's enduring feature, the meaning of that liminality is not constant, especially when viewed through the prism of literary historicism. As the trope gained currency with the increased importance of territory in the construction of collective identities, it evolved in two main directions. On the one hand, once Ottoman Bosnia became more accessible to Western European travelers, especially in the wake of the Austro-Hungarian takeover, its geographical location within Europe—and its cultural dislocation from it—came to be depicted in conspicuously colonial imagery. Here, Abdul JanMohamed's argument about the syncreticism of the Manichean opposition of the colonizer and colonized comes to mind, whereby the other is treated in a complex, "symbolic" way as mediator of European desires and a challenge to simplistic colonialist mentality.[77] Accordingly, travel narratives do not depict Bosnia in a uniform way. As long as it was an Ottoman province, Bosnia was seen as an exotic and gloomy region, dislodged from the historical frame of Europe, and eerily alienated from its affairs. On the other hand, after the Austro-Hungarian takeover and the recuperation of Bosnia by Europe, such literary exoticism was given a new tone, accommodating Bosnia's image as a place unaware of the demands of modernity and safely ensconced in its liminal state. In both depictions, though, when one is in Bosnia, one seems to be nowhere. Yet in both modes, the interplay between cultural rejection and self-reflection that is woven in European representations of otherness confirms a certain ambivalence toward this periphery. Consider, for example, the difference between the following two quotes: the first one by Dr. Germanus, an eighteenth-century European official in Bosnia, and the second by Anthony Rhodes of the early twentieth century:

> The Bosnians looked with curious eyes upon me and I suddenly remembered all the bloodcurdling stories read in fanatical books about Muslim intolerance. I noticed that they were whispering among themselves and their topic was my unexpected presence. My childish imagination flared up in horror; they surely intended to draw their daggers on the intruding "infidel". I wished I could safely get out of this threatening environment, but I dared not budge.[78]

And now Anthony Rhodes:

> My intention was to spend the summer wandering in Bosnia and the Herzegovina where, until recently, Islam was preserved in greater and more unbroken purity than in Turkey itself; a slice of feudal Europe preserved, as it were, by the Sultan in spirits of wine. Beautiful, fair lands they were to me, survivals in some way from a medieval age I longed to discover.[79]

While seemingly incongruous, these depictions, as JanMohamed would argue, draw on a common epistemological structure around which "otherness" is narrated in colonial literature. The first one, politically and ideologically simpler, dissociates Bosnia from anything European, and therefore maintains a grotesque clarity of the boundaries between the familiar and the unfamiliar. Fright, savagery, horror. Nothing in Dr. Germanus's quote initially hints at his sympathy or empathy with the world he is describing. Neither the physical proximity of Bosnia to Central Europe nor its pre-Ottoman past seems germane: The atmosphere is threatening, suspension and suspense go hand in hand, and the abyss between the narrator and "natives" seems unbridgeable. As his childish imagination flares up, however, Germanus conflates the prevailing image of Muslims he had grown up with and the reality he observed. In contrast, Anthony Rhodes needs to deal with Bosnia's Europeanness, its recuperation by and integration into the continental center, yet its estrangement through its Ottoman culture. The irony of his allusion to Bosnia as "a piece of feudal Europe" and "pure Islam," in contrast to the atmosphere Germanus describes of exaggerated depravity and threat, draws attention to a reconciliatory tone toward an otherness that is no longer geographical but historical. Otherness is created in terms of historical distancing (feudal Bosnia versus industrial Europe) and not physical. Although

seemingly nonrelated, the two depictions ought to be considered as stemming from the same supposition of irreconcilable dissimilarity. As Irvin
Schick suggests in his analysis of colonial discourse, "It is the very existence of difference that is operative, not particular differences. Mutually
contradictory stereotypes can co-exist without undermining one another's effectiveness; indeed, they reinforce each other even while they
reciprocally contradict or negate one another."[80]

In both cases, then, Bosnia's liminality emerges as a space native to Europe, yet incongruous with its "civilizational" advancement. The inherent
tension of Bosnia's in-betweenness, of its being at once internal and external to Europe, has given rise to two rhetorically dissimilar, yet epistemologically overlapping, attitudes to Bosnia. On the one hand there evolved an
image of Bosnia as "a step child of the centuries,"[81] a non-nation which,
having no historical identity of its own, has been doomed to survive only in
artificial terms,[82] as the object of external interventions and machinations.
Assigning a primordial quality to culture, this view is fostered most readily
in local, ostensibly Eurocentric writings; it expands the aforementioned depiction of Bosnia as amputated from its evolutionary trajectory, of its dislocation from history thanks to its *islam*—that is, submission—to Islam.
Danilo Kiš recounts the emergence of this image in the following terms:

> Bosnia, that exotic land in the heart of Europe, had until the Napoleonic
> wars been as unknown and foreign as the uncharted side of the moon. Only
> some rare travelers had left accounts as testimonies to its existence, which
> sound like descriptions of a damned island. Pierre DeVille, the French con-
> sul in Travnik (1807–1814), speaks of it as "the land of cannibals," and its
> people as "savages and barbarians" who overflow with "spite and burning
> hatred." One Croatian author, who traveled to Bosnia as if to explore a mys-
> terious and distant continent, describes it in 1858 as "completely barbarian"
> and its people as "simpleminded, insipid, and benighted." . . . This "murky
> land of Bosnia" where the Levant and West collide, Mohammedanism and
> Christianity [clash], and where Balkan Christians coexist by necessity with
> the Ottoman invader, would come to life in the work of Ivo Andrić.[83]

Kiš's observation of the evolution of the typically Orientalist trope of
Bosnia as a "dark province" in Yugoslav literature takes him, rightfully, to
Ivo Andrić, whose thesis of Bosnia's loss of history became a commonplace with quite evident implications for the political culture of Yugoslavia as well.[84] In his Ph.D. dissertation Ivo Andrić writes:

> According to its geographical position, Bosnia should have been the con-
> nection between the countries along the Danube and the Adriatic Sea, i.e.,
> Bosnia should at one time have connected two peripheries and the Serbo-

Croatian element with two zones of European culture. Having fallen to Islam it lost the possibility of fulfilling this, its natural role, and of participating in the cultural development of Christian Europe (to which it belonged through ethnographic and geographic features). Instead, Bosnia became a mighty fortress against the Christian West. Bosnia was to remain in this unnatural position for the remainder of Turkish rule.[85]

In Andrić's view, then, Bosnia's cultural deformity stems out of its disturbance of the assumed natural order of things. The persistence of this view in Eurocentric and nationalist discourse in the former Yugoslavia is suggestive of the ongoing ambivalence toward the Ottoman Islamic legacy. As late as 1989, the Belgrade University political scientist Miroljub Jevtić claimed that "Bosnia has sunk to the lowest depths through the name of Islam,"[86] giving this metaphor a distinct political implication. Throughout the 1992–1995 war, and even in its aftermath, this interpretation seeped into the decisions of nationalist policy-makers in Bosnia and their international supporters.[87]

On the other hand, in the mirror image of this trope, Bosnian liminality is conceived not as an absence of selfhood due to Islamization, but, quite to the contrary, as its dynamic configuration despite, or perhaps thanks to, its harsh historical conditions. In this case, then, the trope does not evoke a sense of loss of identity, but of action and self-affirmation. Regenerated with every new external intervention in Bosnia, liminality is constructed as an identity formed through dialogic workings. This is where the popular motif of Bosnian defiance comes to life as emblematic of Bosnia's geography and its history of disjunction from "centers," East or West. The margin gives meaning to the center, exposes its instability, points to its weakness. The sense of the self is defined and defended through its elasticity and interactivity, and its determination to elude external or internal incursion demands that the Other be filtered, reworked, and sustained by local values. In her 1937 travel journal *Black Lamb and Grey Falcon*, Rebecca West narrates Bosnia, "the European frontier," by likening it to a woman who resists a powerful man (the "Turk," in West's imagery) by yielding:

A man is pleased by her, he makes advances to her, he finds that no woman was ever more compliant. He marvels at the way she allows him to take possession of her and perhaps despises her for it. Then suddenly he finds that his whole life has been conditioned to her, that he has become bodily dependent on her, that he has acquired the habit of living in a house with her, that food is not food unless he eats it with her.

It is at this point that he suddenly realizes that he has not conquered her mind, and that he is not sure if she loves him, or even likes him, or even considers him of great moment. Then it occurs to him as a possibility that she failed to resist him in the first place because simply nothing he could do seemed of the slightest importance. He may even suspect that she let him come into her life because she hates him, and wanted him to expose himself before her so that she could despise him for his weakness.[88]

While perhaps a commonplace of colonial discourse,[89] Rebecca West's deployment of sexual imagery—of the masculine colonizer and the feminine colonized—becomes mainly interesting insofar as it splits, and even inverts, traditional power relations. The external shattering that comes with conquest can obscure internal steadiness. Although in this line of understanding too, liminality is born out of external, not internal, vacillation and motion, the emphasis is placed on the dialogic response to those motions by Bosnian culture. Political penetration into its space leads, as it were, to cultural counterpenetration, and Bosnia stands not as a victim but a translator of other realities that come its way. Its liminality is not a sign of passivity against external motion but of its interactivity. Liminality, then, is a dialogic zone where selfhood is constituted around the notion of defiance, which forms the central narrative tension of the trope. West's notable reference to "the Slav" in the following quote resonates with Slavophilic writings that had, since the mid-nineteenth century, made introspective, spiritual appeals to a single Slavic culture, mentality, and the tragic yet brave Slavic soul.[90] Reinforced by the particularity of the Bosnian experience, the metaphor is spatially determined:

> At last the two lovers [the Turks and Bosnians] had destroyed each other. But they were famous lovers. This beautiful city [Sarajevo] speaks always of their preoccupation with one another, of what the Slav, not to be won by any gift, took from the Turk, and still was never won, of the unappeasable anger with which the Turk longed throughout the centuries to make the Slav subject to him, although the Slav is never subject, not even to himself.[91]

Although originally associated with Orthodox ecclesiastical Slavdom, the idea of Slavic resistance to subjugation was filtered through the multiconfessional Yugoslav context in quite a heterogeneous way. Though the equation of religion and Slavic race maintained its importance in Serbian nationalist writings in particular,[92] the main appeal for other South Slavs was the pathos of martyrdom against historical suffering, cultural deprivation, and economic underdevelopment. Intertwining folk imagery and historical discourse, the traces of such appeals remained tangible even after the pan-Slavic idea lost its currency.[93] Because of the turbulent conditions surrounding the historical culture of Yugo-Slavs, the theme in their context appears in minor variations in reference to their history, reflecting, somewhat deceptively, a shared "national consciousness."[94] For example, under the pressure of institutional discourse and the new national mythology, the theme evolved as central even in the Partisan literature in the aftermath of World War II.[95] Nowadays, after the break-up of Yugoslavia, it has re-emerged in yet another direction according to the situation of each national group.

In the Bosnian context, however, it is important to note that the ubiquity of the theme of Bosnia's defiant spirit ties in with the textured representation of its geographic role as the fault line of civilizations, worldviews, political aspirations, and cultural sensibilities. As long as metageographical binaries continue to inform our understanding of the world—be they sifted through colonial, nationalist, communist, romantic, or other modes of representation—the construction of liminality in reference to Bosnia will maintain rhetorical currency. Consider, for example, the following excerpts of contemporary depictions of Bosnia. The 1993 farcical publication *Sarajevo Survival Guide* addresses liminality with much political piquancy:

> If you play with lines on the map of Europe, you will have to find Sarajevo. It is revealed where lines cross over the Balkans. First you draw a line from Paris, through Venice and then to Istanbul, and it is the closest East that Europe has ever known. A second line starts in Northern Europe, goes between Berlin and Warsaw, through the Mediterranean, and then to Africa. These lines meet over Bosnia and Herzegovina. In fact, they cross over Sarajevo. Here wars began and here wars went on, while its people made love and longed for love. Here merchants sold their goods from around the world and life was both similar and different to the life of the East and the West. It was a life too Western for the East, and too Oriental for the West. Still, it was the life of Sarajevo.[96]

Spatial representations here take on the flavor of historical irony as the cartographic precision of the passage is exercised from a particularly tragic vantage point: the 1992–1995 siege of Sarajevo. The more the city was turned into rubble, the more heightened its topographic liminality and the more enhanced its demographic and cultural vibrancy. Evoking a similar sense of historical loss in the face of the latest destruction of Bosnia, the British historian and journalist Noel Malcolm nostalgically reflects on Bosnia's historical centrality and uniqueness in allowing different empires and faiths to meet, coexist, and collide within its space:

[Bosnia-Herzegovina] was a land with a political and cultural history un-like that of any other country in Europe. The great religions and great pow-ers of European history had overlapped and combined there: the empires of Rome, Charlemagne, the Ottomans and the Austro-Hungarians, and the faiths of Western Christianity, Eastern Christianity, Judaism and Islam.[97]

Looking at the same scenery, but decades earlier, the English traveler Anthony Rhodes registers a similar set of impressions:

From a brief visit to Sarajevo as a child, I could remember the women in their yashmaks, the wooden Turkish houses standing in the fruitful gardens, the mosques abutting on the churches, the campaniles and the minarets, the delicious coffee one gets in any part of the world where the Turk has pene-trated. And then, the plethora of races and religions all living together—the Catholic, the Orthodox, the Moslem, the Protestant, even the Jew.[98]

Or, to stretch the field of vision even further and earlier, the following para-graph is from a 1903 issue of *The National Geographic,* whose reporter, William Curtis, combining his own observations with legends, turns Bosnia—and Sarajevo in particular—into a fantastic and exotic destination:

In Sarajevo the ancient and the modern meet: the East and the West touch hands; the oriental with eternal composure listens to the chatter of the Frenchman and regards the gesticulations of the Italian with supreme con-tempt. The town itself is half Turkish and half Austrian. The old parts look like Damascus and the new part like Budapest, which, in many respects, is the handsomest city in the world. I was told that Sarajevo contained a larger variety of types of original oriental races than even Constantinople, and that in the bazaars may be seen daily examples of every national costume from the Straits of Gibraltar to the Yellow Sea of China; and they all live together in peace and harmony, each recognizing the scruple of the other, permitting him to practice in peace the creed and customs of his faith.[99]

Bosnia is thus always more than its geographical self: It is the site of the confessional split between Orthodoxy and Catholicism; a Christian-Is-lamic frontier; a bridge between the First and Second Worlds. While these writings assuredly stem out of different perspectives on the region, they are nevertheless united in foregrounding "defiance" as a cultural cat-alyst against liminality. Defiance has been represented as the kernel of the Bosnian psyche, a kismet from which there is no escape and that conse-quently manifests itself in the mentality and behavior of its people. In the following quote from Meša Selimović's *Death and the Dervish* (1966), the two interpretive directions of the trope of liminality—the loss of identity and a resolution to go on—intermesh in a poignant reflection on cultural selfhood:

Not a long distance from here [Istanbul] there is a province so backward that you can hardly imagine. Just over there, next to you, almost adjacent to this Byzantine splendor, your brothers live as beggars. We belong to no one, we are always in a twilight zone, always used as someone's dowry. Is it then surprising that we are so poor? For centuries, we've been trying to find and define ourselves, and it seems that soon we will not even know who we are. We are already forgetting what we want because others are doing us the favor of leading us under their banner since we don't have our own. Others tempt us to join them when they need us and then they simply dispose of us. The saddest province in the world, the saddest people in the world. We've lost our face without being able to fake someone else's. We are abandoned without being adopted, which alienates us from everyone, including those who are our own kinsfolk, yet they don't consider us as such. We live in the frontier of different worlds, in the border zones of other peoples' lands. We are always in someone's way, always led by someone else, always guilty to someone. The waves of history break against us, as waves break against the cliffs. We are revolted with those in power, so we've created virtue out of our misery and become noble out of defiance.[100]

Ironic in tone, this passage is a form of meta-representation, a way of transcending the complexity of the trope by interweaving its various binary manifestations: center/periphery; prosperity/poverty; identity/loss of selfhood; power/subjugation; belonging/estrangement. In juxtaposing them, Selimović centralizes the burdens and expectations of an exoticized Bosnia. As the geographical frame becomes increasingly permeated with a desire for salvation from the predicament—an appropriately spiritual effort—"liminality" turns into a metaphor of struggle for collective identity, not of complicity with the discourses that have generated its internal division.

While Selimović opts for Ottoman Bosnia as the historical frame of that struggle against "liminality," seemingly excluding non-Muslims from the quest for cultural salvation,[101] Mak Dizdar, whose *Stone Sleeper* appeared the same year as *Death and the Dervish,* constructs "liminality" around the stećak burial grounds. His representation of Bosnia as pliant on the outside and resilient on the inside allows Dizdar to speak from within the dualist framework. The duality of the trope is enhanced by Dizdar's appeal to the medieval Bosnian ethos. Bosnian selfhood, then, while territorially durable, is continuously produced from within and from without. In emphasizing the Bogomil commitment to the inevitable triumph of good against evil, Dizdar makes Bosnia into a vigilant agent of justice, and the stećak into its central register. Thus, the deployment of Bogomil religious imagery makes liminality a cosmic principle foundational to the fashioning of Bosnian nationhood. In turn, defiance becomes its spiritual force, a technique necessary to resist political pressure. "A Text about Land" highlights this order in the form of a dramatized dialogue about Bosnia:

Once upon a time a worthy questioner asked:
Forgive me who is and what sir
Where is
Whence and
Whither sir
Prithee sir
Is this
Bosnia

The questioned swiftly replied in this wise:
Forgive me there once was a land sir called Bosnia
A fasting a frosty a
Footsore a drossy a
Land forgive me
That wakes from sleep sir
With a
Defiant
Sneer

The originality of the poem, like Selimović's passage above, lies not in the imagery per se, since defiance, pride, even awakening are tropes that appear before and after Dizdar;[102] it lies in his ability to articulate the spiritual potency of those depictions in geographically specific and philosophically universal terms. This marks an important shift in the construction of the trope. As the religious language associated with the formation of national communities—Serb/Orthodox, Croat/Catholic, and Muslim—became equated with national exclusivity, territorial belonging had fallen short of acquiring a common symbolic meaning for all those communities. *Stone Sleeper* gave the land a shared numinous quality, turning it into a rich source of collective empowerment and renewal.

Moreover, in Dizdar's poetic cartography, the stećak lies at the epicenter of Bosnia's in-betweenness: textually, on the margins of ancient manuscripts; topographically, on the brink of primeval forests; culturally, on the verge of forgetting. The manifold marginalization turns the stećak into the navel of Bosnia, the very core of its liminality: "Bosnia's *situation* is reflected in its earliest texts, literary and artistic."[103] The double-entendre of "situation" is worthy of note: According to Dizdar, Bosnian history cannot be dissociated from its geographical location, nor can its culture be comprehended without the stećak as its intertextual testimony. This is the subject matter of the next chapter.

Frontispiece 2: "Man with a hand raised high," Radmilja Cemetery. Photo by András Riedlmayer.

CHAPTER TWO

THE ARCHEOLOGY OF THE STEĆAK

HISTORICAL AND
CULTURAL CONSIDERATIONS

"The necropolis is the reverse side of metropolis."[1]

A relatively recent and glossy publication on the cultural treasures of the former Yugoslavia introduces the stećak in the following way: "The medieval tombstones of Bosnia and Herzegovina are the most original aspect of Yugoslavia's rich cultural heritage. . . . The stećak has been called the most curious necropolis on earth."[2] This comment reflects quite accurately the admiration shown for the stećak, if not in all of Yugoslavia then certainly in Bosnia-Herzegovina. In spite of such enthusiasm for the historical and lapidary value of the stećak, however, the process of understanding its meaning has been uneven and is to this day incomplete. The historical evidence linked to the stećak has gravitated toward several interpretive directions, leading to incompatible hypotheses regarding its origins and symbolism. In light of such dissonance, this chapter will try to situate the archeology of the stećak within the interpretive frames that have polarized theories about it in both scholarly and lay circles. Not being in a position to either validate or challenge them, the chapter will present the findings only insofar as they have left an imprint on the cultural sensibilities of contemporary Bosnians in relation to their medieval past. In that sense, while on the surface this chapter centers on the stećak as the subject matter of history and archeology, it also seeks to address the stećak as a subject matter of cultural memory. It needs to be emphasized that history writing and cultural imagination are delineated here primarily as analytical categories, but that it is precisely through their interweaving in several discordant ways that identity formation in modern Bosnia-Herzegovina began, and continues to take place even as I write.

The first serious interest in the stećak seems to have been expressed by a Slovenian translator in the service of the Austrian Emperor Ferdinand I during his journey through Bosnia in 1530. Though mentioned in many later writings as well, the stećak became the focus of a concerted scholarly effort only in the wake of the Austro-Hungarian occupation of Bosnia-Herzegovina in 1878. This colonial initiative to address the stećak's history and value is situated within two vital processes for the people of Bosnia-Herzegovina: a subjugation to the second imperial occupation on the one hand, and the age of national awakening among its South Slav kinsfolk on the other. Both processes were to leave a lasting imprint on the historiography of the stećak and its reception in Bosnia-Herzegovina and beyond.

In the aftermath of World War II, the stećak's uniqueness was placed in the limelight through systematic archeological and ethnological research administered by the Yugoslav office for the protection of cultural monuments. More specifically, the 1950s witnessed a dynamic and comprehensive cataloging process involving documenting, classifying, and arranging the physical evidence about the stećak. In addition to meeting the challenge of cultural preservation against the effects of rapid industrialization in Bosnia-Herzegovina, this archival effort to centralize knowledge about the stećak was deeply intertwined with a need to reconnect more profoundly with the medieval and "forgotten" past. Speculations about the stećak's origins and imagery were raised in reference to a more general quest to understand the culture that had created and sustained this form of funerary art, a culture that had, by and large, faded away during the Ottoman administration of the region. The recovery of memory thus became a matter of a systematic, archival effort commensurate with a more historicized understanding of collective identity in the socialist Bosnia-Herzegovina.

THE PHYSICAL EVIDENCE

Drawing upon archeological explorations, the basic definition of the stećak has become unavoidably phenomenological, presenting and describing its distinctive features rather than merely stating its meaning. According to that perspective, the stećak is a massive limestone monolith distinguished by rich figural and scenic imagery. It is now generally accepted that the stećak was a common type of tombstone in pre-Ottoman and even early Ottoman times among all confessional and social groups in medieval Bosnia-Herzegovina, betraying class and status only in lapidary representations.

According to the data accumulated through the concerted cataloging and cartographic effort of post–World War II Yugoslavia, Bosnia-Herzegovina is home to 2,612 stećak cemeteries of varying size and composition. The total number of stećaks amounts to roughly 59,000. However, Bosnia-Herzegovina is not the only territory where the stećak is found. Some 12 percent of the overall number of stećak cemeteries are in other regions of the former Yugoslavia (primarily southern Croatia, Montenegro, and Serbia), although there the stećak is neither as ubiquitous nor as visible a type of tombstone. Taken together, the number of stećak cemeteries in the former Yugoslavia stood at 2,988, while the individual stećaks were numbered at 66,663.[3]

Notwithstanding the scantiness of historiographical data, it needs to be noted that the cataloging process was never free of controversy. The search for the stećak occasioned definitional revisions as to what constitutes a stećak, so much so that the multi-team fieldwork conducted over a period of several years led to discrepant criteria of enumeration based variably on time period, shape, material, location, and imagery. Added to such inconsistencies was the problem of appellation: During the onerous fieldwork in various locations, it became obvious that the stećak was known by many different names of unrelated etymologies. Moreover, the very term stećak (literally, a "tall, standing stone"), although common in urban argot, proved to be rather uncommon in regional dialects. Bearing no etiological value, the term's popularity among the city elite points paradoxically to its homogenizing and somewhat imprecise connotations.[4] In contrast, the communities living in the vicinity of the medieval graveyards refer to the stećak in a number of different ways, each of which sheds light on rich local folklore. For example, in some areas of Herzegovina and Dalmatia the stećak is spoken of as *mašhet,* a word deriving from either the Italian *massetto* (rock), or the Turkish *meşhet* (tombstone to a fallen hero).[5] In Bosnia, the stećak is frequently referred to as *mramor* (marble), while in Serbia and Montenegro as *usadjenik* (literally, implantation). Conversely, the internal references, consisting mainly of the epigraphs and signatures, suggest that in medieval times the stećak was referred to as *kam* (medieval for stone) or *biljeg* (mark, imprint). Collectively, folk traditions occasionally refer to the necropoleis as "Greek cemeteries," "Hungarian cemeteries," and/or "cemeteries of the wedding guests," but nowhere do there seem to be paronomastic references to dualist Bogomilism, with which the stećak is commonly associated.[6] Rather than a shared etiology or familiarity with the visual language, these terms seem to reveal local beliefs that evolved, in posterity, from living around the stećak; this further testifies to the local people's gradual estrangement from the context that actually produced the stećak and its imagery.

The dating of the stećak, based mainly on stylistic comparisons, poses certain problems as well. The late nineteenth-century English archeologist Arthur Evans, though a champion of the Bogomil hypothesis of the stećak's origins, saw them as descendants of Roman sarcophagi comparable to the rugged Roman stones found in York, England.[7] Some earlier studies suggest that the stećak has strictly Slavic origins of roughly the eighth century, but the fact that it is not found in other Slavic cultures renders that suggestion insubstantial. Equally apparent are the lacunae in the theories that locate the stećak within the Hunnish, Vlach, or Greco-Roman styles of burial architecture.[8] In spite of ongoing speculations, most scholars have now accepted that the stećak is a distinct trait of medieval Bosnian funerary architecture, and that neither its style nor imagery derives from only one source or stylistic background.

It is also generally held that the stećaks were erected in the period between the thirteenth and sixteenth centuries, although some divergences exist within that view as well. For example, Wenzel limits that time span to the 14th and 15th centuries on the basis of some important visual clues found on decorated tombstones.[9] Bešlagić, on the other hand, uses external evidence to argue that the stećak was a relatively common type of tombstone in the periods between the late tenth and sixteenth centuries—namely, prior to the establishment of the independent Bosnian state under Ban Kulin (1180–1204) and well after the Ottoman conquest in 1463. In his view, although the stećak had existed sporadically before the reign of Ban Kulin, it was the economic empowering of the Bosnian nobility that led to the stećak's increasing popularity as a burial stone. As Bosnia consolidated mercantile relations with Ragusa and other Mediterranean countries by exporting its rich mineral resources, its feudal lords became more prosperous and active in both economic and cultural terms. The earlier practice of building miniature wooden sarcophagi and tombs was now replaced with stone formations intended mainly as post-mortem sites for wealthy landlords. The grandeur and the location of most cemeteries (but certainly not all), as well as the epigraphic formulae (such as "Here lies XY on his land . . .") suggest an increase in ornate family gravesites rather than the common folk's burial grounds.[10] But under King Tvrtko I (1353–1391)—who called himself the ruler of Bosnia, Dalmatia, and Raška—the state's political borders strengthened and expanded, and it was within these borders that most cemeteries were erected, now both for upper and lower classes. With no other expression of monumental architecture or emerging epic literature, the stećak cemeteries became the focal medium of funerary art and architecture in medieval Bosnia-Herzegovina.

The stećak has been classified and studied on the basis of three main criteria: form, school, and decorative motifs.

Form

Regarding the form, the stećak has been roughly grouped into horizontal and upright stones, and these are further subgrouped according to more specific architectural features into tablets, caskets, tall caskets, and sarcophagi.[11] However, as Wenzel argues, some of these categories are misnomers in translation because the stećak most commonly is a solid block and not a hollowed tomb implied by most of these terms. For example, the term sarcophagus is particularly problematic since it is used to translate the word *sljemenjak*, a peak-topped stećak that has no immuring function or connotation.[12]

School

The second method of classifying the stećak is in reference to the place/school of production. The Herzegovina school, located around Stolac (the hometown of Mak Dizdar), is regarded as superior in both composition and productivity over the school that is associated with central Bosnia and its environs.[13] Rich in limestone, Herzegovina was a particularly fertile region for the stećak industry, and it is there that one observes the most elaborate motifs carved in impressive limestone monoliths. In addition to figural and scenic representations, the Herzegovina stećaks are distinguished by their stylized columns, arches, and arcades, all of which point to the high level of artistry and skill that went into their production. Occasionally, of course, the representations betray the hand of an artisan still in the making; but even then, the overall effect of the decorative language is one of unbroken movement, of the celebration of life rather than the austerity of death. In that sense, the Herzegovinian artisans are highly regarded for communicating the dynamic interweaving of experiential and imaginary realms in their stone incisions.

Due to the scarcity of other relevant sources, however, it is not certain to what extent this imagery is to be understood in allegorical terms, and to what extent it is inspired by the lives of the deceased and those who mourn them. Given that similar images recur on tombstones that are distant in both time and location, it may be safe to assume the existence of a shared pool of symbols that allowed for immediate recognition of meaning by both the artisans and the mourners. Moreover, the artisans—particularly the more famous ones like *dijak* (scribe) Semorad of the Stolac region— were known for their specific styles of craftsmanship and skill, which is why similar images and combinations of symbols often bear the same signatures. This suggests that the images were not always commissioned by the family of the deceased but were sometimes left to the lapidarist's discretion;[14] thus it is only in the inscriptions that detailed references can be found to the individual buried under the stone and the cause of death. Such statements of trust in the artisan's skill also addresses the issue of originality: As most art historians of the Middle Ages point out, the medieval artisan was unlikely to exercise a degree of creativity that would set him apart from conventional modes of representation.[15] In the case of stećak imagery, creativity is likely to be measured in terms of the artisan's ability to visually integrate his knowledge about the deceased with the myths of the hereafter. The mediation between the dead and the living is thus objectified in his improvisations. Since the artisan serves an interconfessional audience, it is in the imagery he selects rather than the epitaphs (even formulaic ones) that cultural contiguity most clearly takes place. This shared pool of symbols, mediated by the artisan in the process of carving, opens up to the aesthetics of inclusion rather than exclusion or post-mortem solitude. The death of an individual solicits collective participation in bereavement and remembrance by means of a shared funerary imagery. Since there are no two identical destinies and consequently no lapidary duplications, this shared symbolism is always singularized when the reality of death is inscribed in its stone simulacrum. The lapidarist's skill of shaping the stone into a site of remembering is subject to the community's acceptance of the stećak as a meeting ground—in experience and representation—of myth and reality. In that sense, the appreciation of the stećak's aesthetics from a contemporary vantage point must take into account the interplay between the community in mourning, the lapidarist's subjectivity, and the shared language of symbols.

Decorative Motifs

Naturally, decorative language marks the third criterion of stećak classification. Wenzel points out that of the overall number of registered stećaks, the great majority of them—some 50,000—are undecorated. Around 10,000 stećaks, on the other hand, bear figural and scriptural motifs, all derived from a relatively limited repertoire.[16] Yet despite this fact, one must approach stećak symbolism without a predetermined dictionary. Symbols can be suggestive of a plurality of meaning and their specific contexts can reveal a variety of concerns and subjectivities. Though one would expect certain fixed patterns in lapidary language, it seems that the safest route to decoding this language is in combining the questions of "how" the visual symbols are enacted with "what" they suggest or translate into. This approach is necessitated by the fact that the visual text is at once a method of alienation and familiarization: Whereas the images are scooped from a shared brew of values, they visualize stories about an individual's rite of passage from this life into the next, which makes the symbols at once worldly and eschatological, individual and collective, real and imaginary. That there is a relatively small repertoire of stećak motifs should not concern us in light of the fact that there is an infinitely larger pool of visual combinations that mediate between what is experienced in this life and what can be projected onto the next. This is especially relevant in view of the argument that all Bosnians, irrespective of religious persuasion or ethnic background, used the same sepulchral language. The existing decorations therefore ignore religious, ethnic, or class differentiation and draw attention to a shared burial praxis despite differences in belief about the relationship between this world and the hereafter. Moreover, it seems that the visual vocabulary expanded in response to major historical upheavals in the region that may have left important imprints on the social practices of commemoration. A turning point is associated with the wake of the Ottoman conquest. Wenzel concludes:

> The decorated *stećci* appear as a phenomenon within a relatively narrow range of time. This was a crucial historical period. It began after the battle of Kosovo in 1389 and the fall of Serbia to the Turks, spanned the short emergence of Bosnia as an independent kingdom, and finished in the earlier years after the Turkish conquest of Bosnia. Only a few shapes of tombstones, such as crosses and steles, carry on well into the Turkish times. It would seem that the earliest decorated tombstones were erected by members of a feudal aristocracy, and that the custom was later adopted and the decoration much elaborated by certain groups known as Vlachs who were organized on a tribal, non-feudal basis. The Vlachs, having been economically strengthened as a consequence of their dealings with the Dubrovnik traders, adopted this custom in imitation of the upper classes. It is quite likely that other, non-Vlach inhabitants of Bosnia and Hercegovina adopted the same custom for the same reason.[17]

In that sense, the visual evidence as read by Marion Wenzel reinforces the theory of the stećak's polyvalent aesthetics in several ways: First, it locates the practice of decorating the stećak at a crucial phase in Bosnian history—the arrival of the Ottomans; second, it traces the repatterning of class and economy in medieval Bosnia on the basis of the stećak's decorative detail; and third, it points to the fact that the popularity of the stećak did not disappear immediately after the Ottoman consolidation in Bosnia-Herzegovina but continued even among the converts to Islam. These arguments certainly augment the appreciation of the stećak as a distinctly Bosnian phenomenon shared by all confessional and cultural groups. Furthermore, they present us with the stećak inside rather than outside of history insofar as they offer insights into its subjection to the social and cultural flux, rather than its representational paralysis. "Carved into stone," that metaphor associated with imperviousness to historical change, is challenged by the very act of carving that enacts the change.

Writing the Stećak, Reading the Stećak

The above criteria for studying the stećak have proven to be insufficient; more ink needs to be spilled before scholars arrive at a comprehensive understanding of it. In the future, research on the stećak ought to be more intimately tied with research on medieval Bosnian history at large, and, as such, predicated on the availability and soundness of the sources through which medieval culture is transmitted. Moreover, though a material legacy of medieval culture, the stećak's merit as an enduring source of knowledge cannot be ascertained. To begin with, as a structure composed of a complex system of signification, the stećak ought to be treated as a "text" that points to different social, historical, and aesthetic conditions surrounding its production and reception. In fact, most art historians argue that the medieval appreciation of artisanship is inseparable from the appreciation of how useful and functional the object of art is. Such matters are decided externally, in reference to the beliefs and practices of the community, rather than by the object itself.[18] In that sense, nothing, or very little, about the stećak should be considered autonomous from other forms of medieval Bosnian creativity, despite the stećak's physical disconnectedness from other sources. Though a befitting window into the funerary practices of medieval Bosnians, the stećak's lapidary content encapsulates several poorly understood cultural values, such as the attitude toward death, the cosmological tension between the world of the living and the world of the dead, and the myths and rituals that sustain the community's relationship with its dead.

Yet in spite of this referential value, decoding the stećak's symbolism cannot eliminate the gaps in our understanding of any of these beliefs or practices. Furthermore, the stećak's historical presence in the Bosnian and Herzegovinian landscape has imbued it with a complex representational value in both local and general terms, so much so that the numerous necropoleis across the country often reveal quite unpredictable variances in both form and content, despite their shared qualities. These interpretive complications hint at the depth of contemporary estrangement from medieval culture, but they necessarily deny linearity to any narrative, historical or other, aimed at telling us what the stećak is all about.

Therefore, even prior (or in addition) to examining the stećak for its structural features as discussed above (form, school, imagery), it ought to be approached as a "primary text"—that is, a raw source that communicates, both linguistically (epitaphs and inscriptions) and nonlinguistically (images, architecture, layout), certain unfiltered aspects of medieval Bosnian culture. As any primary text associated with this (or any other) epoch, the stećak is subject to both textual and intertextual concerns, and as such should not be treated as independent or self-referential. Its singularity as medieval art, although widely acknowledged, cannot be divorced from the exegetical inconsistencies associated with the reading of related sources. Consequently, any attempt to understand the stećak without examining the conditions that created it is bound to be incomplete. Per contra, any attempt to understand medieval culture without reference to the ways in which the stećak has framed and been framed by the Bosnian landscape is destined to fall short of addressing the complexity of that epoch and the construction of its meaning in modern times. Yet in many ways the crux of the problem in reconstructing medieval Bosnian history lies in the unavailability of sources that could provide a key to the stećak's origins and imagery. Unlike the study of funerary architecture in many well-documented cultures of both antiquity and medieval times, the cultural beliefs and practices of medieval Bosnia-Herzegovina are poorly understood by both medieval observers and contemporary readers. There is a complete lack of local narrative sources regarding social and cultural formations in this period. The only extant sources are a few Gospel manuscripts, gravestone epigraphs, and a variety of charters whose complete authenticity has partly been questioned.[19] Even as the nineteenth century galvanized other South Slavs into defining their national and cultural identity through history writing, the Bosnian intelligentsia remained rather disengaged from that process. As Sima Ćirković argues, sources and interpreters of medieval Bosnia came from outside, for several centuries at least. While this fact does not cast doubt on the plausibility or reliability of these sources, it does highlight the fact that often impressionistic, even second-hand, insights and ulterior motives should not be ruled out in assessing the scholarly findings.[20] In most cases, their points of departure were Catholic archives according to which medieval Bosnia-Herzegovina was indubitably a land of dualist heresy. It is thus through this external frame of reference that scholarly opinions were formed about medieval Bosnia before any thorough examination of the sources in situ was launched.

It is perhaps even more important to acknowledge that the link between contemporary and medieval Bosnian culture has been broken in many significant ways. Centuries of external domination dispossessed modern Bosnia of its medieval anchor, creating a rupture in cultural selfhood despite the stećak's enduring presence in the country's landscape. By the late nineteenth century, only a handful of scholars—mainly foreign travelers through Bosnia-Herzegovina—showed interest in studying the stećak. It is only in the wake of the Austro-Hungarian occupation that a deeper interest in its historical function and lapidary value was generated. As a colonial initiative for the "rehabilitation" of Bosnian-Herzegovinian culture, the Austrians founded Zemaljski muzej—the National Museum—in Sarajevo, one decade after their 1878 occupation of the country, with the intention of recovering the local culture from the obscurity and silence endured under Ottoman rule. The colonial administrator in Bosnia-Herzegovina, Benjamin Kallay, expressed that endeavor in the following terms: "Austria is a great Occidental Empire charged with the mission of carrying civilization to Oriental peoples . . . What we have tried to do [in Bosnia] is build the new upon the old, . . . to retain the ancient traditions of the land vilified and purified by modern ideas."[21] But Bosnia presented the Austrian colonizer with a dilemma as to what constitutes the other: the Ottoman, the Bosnian, or both? As the two categories converged in the formation of Bosnian Islam (so much so that Bosnian Muslims were often referred to as *Turci* and/or *Turkuše* [Turkicized]), the Austrian colonial project needed to take into account the full reality of the Ottoman legacy, epitomized both in local Islamic culture as well as the social relations formed through the Ottoman *millet* system. To secure the colonial rule meant addressing a multifaceted task: First, consolidating Bosnian Muslims in their European roots without denying them rights to cultural distinctiveness; second, steering Bosnian cultural sensibilities away from the Croats, with whom the Bosnians now shared a colonial ruler; and third, keeping away the Serbs, whose liberation from the Ottomans occasioned nation-building pretensions over Bosnia-Herzegovina as well. In their efforts to hamper bonding among the South Slavs, the Austro-Hungarian goal in Bosnia-Herzegovina was to promote a search for selfhood within the local heritage, emphasizing aspects of culture and history that stood out as singularly Bosnian. Pre-Ottoman Bosnia-Herzegovina proved to be a heritage that could suit all three confessional groups while heightening

Bosnian "difference" from their South Slavic neighbors. The archeological effort concentrated heavily on the stećak as the material legacy of medieval times. Thus, the stećak's transition from being a neglected mausoleum to becoming a museum in small is a critical stage in its history, signaling a repositioning of Bosnians toward their history and culture. Identified as the foundation stone of Bosnian identity, the medieval burial stone was turned into the cornerstone of modern national rebirth.

For several decades the National Museum and its publication "Glasnik" (Voice) functioned as the bastions of preservation and representation of the stećak. Seen in a wider perspective, this museal intervention by the colonial ruler into the Bosnian past clearly had political underpinnings. Since Bosnia needed to be rescued from the Ottoman grip, it had to recover its European/Christian roots. That process necessitated a search into the past for vestiges that predated the Islamic legacy. The National Museum was set up as a cultural lighthouse, illuminating the aspects of the past eclipsed by centuries of Ottoman dispossession. It was assigned the function of representing the archeological process of unearthing, of digging out the cultural layers so as to trace an ethos fractured by the passage of time yet deeply grounded in local soil. The establishment of *ius soli* became linked with the stećak and the recovery of memory.

It happens that the museum, in fact, served a didactic function of drawing attention to sundry aspects of culture that were now threatened with being forgotten in the age of national awakening. As the Ottomans retreated, the people of Bosnia-Herzegovina were caught up in the wave of national awakening sweeping over the Balkans. As discussed in the previous chapter, the age of nationalism imposed its own dialectic of memory and forgetting, and the internal lines of division among the three main confessional groups of Bosnia-Herzegovina (Muslim, Orthodox, and Catholic) occasioned a fragmentation of memory. With collective memory divided, history was turned into a battleground of contesting national myths, each of which negated the participation of the other(s), except in ideological terms. Remembrances became selective, mutually distrustful, and exclusive. Furthermore, Serbian and Croatian memories nurtured centripetal affinities for Serbia and Croatia respectively, while most Muslims (except for the intellectuals who embraced Serbian and Croatian ideologies) were nostalgic about a transnational *umma* as once secured by the Ottomans.[22] In such a climate of forceful internal partition, the vestiges of the past that suggested cultural interweaving or even unity fell through mnemonic fissures of each community. The Austro-Hungarian "museal glance" emerged as an attempt to counteract and reconfigure the tripartite itinerary of cultural memory. Paradoxically, it is under these circumstances that one observes the legitimizing function of

Figure 2.1: Stećci in the frontyard of the National Museum in Sarajevo. Photo by A. Buturović.

the museum that Andreas Huyssen aptly characterizes as "fundamentally dialectical": "The museum serves both as burial chamber of the past—with all that entails in terms of decay, erosion, forgetting—and as a site of possible resurrections, however mediated and contaminated, in the eyes of the present."[23]

Of course, the question of Austro-Hungarian political motivation in counteracting cultural and national divisions in Bosnia and Herzegovina is of great importance. After all, as Huyssen further postulates, the museum as institution is never free of the discursive context that produces it: In the case of the National Museum in Sarajevo, reaching back to local culture as a foundation and canon for a modern sense of belonging suited the Austro-Hungarian imperial interests in diminishing the popularity of the Serbian cause in the region and in downplaying the cultural ties between the Empire's Croatian and Bosnian subjects. In that sense, promoting an interconfessional Bosnian culture and nationhood—*Bošnjaštvo*—was a strategic move to contain, in both political and ideological terms, the nationalistic zeal pouring into Bosnia from neighboring Serbia and Croatia. Unfortunately for the Austro-Hungarians, their timing was bad and the ground barren: The *Bošnjaštvo* project gained no followers among either the Catholic or the Orthodox population, which had already been engulfed by national awakening. Instead, *Bošnjaštvo* became popular mainly among those Muslims who feared confessional assimilation by their Christian neighbors on either side. Paradoxically, the very same project that had been designed to singularize Bosnian national culture became instrumental in sharpening confessional cleavages insofar as it activated the sentiments of Bosnian Muslims into a resistance against assimilation into the Serb and Croatian national projects.[24]

As *Bošnjaštvo* in its original sense died a quiet death with the demise of the Austro-Hungarian empire, the medieval past that had served as a vehicle to ground the project in pre-Ottoman history lost its discursive role as envisioned by the Austro-Hungarians. Nevertheless, the stećak's potential to be integrated in the historical imagination never fully disappeared: As physical witness to the singularity of Bosnian medieval culture, the stećak remained an important subject matter in foreign and local evaluations of Bosnian ethnohistory. Accepting the position—based largely on Catholic sources—that medieval Bosnians were dualist Bogomils (locally also referred to as "Patareni" and "Krstjani"),[25] the initial theses advanced an image of medieval Bosnia as a land situated between, and torn by, Catholicism and Orthodoxy. Frequently employing dualist metaphors of evil and good, loss and redemption, visible and hidden practices, scholarly studies as well as popular accounts fostered the image of the stećak as a symbol of resistance and purity. As a matter of fact, Alojz Benac argues that the first far-reaching publicity given to the "Bogomil question" had happened before the Austro-Hungarian advent—that is, in the 1875 travel memoirs of the English historian Arthur Evans, *Through Bosnia and the Herzegovina on Foot*, which dedicates a large section to the hidden purity of medieval Bosnia that now yearned to be discovered.[26]

Though a subject worthy of study in its own right, the European colonial imagining of Bosnia-Herzegovina, of which Evans is a fine example, deserves some attention here as well. Despite the fact that Evans is English and thus not representative of Austro-Hungarian colonial policies in Bosnia-Herzegovina, his overall motivations are situated within the larger Western/Christian European view of the Ottoman presence in the Balkans. In addition to a simple admiration of the "picturesque costumes and stupendous forest scenery"[27] of Bosnia-Herzegovina, Evans's writings alert us to the discursive subtext of the European journeys into the Ottoman lands of the time. As postcolonial theories propose, the colonial imaginings of "the other" are discursive constructions indicative of not just perceptions of the other, but the colonial self-formation and self-definition as well. In that dialectic, as Irvin Schick suggests, "the other plays a determining role as the antithesis, an embodiment of characteristics disavowed by the self that thereby paradoxically mirrors the self."[28] But given the specificity of each colonial encounter and the complexity of its literary codification (such as genre, images, language), this dialectic is carried out with different ethical imperatives in mind. In that sense, Evans's depiction of Bosnian culture can both subvert and confirm Schick's observation in many significant ways. As an Englishman exploring the outer frontier of "civilized" Europe, Evans never loses sight of the Ottoman other as the main alterity of his travel narratives: "If this book should do anything to interest Englishmen in a land and people among the most interesting in Europe, and to open people's eyes to the evils of the government under which the Bosniacs suffer, its objects will have been fully attained."[29] As a point of comparison, it is worthy of note that this view was typical of Western observers of Bosnia: A 1903 issue of *National Geographic*, apparently keen on presenting the new, re-Europeanized Bosnia to the American reader, writes:

> While subject to the Turks Bosnia practically vanished from the current of civilization until 1875, when, exasperated by extortion, robbery, rapine, murder, and religious prosecution, the people rose in rebellion. The powers of Europe placed them under the protection of Austria, which has given the most remarkable exhibition of administrative reform known to modern history, and has demonstrated the possibility of governing alien races

by justice and benevolence. . . . Today human life is as safe in Bosnia as it is in Illinois. . . . Through all the centuries that Bosnia was controlled by the Turks, the people were without morality, education, arts or sciences, and their industry was limited to the supply of their wants.[30]

But this very same Bosnia proves to be a twilight zone, not a simple illustration of the "Turkish yoke," which constituted the central trope in Western writings on the Ottoman legacy in the Balkans. In addition to the Turkish "other," Bosnia presents a more careful European observer—Evans is one of them—with another "other": the Bosnian Muslim, who stands neither among the Turks nor among Europeans per se. The belief that Bosnian Muslim is a liminal category that once belonged to the European self but is no more is what prompts Evans to create a parallel text with a different kind of representation. That parallel text thematizes Europe's "uncivilized" legacy and the history of intolerance that allowed for such an alteration of the self. The Bosnian Muslim makes Evans question the image of an ever homogeneous, morally superior Europe: "There never was a clearer instance of the Nemesis which follows on the heels of religious prosecution. Europe has mainly to thank the Church of Rome that an alien civilisation and religion has been thrust in their midst, and that Bosnia at the present remains Mahometan."[31] Whereas Evans's observations can be assessed as a typical example of colonial feelings of moral and cultural superiority over the (Ottoman) other, they are also a good illustration of the internal tensions that challenge the images of unbroken European selfhood. Just as there has never existed a homogeneous other, Evans implies that there has existed no singular self capable of sustaining the myth of a linear, uninterrupted collectivity within Europe's borders in the face of perpetual conflicts and persecutions. In current critical thought it is Michel de Certeau who alerts us to this complex unfolding of European history (albeit not always in an area-specific way), arguing for a lack of homogeneity in Europe's self-formation:

> There is both continuity and discontinuity, and both are deceptive, because each epistemological age, with its own "mode of being of order," carries *within itself* an alterity every representation attempts to absorb by objectifying. None will ever succeed in halting its obscure workings, or in staving off its fatal venom.[32]

Evans's double discourse—one addressing outer alterity, the other inner alterity—can be well assessed in light of JanMohamed's division of colonial literary production into two main categories touched upon in the previous chapter: the "imaginary" and the "symbolic." In JanMohamed's view, though all colonial literature valorizes the culture of the colonizer, a difference does exist in the ways certain colonialist authors configure the dialectic of the self and other. In the "imaginary" literature, the native population is degraded as essentially incomprehensible and consequently immobile in its otherness. This style of representation is narcissistic as it entraps the two worlds in a permanent and fixed opposition allegorized as the "good" colonial self versus the "evil" other. Conversely, the "symbolic" literature posits the native as a mediator of colonial desires in an attempt to understand the unknown and to "reflect on the efficacy of European values, assumptions, and habits in contrast to those of the indigenous cultures."[33] In other words, while exploring the possibility of understanding (and domesticating) the unknown world, the "symbolic" literature occasions a need for self-critique. This mode of representation of the other is more dialogic than the "imaginary" literature insofar as it consents to a certain degree of understanding. Seen from that perspective, Evans's writing reveals traces of both modes of representation. For him, the Bosnian Muslim incarnates the history of Europe's intolerance, and this inevitably makes Evans pause—albeit reluctantly and sparingly—to question his view of the Ottoman other. While condemning the Ottomans for their "backwardness" and "brutality," he commends them for being more religiously tolerant than medieval Europe.[34] Thus, it comes as no surprise that he dedicates a large section to the medieval history of Bosnia: The Bogomil/Bosnian tragedy is thematized as a memento mori of the collective value system, so an urgency to recuperate it becomes an imperative with both political and ethical overtones. He writes, "Bosnia was the religious Switzerland of Medieval Europe, and the signal service which she has rendered to the freedom of the human intellect by her successful stand against authority can hardly be exaggerated."[35] Rendered in similar ways by Rebecca West, Anthony Rhodes, and other Western European travelers in the region, this didactic configuration of Bosnia as a site on which aspects of Europe's internal dialectic of good and evil were played out further allegorized the Bogomil tragedy as Europe's "civilizational" responsibility.

Many subsequent writings reflect the same attitude: The stećak is testimony to the enigmatic charms of the oppressed Bosnian culture, now valued mainly for its simple cryptic imagery and vernacular inscriptions. It continued attracting scholars and writers from around Europe who offered new insights into its historical and cultural relevance for European history at large. The "Glasnik" of the National Museum remained the most important medium of promoting and disseminating the accumulated archeological knowledge about the stećak, sustaining interest well into the mid-twentieth century and beyond.

Locally, interest in the stećak occasioned a rekindling of collective memory and a rebonding with the medieval past. Significantly, this process went hand in hand with a tardy and turbulent process of de-imperialization, one of whose facets was the formation of a critical academic (and popular) stance vis-à-vis the history of double imperialization. In that process, the Ottoman and Austro-Hungarian imperial mentalities were also weighed against their attitude toward the Bosnian medieval heritage. Just as the colonizer once formed an opinion on the subject's alterity, the liberated subject turned the table around and began assessing the colonizers' value systems. The Austro-Hungarians became appreciated for exerting efforts to recover the cultural legacy of medieval Bosnia. The Ottomans, on the other hand, who had shown no special interest in medieval Bosnian culture, were denounced for alienating Bosnians from their historical experience and for manufacturing an identity crisis to suit their political interests. Alojz Benac, a former director of the National Museum in Sarajevo, articulated that perspective in the following terms: "Under Turkish domination, the Bosnians and Herzegovinians themselves were in no position to study their art treasures and present them to the outside world. . . . Centuries of Turkish rule impeded the *normal development* of these countries."[36] Resonating quite distinctly with Ivo Andrić's thesis on the Bosnian loss of history,[37] Benac's statement also reflects the Austro-Hungarian vision of Bosnian history as a linear evolutionary process situated within the European (and Christo-Slavic[38]) system of values.

Such a vision inextricably linked the recovery of memory with the ideology of belonging, and the reaction to the two imperial interventions shifted the emphasis from the historical forces that orchestrated their respective positions vis-à-vis the medieval past to the question of civilizational mentality. In this scheme of things, opposing Austrian "sensitivity" for indigenous Bosnian culture to the Ottoman "indifference" (or "ignorance"?) was configured as a show of Austrian solidarity rather than assessed for what it truly was: a colonial strategy of subjugation disguised as a mission of cultural progress. The recuperation of the medieval heritage, in view of the Bosnians who saw European ideals as their own, was conceived in both diachronic and synchronic terms. In other words, it was not sufficient just to patch up times modern with times medieval into a narrative of continuity, but also weave them back into the European cultural fabric at large. "The art of the stećak," concludes Benac, "has an authentic and distinctive style which assures it of a place in the cultural picture of the Balkans and of Europe."[39] Such an assertion of belonging, then, prompted many local medievalists to contrast the two colonial interventions in Bosnia-Herzegovina—Islamic Ottoman and Christian

Austro-Hungarian—on the basis of their attitude toward the stećak: While the Ottomans made Bosnians forget the stećak, the Austrians helped them retrieve it from oblivion. The dialectic of memory and forgetting was thus framed as a clash between two different and seemingly irreconcilable imperial systems, both foreign but only one sympathetic to "what" and "where" Bosnia ought to belong, ideologically and spatially.

Outside scholarly circles and the urban elite, however, the stećak was well integrated into village life. Bearing no explicit symbolic or historical relevance in the "official" national memory of any community—Serb, Croat, or Muslim—it was left to assimilation in nature and by nature. Stripped of its historical framework, it became absorbed by the landscape and reduced to a ruin sustained by nature and the people who lived in its environs. In his study on the collective memory of France, Pierre Nora suggests that the places of memory associated with a national culture are anchors for the present only insofar as they are representations through which that past has been remembered. Modernity transforms them from being repositories of unmediated recollections to being evocations, or mirrors, in which we observe ourselves without ever having direct insight into the lived experience.[40] Taking a cue from Nora, the contemporary Bosnian sees the stećak as a "lieu de mémoire," a site that evokes a sense of continuity, an atmosphere of belonging, but provides no lived experience. Conversely, for the medieval Bosnian the stećak was a "milieu de mémoire," a place permeating everyday life and thus a fountain of living memories. To produce a meaning for the stećak nowadays, then, requires acknowledging that memory is "always embodied in living societies and as such in permanent evolution, subject to the dialectic of remembering and forgetting, unconscious of the distortions to which it is subject. . . . [It] is always a phenomenon of the present, a bond tying us to the eternal present [whereas] history is a representation of the past."[41]

This paradigm, though probably operative in some contexts, can mislead us into generalizing about the nature of the split between modernity and tradition in many places and cultures where that split is neither as sharp nor as relevant. Even in the French case, Jay Winter has persuasively shown that the sites of memory of World War I persist as active places of mourning, and although they highlight a typically modern sense of dislocation and paradox, they are nevertheless phrased in very traditional tropes. He argues that the enduring presence of these tropes is directly linked to the bereavement expressed around the sites of memory of the war and its aftermath.[42] In that sense, the experience of loss and death adds a new dimension to the collective (and indeed individual) memory as it reaches into the traditional modes of mourning. The assumed hiatus between traditional and modern ways of remembering is often effaced by the ways in which actual experiences of loss are narrated. In a similar vein, when in the 1990s Bosnia-Herzegovina was subjected to medieval-style savagery euphemistically qualified as "ethnic cleansing," its extreme Serbian (and in comparable ways Croatian) nationalist choreographers utilized anti-modern tropes of sacred blood and sacred soil to animate highly modern agendas of political, military, and psychological mobilization. It is well recorded that Serbian nationalists, for example, conflated modernity and tradition in the different aspects of warfare, from using weapons of mass destruction (for medieval-style sieges of towns) along with individual execution and torture, through running highly efficient concentration camps, to subjecting their fighters to ritual baptism before they went off to slay, loot, and rape non-Serbian victims. For the victims, the loss of land and material culture necessitated the employment of both traditional (folk songs, dress, customs) and modern (cyberspace, CD ROM, television) methods of truth-telling and remembering so as to keep a sense of identity against the assault.[43] The fact that the people had recourse to traditional expressions of loss and grief challenges Nora's statement that "there is no such a thing as spontaneous memory."[44]

To return to our subject matter, in quite a different but equally illustrative way, the stećak's integration into the life of its surrounding villages can serve as a basis for proposing a third model that would interweave Nora's dual approach to the historical and national object. It is a model according to which lived experiences of the past are never fully erased from the object, and the object, conversely, can never be freely relegated to the past. This can be termed a pentimento of memory: Although the object is continuously recoated with new experiences of temporality, the base coat always shows through. Whereas none of the new coats of meaning can retrieve the original memory, all can lay claim to having interpreted it in one way or another. That the stećak remains alive mainly in the legends and ritual practices of the communities sharing the land with it signals this shift to the third model discussed earlier: the stećak being both place and site of memory. Although the ideas and practices that gave birth to the stećak and its imagery are no longer alive, the stećak continues to function as a site of ritual and narrative evocations. For example, ethnographers record frequent visitations to the stećak for its supernatural, mainly healing powers related to either the harvest season or the cattle's reproductive cycles. In certain highly agrarian communities, the stećak is said to cure infertility not just in cattle but in young women as well. In wedding ceremonies and athletic rituals, it serves as a place of blessing, a *baraka* that is neither divinely bestowed nor divinely sustained but fully embedded in the dynamics of the tradition. Highly localized and cryptic, most of these mythic underpinnings suggest the importance of nurturing a bond of intimacy with the surrounding gravesites because of their unbroken connection with tradition. This results in the community's active need to sanction, in both prescriptive and descriptive terms, the code of behavior in and around the cemeteries. The stories and legends transmitted about the cemeteries dictate a sense of neighborly ethics and awe, allowing the communities of the dead and the living to coexist and interact. Though ruled by different norms, their spaces feed on an atmosphere of mutual dependence and safekeeping. The gravesites are thus kept alive by being conferred a semi-numinous status. Not regarded as sacred ground per se by its neighbors, whose sense of the sacred has been reconfigured—both materially and otherwise—in the course of time, the stećak is infused with an aura of numinosity maintained by an interplay between local memory and social mores. Each graveyard is a narrative site kept alive both through generations of storytellers and through ritual. In that sense, the land held in the possession of the dead simultaneously functions as a *poietic* ground joining collective imagination, ritual practices, and local value systems.

Significantly, confined to local praxis and sustained by the economic and social formations of the people who share land with it, the stećak's numinosity is area-specific. Being of nature as well as man-made, the stećak's ritual meaning remains inextricably linked to the land on which it stands. Stretched through time and implanted in the landscape, the stećak has, paradoxically, become an object in time and space but also a site outside time and space, a phenomenon partly liberated from the historical dialectic that had governed it. This fate of the stećak exemplifies what Roland Barthes observes about myth as it passes from history to nature. In so doing, Barthes explains, "myth organizes a world which is without contradictions because it is without depth, a world wide open and wallowing in the evident, it establishes a blissful clarity: things appear to mean something by themselves."[45] Consequently, the process of rapid change brought about by industrialization and modernization took a toll on the stećak: As the migratory patterns from countryside to the cities increased, the communication between the living and the dead weakened. Furthermore, a physical threat was posed in places where the stećak started to be uprooted, along with the soil in which it was planted, so as to make space for railways, highways, and urban amenities.[46] Paradoxically, however, while modernization threatened the survival of the stećak in its natural setting, it is also thanks to modernity's impact on identity formation in Bosnia-Herzegovina that the stećak's preservation was made possible. The very same development that domesticated the feral landscape that had been home to the stećak for so many centuries turned it into the central motif of historical imagination, and consequently the object of a pedantic cataloguing process. In many ways, then, the stećak's location between modernity and tradition, memory and forgetting, history and myth has made its place in Bosnian culture at once allegorical and real.

THE STEĆAK, THE BOSNIAN CHURCH, AND THE BOGOMIL HYPOTHESIS

As has been noted earlier, many scholars of the Middle Ages and the Balkans have attributed Bogomil origins to the stećak. Significant for this study is the fact that Mak Dizdar too accepted this proposition, turning it into the very basis of his poetry and lapidary exegesis. Although nothing in the names of either the tombstones or the cemeteries suggests a dualist Bogomil connection, there have been other important sets of evidence that have steered discussion of some early scholars of medieval Bosnia in the direction of Bogomil dualism.

The Bogomil hypothesis is closely associated with the examination of *bosanska crkva,* the Bosnian Church, which functioned as the central institution in medieval Bosnian society. Three main theories have ensued from scholarly investigation of the extant sources: First, that the Bosnian Church, founded in schism to both Catholic and Orthodox establishments, espoused dualist teachings—akin primarily to Bogomilism of Bulgaria and, in broader terms, to medieval European Manicheanism;[47] second, that the Bosnian Church was essentially Eastern Orthodox in teaching, and was therefore attacked by the pope primarily in the context of Orthodox-Catholic antagonism;[48] and third, that the Church was independent of both Catholic and Eastern Orthodox influences, fostering a simple form of Christianity permeated with pagan Slavic symbolism and folk legends. In that sense, it was neither "heretical" (that is, dualist) nor mainstream (that is, Catholic or Eastern Orthodox), but local. In support of the third position, the revisionists, lead by the medievalist and Balkanologist John Fine, argue that the Bosnian Church coexisted with other forms of Christianity in the region, and cannot therefore be treated as the sole source of religious authority.[49]

As expected, the differences in scholarly position derive mainly from the ways in which the medieval sources have been handled. Many serious gaps in the primary material were frequently ignored in favor of situating medieval Bosnia into a well-documented history of medieval Europe at large. The result was an acceptance of the authority of Catholic and Orthodox documents without taking into account the fact that local Bosnian sources—whatever was left of them—could offer different insights and clues. Unfortunately—except for the stećak, several Gospel manuscripts, and a few charters—medieval Bosnians left few vestiges of their pre-Ottoman past for posterity. It is thus under these circumstances that the Bogomil theory was conceived, and then well received, in both scholarly and lay circles in Bosnia and abroad. The following is a brief summary of the arguments that went into the making of the Bogomil theory.[50]

The basis of the theory lies in a series of Catholic (papal and inquisitional) and Byzantine sources that identify the eleventh century as the time when Bogomilism spread within Bosnia. Named after its founder Bogomil (literally, "dear to God")—a village priest turned wandering preacher during the reign of Bulgarian king Petar (d. 969)—Bogomilism became the prevalent religious teaching in medieval Bosnia. Most Catholic sources concerned with the dissemination of dualism in Europe make mention of Bosnia as a land in which Manichean heresy found strong roots and devout followers, so much so that it became the official teaching of the Bosnian state in the early twelfth century. In 1180, the sources suggest, as Bosnia began asserting its political and economic power under Ban Kulin, the Catholic rulers were deeply worried about the religious situation in this land. In their correspondence with the pope, they accused Ban Kulin of disseminating heresy, referring to it as "Patarenism" (after Italian dualists), "Bosnian Christianity," or "the Bosnian Church." For example Vukan, the ruler of Dalmatia who supported Hungarian pretensions over Bosnia, says the following about the matter:

> Significant heresy is seen to sprout in the land of the King of Hungary, namely Bosnia, in such numbers that Ban Kulin himself, his wife, and his sister, as well as many of his relatives, have been seduced by the sin, and he has led more than 10,000 Christians into this same heresy.[51]

Needless to say, speculations that dualism, rather than trinitarianism, governed the belief system of the Bosnian population, including their king, deeply worried the pope(s). Over the next two centuries three major expeditions were launched against Bosnia: in 1203, against the Bosnian king Ban Kulin; in 1340 (not an armed campaign but a peaceful Franciscan mission) against King Stjepan Kotromanić; and in 1459, against King Stefan Tomaš. Notably, in all three cases the Bosnian rulers are said to have accepted Catholicism, at least nominally, but the repeated missions and the ongoing concern about the religious situation in Bosnia indicates that the renunciations accomplished through these expeditions bore no lasting effect on the practices of the common folk.

In 1461, Cardinal Torquemada ordered three Bosnian noblemen of dualist persuasion to Rome for interrogation. This was their second subjection to inquisition, which probably suggests that the first interrogation,

conducted locally by the Franciscans, must have assured the Catholic offi-
cials that they indeed had dualists in custody.[52] A trip to the Vatican was
intended as final renunciation. Drafted under the title "Fifty Points," the
document lists fifty articles of dualist belief that were allegedly condemned
by the three noblemen. The document, believed to be fully authentic, has
been very influential in scholarly reconstruction of the religious doctrines
circulating in medieval Bosnia. Though its usefulness is now being questioned, the document serves as an important key for understanding the
main aspects of "Manichean heresy" as practiced by medieval Bosnians.

Of course, the term "Manichean" is to be neither singularly understood
nor interpreted, and Bogomilism is but one of the Western diffusions of
dualist teachings that had originally sprung up in the Near East among
Paulicians and Messalians. What unites the dualists is a bifurcation of the
universe into the corporeal realm of Satan(ael) and the spiritual world of
his brother Jesus.[53] It is Sataniel who created this world (including, out of
clay, Adam) after his expulsion from Heaven. Because of his persistent dis-
obedience to his Father, Sataniel's creative powers were eventually with-
drawn from him, but he was allowed to remain the (sole) ruler of this
world. There, however, he kept on deluding humankind by sending false
prophets to lead them astray. Tired of Sataniel's wickedness, 5,500 years
after the creation of the world God plucked from his heart another son by
the name of Jesus, whom he sent to the Earth as a true spiritual guide to
humankind.

In the ancient Zoroastrian teaching that serves as a philosophical basis
for Christian dualism, the world is composed of the principles of dark-
ness/evil and light/good, and it is only through firm ethical commitment
to the forces of light that salvation can be attained. In subsequent Christian cosmology, Jesus and Sataniel are allegorized as the primordial
light/soul and darkness/body. While Sataniel is given chronological priority as God's firstborn, to Jesus belongs ethical priority, and it is in his
name that the corporeal world must be condemned.

Bogomil cosmology carries important social and ritual implications.
As duality becomes the ontological reality of all creation, commitment to
inner purity as against outer impurity determines the actions of all individuals. Scripturally, for example, the Old and the New Testaments are
counterposed on the account that the former text is of Sataniel's author-
ship (he is thus also referred to as the Wicked Lord of the Old Testament,
and/or as YHWH), while the latter is Jesus's prophetic recital. In ritual
prayers, therefore, the Old Testament is fully rejected. Furthermore, corporeality is avoided through poverty, humility, confession, and prayer.
Such a lifestyle, while revolving around family and community, is doctri-
nally dissociated from any organized ritual, since the workings of the

church are believed to be orchestrated by Sataniel. Correspondingly, ob-
jectifying belief through church, relics, the crucifix, and icons leads to pollution and self-delusion. We learn from different writings on Bogomil
dualism that their diet excluded meat and wine; that their rituals had a
strong family focus; and that they were engaged in passive resistance
against hierarchies as exemplified institutionally by the church and eco-
nomically by feudal landlords.

The Russian historian Alexandar Solovyev, one of the most dedicated
supporters of the Bogomil theory, had a strong influence on Bosnians'
scholarly and popular attitude toward their medieval past (Mak Dizdar
himself, though aware of the debate about the Bosnian Church, seems
greatly influenced by Solovyev in his own readings of medieval Bosnian
texts). Though subtle and comprehensive in exposition, Solovyev's critical strategy is straightforward: Both archeological and narrative sources
are read as evidence of Bosnia's Bogomil character. Using Byzantine
sources to trace the dissemination of dualist teachings from the Near East
through the Balkans to Western Europe, Solovyev zeroes in on the texts
that identify the Bosnian Church as the bastion of Balkan Bogomilism.
With such textual background in mind, he approaches the stećak as an
embodiment of dualist faith and practice. Here are the main points of his
theory as summarized (and also challenged) by Alojz Benac:

> Solovyev holds that the frequently occurring half moon and star symbols
> have their source in the esoteric belief of the Bogomil Church that the sun
> and moon are heavenly ships, "dwelling-places of the souls of the righteous
> before their entrance into paradise." This ancient Manichean and Pauline
> doctrine was deep-rooted among the Bosnian Bogomils.
>
> Still according to Solovyev, the Bogomils, like the Catharists and other
> Neo-Manicheans, rejected realistic images of the Crucifixion, but revered
> the Cross itself and represented it in three forms: (a) anthropomorphic or
> theomorphic; (b) the Greek Cross, and (c) the Cross of Light, i.e., a cross in-
> side of a solar orb. The theomorphic cross symbolizes Jesus Christ himself
> who, "extending his arms in the sign of the cross, vanquished death." Christ
> is also the sun which after the Last Judgment "will shine for all eternity."
>
> Solovyev attaches deep symbolic meaning to the stag in the Bosnian re-
> liefs. He interprets it as a symbol of the righteous soul, and that, in his opin-
> ion, is why it occurs so frequently. The stag hunt, then, symbolizes the soul of
> a man "pursued by the spirit of evil (horseman) and by sins (the hounds)."
>
> The shield motif is explained by Psalter. For the Lord Himself "is my
> strength and my shield."
>
> The round dance, Solovyev tells us, is a sacral motif for the Bogomils.
> And the man with the outstreched arms "denotes the deceased who draws
> closer to Jesus Christ by taking the form of the Cross."[54]

If dualism as suggested by Solovyev and others was indeed the main religious tradition of medieval Bosnia, it is hardly surprising that eliminating it ranked so highly on the papal list of internal affairs. Although Bosnian Bogomils were clearly within the Vatican's reach, the campaigns to set them straight were not nearly as successful as they were against the Bogomils' more Western brothers-in-faith, the Cathars.[55] It is thus a great paradox in Bosnian history that, despite a series of Catholic missions and crusades launched to rid Bosnia of dualism, the fate of this teaching was sealed only after the fall of Bosnia under the Ottomans in 1463. This was not a result of forced conversion to Islam: On the contrary, the Islamic law, based on the Qur'anic verse that there is no compulsion in matters of faith (Q.2:256), explicitly forbids forceful conversion of the "People of the Book" (Jews and Christians). According to some accounts, a relatively rapid and en masse conversion to Islam did take place, to the surprise of the Ottoman authorities themselves.[56] These accounts gave rise to a myth that converting to Islam was a voluntary and unidirectional act of all members of the Bosnian Church, that is, the Bogomils. However, most Ottoman cadastral documents show that conversion did not happen at once but in an ebb-and-flow process over a long period of time and across different trajectories (from and to different religions and denominations). Moreover, some documents mention the survival of the church elders in certain parts of the country even into the late sixteenth century.[57] The increasing evidence that the Bosnian Church gradually lost followers to *all* faiths, not just to Islam, became the focal point of revisionist writings of medieval Bosnian history. It is therefore to John Fine, the leading reinterpreter of medieval Bosnian history, that I now turn my attention.

Although the Bogomil theory was partly challenged even before John Fine, his is the most systematic and well-documented articulation of the Bogomil theory's inconsistencies and problems. In his *The Bosnian Church: A New Interpretation,* Fine addresses the use and abuse of the sources: Whereas Catholic sources have always been given priority, Fine contends that they have been read at face value and in conjunction with sources that do not directly relate to Bosnia. This methodological objection leads him to eliminate larger comparative issues in favor of broadening the set of questions concerned with Bosnia itself. Furthermore, he argues against comparative readings in the instances where comparativism ignores important sociological issues (such as the religious practices of Bosnia's peasant society versus those of the ruling elite elsewhere). Not only does this wider perspective confirm the fact that the dynamics of a religious teaching is determined on the ground and not in scriptures, it also underscores the fact that much of medieval religious practice is lost and unlikely ever to be fully recovered. Having thus in mind the richness as well as the shortcomings of the primary material, Fine identifies three main sets of sources pertinent to the examination of the Bosnian Church that should be read in conjunction with each other: South Slavic records (charters, documents, transactions); Catholic sources (Papal, Franciscan, and Inquisition); and the archeological material (Bosnian Gospel manuscripts, cemeteries, churches). Complementary, but not fully explored yet, are Ottoman cadastral documents *(defters)*.[58]

Although traditional scholarship accepts unproblematically the Catholic characterization of Bosnia as a land of dualist heresy, John Fine draws attention to the lack of precision and frequent inconsistencies in Catholic texts' usage of the term "Manichean heresy." This leads him to suspect the extent of their knowledge of the situation "on the ground." Fine here ventures beyond the first layer of meaning to propose that, although a dualist teaching is likely to have been present in the region, it was neither the official teaching of the Bosnian Church nor the most influential one, but a phenomenon that coexisted with other forms of Christianity. In other words, identifying Bogomilism with the Bosnian Church—as it is commonly done in Catholic sources—is a serious historical misinterpretation. While Catholic and Eastern Orthodox practices in the region were easy to record, access to other teachings and rites was obstructed by several significant problems: language difficulty, physical accessibility, bias, lack of doctrinal debates in the Bosnian Church, and so on. These obstacles, and probably many more, stood between the papal legates and the followers of the Bosnian Church. Consequently, when considered together rather than independently, the Catholic sources do not show a level of involvement and understanding commensurate with the extent of their authority in the region. Concludes Fine, "It also should be pointed out that even though it is likely that there were at least two different movements in Bosnia—the Bosnian Church and a small dualist heretical current—the papal correspondence—through ignorance, design or lack of interest—generally makes no distinctions and lumps all deviants together as 'heretics.'"[59]

But Fine is careful, rightfully so, not to place the burden of misinterpretation only on the Catholic Church. The scarcity and inconsistency of circumstantial evidence that resulted in the Catholic alarm about Bosnia was magnified by the fact that confessional loyalties in medieval Bosnia were neither steady nor ardent, as in many other parts of Western and Eastern Europe. On the contrary: Catholic, Orthodox, and Ottoman observers record considerable shifts in religious affinities throughout this period. Bosnia was distinguished not only for its multiconfessional profile, but also for the fact that this profile was sufficiently relaxed so as to occasion conversions in different directions over a period of several centuries, the most important of which were to occur under the Ottomans in the sixteenth and early seventeenth centuries.[60] Even if vicissitude in religious loyalty was motivated by complex political and other factors (including religious persecution), such flux nevertheless alludes to the fact that interconfessional boundaries were both flexible and porous, and thus generative of a shared set of values that transgressed and challenged confessional exclusivity. Viewed in that light, the stećak can be singled out as the most visible testimony to dynamic cultural interpenetrations.

However, although persuasive and thoroughly analytical, Fine's conclusions are yet to find full acceptance in Bosnian historiography and cultural imagination. The most popular view in Bosnia still holds that the rapid conversion to Islam by the followers of the Bosnian Church was a result of its heavy and systematic persecution by Catholic and Orthodox establishments. The argument that medieval Bosnians were predominantly Bogomil before becoming Muslim lays emphasis on the ritual and doctrinal affinities between the two religious systems—Islam and Bogomilism—particularly in the ways in which they define sacred space and sacred time. Iconoclastic, both religions simplify ritual life into an unmediated relationship between human beings and God. In this sense, the institutional hierarchies that in mainstream Christianity led to a sharp differentiation between the concepts of sacred and profane are replaced in Islam and Bogomilism by the sanctity of all space. Furthermore, since Islam posits itself as a return to the original monotheistic teachings lost in the corruption of Jewish and Christian institutions, the Bosnian Church's exegetical authenticity and purity further emphasize a spiritual affinity between the teachings of Islam and Bogomilism. Transition from Bogomil to Muslim rituals is in this sense reckoned as a continuation, not interruption, of religious practice. Though politically motivated, the cause of mass conversion is thus perceived as intrinsically driven.

One can easily perceive the main merit of this argument from the Bosnian Muslim perspective: In accounting for the complex formation of the Bosnian Islamic community, this argument identifies doctrinal compatibilities between the two religious systems as a motivating force behind voluntary and mass conversion. The emphasis is placed on simplicity, inner purity, and nonconformity as some of the "essential" traits of Bosnian culture, carried over in different forms from medieval times through Ottoman times to the present. But this argument, embedded as is it in the historical imagination of contemporary Bosnians, fails to account for the fact that conversion was a multidirectional process that had begun even before the Ottoman arrival within different Christian denominations, and that the shaping of the Bosnian Muslim community took place over the course of two centuries rather than in one forceful wave. It is not the purpose of this study to problematize in great detail the popularity of this argument, but it seems reasonable to assume that its persistence lies in the national climate of modern Bosnia-Herzegovina. If "communities are to be distinguished not by their falsity/truth, but by the style they are imagined,"[61] it is highly unlikely that either Serbian or Croatian historical imagination would be comfortable with accepting the arguments of their populations' willing conversion to Islam. In both cases, and particularly so in the case of Serbian national identity—which explicitly defines itself against the Muslim/Turkish other—the idea of conversion to Islam amounts to cultural apostasy and damages the image of unity against the "Turkish yoke." Conversely, for the Muslims of Bosnia-Herzegovina, whose historical and cultural identity was shaped by Ottoman Islamic culture for more than four centuries, conversion is explained in teleological terms. In this case, historiography and cultural imagination work together, insofar as they relate the medieval and Ottoman past in connective rather than disruptive ways, that is, in terms of preservation of cultural values and not their loss.

Thus, the argument of the Bogomil character of the Bosnian Church has discursive overtones. It is a narrative that establishes Bosnian identity as separate from Croatian and Serbian ethnogenesis. The myth of origin places Bosnia in a space that lies between Catholic Croatia and Orthodox Serbia. Resting between these historically more powerful national cultures, Bosnia is constructed in this myth as an ethical middle ground of resistance and nonconformity to the black-and-white dialectic of the "self" and the "other." The Bogomil story imbues the universe with a perpetual tension between the forces of evil and good; therefore, depicting Bosnia as the middle ground in which the universal paradox is both understood and enacted underscores the importance of preserving its cultural and geographical identity.

As mentioned earlier, many Yugoslav writers fostered this view of medieval Bosnia and its Bogomil fate. The great Croatian essayist Miroslav Krleža hails its suppressed voices. In his view, by rejecting the existing hierarchies, Bosnia challenged the very foundations of the medieval European justice system: "[These hands] express a challenge, supported by all the moral sanctions of the age, a refusal far more radical than those of Wycliffe, Huss or Luther, to recognize any moral authority."[62] Infused with such a system of representation and signification, the popular imagination was quick in turning the mythos of Bogomil strife into the very foundation of cultural identity. In literary and artistic treatments of Bogomil themes (by such poets as Skender Kulenović, Vuk Krnjević, Svetlisav Mandić and Mak Dizdar, and artists like Dževad Hozo and Mersad Berber), the aspiration was not to verify the historical truth, but to present an axiological understanding of the medieval past. This was a way of resuscitating the memory—to whose damage, ironically, the stećak stood as an enduring witness. Such artistic and literary endeavors can perhaps be best explained in terms of David Price's "poietic history":

> Rather than being held captive by the conventions of epistemology, [the novel of] poietic history provides the perfect discursive space for examining the past by presenting a series of representations of concrete particulars to universal conditions facing every generation. . . . In other words, to comprehend fully the reality of the past we must participate in the process whereby individuals, peoples, and entire cultures and societies figured their futures through imaginative projections of their wills.[63]

But unlike the novelists whom Price discusses in his study, Mak Dizdar and other literary authors and artists situate their own reading of the past within the dominant historical view, that is, without constructing a counter history. Their most significant contribution lies, then, in an attempt to foreground this historical epoch at the expense of the existing national histories, give it a new symbolic value, and thus add a new force to the set of historical conflicts that are said to have shaped medieval Bosnian culture. Dizdar's role in that national rewriting process is central. Contrary to the official national division of Bosnia-Herzegovina, his poetry unifies these three groups around the stećak's imagery and epitaphs. This alternative national sentiment centralizes the Bogomil story as a shared, spatially determined "subjective antiquity." In that sense, Dizdar stabilizes and appropriates the mainstream historical view by establishing continuity between the past and the present, intimating its relevance as a set of personal narratives silenced under the stećak but carved into stone. The stećak thus functions as a stage on which a common national drama is enacted, and its persistence in collective memory signals that all Bosnians, regardless of their present-day national divisions, are involved in its production. Dizdar once explained: "For me, the stećak is but an inspiration to address in poetic terms the existential questions pertinent to all historical epochs. Hence a misconception that my poetry is only a representation of medieval times, or any other for that matter."[64] So if the medieval past is a well from which Bosnian culture derives its identity, then the stećak is its incarnation and a lyrical inspiration without which that identity is doomed to oblivion.

Frontispiece 3: "Vine and its Branches," Radmilja Cemetery. Photo by András Riedl-mayer.

Chapter Three

The Ancestral Voices Speak

Mak Dizdar's *Stone Sleeper*

The previous chapter explored the place of the stećak in the Bosnian historical and cultural imagination. The meticulous process of cataloguing the tombstones and classifying them according to different criteria of monumental art and architecture speaks to the politics of memory in both imperial and postimperial times. Disrupting the stećak's existence as a rural ruin invested with a rich legendary repertory, the archival process set the stage for an appreciation of the stećak's distinctiveness in European cultural history. Situated at a crucial juncture in Bosnia's colonial experience, it paved the way for the stećak's treatment as a historical and cultural treasure, but it fell short of imbuing it with symbolic importance in the Bosnian national imagination.

It is Mak Dizdar who prompted Bosnians to reappraise the meaning of the medieval tombstone and to align cultural selfhood in its direction. The evocative power of his poetry, in contrast to the dry scholarly discourse in which archeological descriptions of the stećak were expressed, immersed Bosnians, both individually and collectively, in the discovery of their "forgotten" past. *Stone Sleeper* is neither purely demonstrative nor overtly prescriptive. Rather, it is configured as a process of disclosure that, much like an archeological enterprise, unfolds as a gradual and fragmentary recovery of memory and a piecemeal unmasking of the enigma surrounding the artifact. Dizdar suggests that *Stone Sleeper*, as a funerary text, must not be treated as a finished product. Set against cultural amnesia and the squalls of national history, it invites the reader to brush off the dust from the lapidary text and assign it a meaning that, neither clear nor finite, sways the collective self-identification into a new direction. Although *Stone Sleeper* speaks about the dead, it is not poetry of mourning because it does not assume either the traditional or modern psychology of elegiac genre. Despite such a formal discord with conventional elegy, however, *Stone Sleeper* initiates a literary communication with the dead, not in an attempt to transform grief into consolation—as is commonly intended in traditional elegies[1]—but to make the medieval deathscape culturally and historically relevant for the living. This attempt expands the literary boundaries of *Stone Sleeper* in that it brings the medieval dead into the Bosnian imagination and establishes a relationship of reciprocity previously lost to both history and memory. In this sense, *Stone Sleeper* aims at a recovery of memory, and through memory, at a more comprehensive spatial and temporal sense of belonging. The pathos of mourning yields to the ethos of remembrance, thanks to which cultural selfhood can be reconfigured. This certainly aligns *Stone Sleeper* with the poetry of postcolonial recuperation and national self-affirmation, more than with traditional elegy.

In treating the stećak as a reservoir of aphorisms that evoke cultural unity despite an ongoing political pressure to disunite, Dizdar extends the stećak's metonymic function. The stećak, in his view, is not just a medieval ruin made meaningful internationally through colonial archeology, and locally through folk wisdom. It is not just a cryptic artifact that adds to the fascination with pockets of medieval Europe. It is a dynamic cultural text, rich with visual and linguistic signs whose decoding can be decisive for the reunification of national selfhood. The stećak draws upon a polyphony of voices that can be released only when the collective focus shifts from archival to cultural memory. To that end, Dizdar treats the burial grounds as a stage on which shared cultural symbols are propped and a national drama is enacted. Constructed subjectively as well as objectively, this drama evolves in both emic and etic terms, insofar as it derives from Dizdar's participation in its performance on the one hand, and from his efforts to articulate its pedagogy on the other. Poetry is thus authorized to recuperate the wisdom of the medieval past by listening to the stećak's silence and identifying its constitutive elements. Historical arguments, archeological findings, folk wisdom, poetic imagination, political conditions, all intertwine in a textured production of poetic meaning.

Negotiating a position both outside and within the framework of the imaginary stage, Dizdar maps the physical and symbolic boundaries of cultural selfhood. He elucidates popular legends and enriches scholarly findings about the stećak with new poetic sensibilities. *Stone Sleeper* is thus a form of ethnography as well as mythography, achieved by one man's incisive intervention into the historical imagination of the Bosnian people. The implications of Dizdar's framing of a *communitas* opens up to theoretical discussions about ethnicity and the agency of its making: As the creative impulse of one poet brings together a politically divided community, we are alerted to the variety of processes in which ethnicity and nationhood can be re-imagined and articulated. If, as theorists tell us, ethnicity is a relation among people who (believe that they) share cultural unity and continuity, including language and religion,[2] then *Stone Sleeper,* in its production and reception, demonstrates the power of poetry to reunite the national culture in a way analogous to great national epics.

Interestingly, most literary critics in the former Yugoslavia have remarked that Dizdar's interest in Bosnian medieval history is unfettered by political and national concerns, which otherwise perturb the writings of most of Dizdar's contemporaries. Dizdar's poetic reflections on the stećak have been viewed as a preoccupation with human nature in general, not with "the political or national myths," as if "human nature" is a reality that resides outside the arena of political culture. Writes one commentator: "In the torrent of national historicism that floods our contemporary poetry, *Stone Sleeper* does not subscribe to either apologetic views of the past or to national narratives which commonly contain more politics than poetry."[3] What is worthy of note in this comment—shared and quoted by other acclaimed critics of Dizdar[4]—is a sense of relief in dissociating Dizdar from the seemingly assertive and unsophisticated tendency of many Bosnian writers to espouse narrow national causes in their works. But as I argued in Chapter One, Dizdar's innovative appeal to the past does not signal his detachment from national imaginings: On the contrary, it is his ability to enrich the conventional patterns of literary representation with a new and incisive construction of Bosnian nationhood that sets him apart from other literary authors.

Dizdar's intervention in the collective imagination is manifold: One, he moves the national clock to the period commonly tossed aside as inconsequential for the issue of national belonging. In so doing, he bypasses the existing national categories of Bosnia-Herzegovina—Serb, Croat, and Muslim—implicitly rejecting the internal partition that is demanded by the institutional discourse on nationhood. Two, he spatializes Bosnian identity by situating it topographically around the stećak gravesites that point to the culture's implantation and naturalization in the landscape. And three, Dizdar turns away from the kind of epic and/or novelistic narration of belonging that exalts national traits as primordial, exploring instead eclectic poetic patterns to create an intertextual tapestry of ordinary voices, images, and biographies that lie embedded in Bosnian soil. While some elements of the epic apparatus are present in *Stone Sleeper*—folk lyric, magic, eschatological invocations, and stories of battles—the overall tone is neither lofty nor didactic, but serene and respectfully human. Unlike the epic world, which is, according to Mikhail Bakhtin, "constructed in the zone of an absolute distanced image, beyond the sphere of possible contact with the developing, incomplete and therefore re-thinking and re-evaluating present,"[5] the world of *Stone Sleeper* establishes between the sleepers and the speakers a poetic freeway along which the past is heeded, the present evaluated, and the future envisioned. The effect is polyphonic, not in terms of ideological dissonance but as a biographical mélange derived from epitaphic messages, and narrated in reference to Bosnian Bogomil mythology. In referring to *Stone Sleeper* as polyphonic, I am skewing Bakhtin's terminology to promote an anti-Bakhtinian argument: Since Bakhtin associates polyphony with the novel and, in contrast, poetry with monologue,[6] it seems incongruous to speak of a book of poetry—*Stone Sleeper*—as a polyphonic text. Yet, insofar as it summons the simultaneity of voices that interactively weave into the fabric of Bosnian culture—rather than limiting itself to the centralizing voice of the poet— *Stone Sleeper* certainly encourages a dialogic communication with the past. In guiding the collective memory through these seemingly familiar moments and locations and phrasing them in condensed, rhythmical lyrics rather than grand, sermonic diction, Dizdar provides his readership with an immediate and exigent sense of national history. He offers vignettes, not a report, about an era gone by. His poetic framing of the historical and physical space enunciates a new possibility for collective identification that indirectly expanded the political narrative of communist Bosnia-Herzegovina. Drawing on the medieval landscape to make topical points about the historical backdrop of Bosnian cultural diversity enables Bosnians to reach out to their shared medieval ethos as a way of affirming the axiomatic link with their land and their ancestors, without denying the divisive legacy of imperial history.

Thus, what is generally interpreted as Dizdar's metaphysical interest in human life is his mastery of constructing a new location as the cradle of national culture that provides all Bosnians, irrespective of their official national groupings or their attitudes to imperial legacies, with a sense of common beginning, cohesiveness, and continuity. Dizdar unites Bosnians in the poetic event that retrieves the visual and social symbols of the funerary text, and intimates that they are both germane to and persistent in contemporary culture. Historical questions surge as both allegorical and real, and the medieval deathscapes proliferate meanings that perpetuate a sense of unity and continuity between and among ethnoreligious diversity. Dizdar's commentators seem to have overlooked this crucial interface between nationhood as understood in the historical and political sense and nationhood as a semiological complex that can both dissuade and stimulate a sense of belonging. Dizdar manufactures this interface by approaching the stećak as a phenomenon standing both within and outside his cultural values, which allows him to both engender new and confirm old expectations about the funerary text. Useful here is Homi Bhabha's characterization of such interfaces as a field of tension between the pedagogical and performative dimensions of nationhood, without which no national narrative can be sustained:

> The people are the historical "objects" of a nationalist pedagogy, giving the discourse an authority that is based on the pregiven or constituted historical origin or event; the people are also the "subjects" of a process of signification. . . . In the production of the nation as narration there is a split between the continuist, accumulative temporality of the pedagogical, and the repetitious, recursive strategy of the performative.[7]

Dizdar builds the pedagogy of the stećak around several semiological clusters: folk tradition with its legendary repertory and talismanic knowledge; scholarly findings instigated by Austro-Hungarian colonizers and carried over, in Dizdar's times, by the Yugoslav cultural institutions; his own repeated pilgrimages to and ritual meditations at the stećak cemeteries; and his assiduous research on lapidary imagery and medieval language published in a prose collection entitled *Stari bosanski tekstovi* (Old Bosnian Texts). In toto, they form the eclectic basis of Dizdar's poetic configuration of Bosnian nationhood, which reassesses the pedagogy of Bosnian political and cultural history. If the pedagogical lies in the poetic articulation/narration of Bosnian nationhood, the performative relies on its reception. Dizdar's effort to overshadow the ethnonational partition of Bosnia with this alternative and integrative pedagogy necessitated encoding it in the social space of contemporary readership. The book's instantaneous success led to his characterization as the greatest poet that Bosnia has ever produced. Meša Selimović commented on the overwhelming popularity of *Stone Sleeper* shortly after its publication in the following way:

> Mak mastered the greatest challenge of poetry, something that very few poets can accomplish. He formed a genuine, spontaneous bond with the tradition, revived the ancient language and found in it contemporary value, and he enriched the sum and substance of medieval inscriptions with contemporary sensibilities and thought. These kinds of innovations make an era.[8]

In a similar vein, the critic Midhat Begić comments:

> Stone Sleeper is a unique piece of Bosnian literature in Bosnian language . . .
> it absorbed into its pages the entirety of the literary—especially poetic—
> and cultural heritage of Bosnia-Herzegovina, creating a linguistic harmony
> between the folk spirit as expressed in lapidary texts and folk poetry as it
> evolved in their environs.[9]

In the absence of shared commemorative attendance to the stećak, or any other collective vigilance over the medieval deathscape—except in highly localized and mutually disconnected forms—the act of reading Stone Sleeper assumes the function of ritual remembrance of the dead. Their voices resurrected through Dizdar's poems, the dead enter the memory of the living, prompting them to reassess their attitude toward the medieval past. The textual conflation—medieval funerary and contemporary poetic—generates a space in which the dead and the living can reinstate a bond of kinship and, above all, sustain a connection where there once was rupture. This recuperative process, in addition to producing a fascinating poetic tapestry, raises important questions about textual mediation in the construction of nationhood. It attests that authentication of the medieval voice is inevitably a dialogic issue, based on the one hand on extensive but filtered understanding of medieval history, and on the other, on the role of contemporary Bosnian readership in the performance and preservation of medieval culture. The two interrelated agencies—of the poet in recuperating the voice of the dead through his verse, and of the readership in reiterating their words—strengthens the feeling of consanguinity between contemporary Bosnians and their medieval ancestors, and opens up a new horizon in the historical imagination.

As stated earlier, in his search for meaning Dizdar drew on several pools of information. In agreement with the dominant scholarly opinion as articulated by the Russian historian Alexandar Solovyev, Dizdar postulated the predominantly Bogomil origins of the stećak. It was his conviction that the linguistic and visual texts carved in tombstones reflect Manichean cosmology and praxis. In contrast to the strictly monotheistic pinnacle of truth, the dualist truth is twofold: light and darkness, corporeality and spirituality, loss and redemption, and victory and loss, constitute perennial but alternating binaries. The autocracy of the monotheist God in normative Christianity is destabilized through the existence of a second source of power, the evil Sataniel, keen on dethroning the good God and seizing the reins over the world. Human beings can never fully grasp the truth about the cyclical cosmic struggle: Caught between good and evil, the best they can achieve is to do good deeds and pray to the good God to return them to the realm of heavenly peace from which they were expelled. Still, the Bogomil God is not the agent of redemption. He offers compassion to those who commit their lives to justice, turning every individual into the agent of his/her own salvation.

Since it was not sufficient to treat funerary motifs as having a purely religious value, mythology required adaptation to real life in order to become an effective national pedagogy. Because Manichean symbols are potentially applicable to all narratives of oppression and insurgency, Dizdar was keen on particularizing the dualist teaching to Bosnian cultural and political conditions. Drawing upon the religious teaching went hand in hand with meditating on its effects on society and culture. The lack of textual and other sources of the period that could attest to the integration of dualist beliefs into the social fabric of medieval Bosnia necessarily turn Dizdar's enterprise into mythography as well as ethnography. In *Stone Sleeper,* the stećak's lapidary motifs are animated through scholarly and folkloric understanding of the Bogomil religion. In turn, as Dizdar transforms the spiritual realm into the political, the medieval Bosnian ethos as conjured by *Stone Sleeper* echoes the mutable structure of the universe: Pretensions to omniscience and omnipotence are discarded as foolish and authoritarian. Cosmic flux, expressed elementally as the shift from night to day, demands that claims to absoluteness be rejected in all forms of life. Since flux is played out at both the spiritual and the political levels, the leitmotif of defiance—to theological autocracy and political oppression—is correlated to mythic episodes in funerary texts and motifs. A poem in an anthology published prior to *Stone Sleeper* enunciates the message as follows:

So even if they beat me defeat me	Pa ako me biju i ubiju i tijelo bace vranu mome gavranu
and toss my body to my crane to eat me	Ako me objese u aleji mojoj aleji na granu moju granu ako me
or hang me in a valley, my valley on a tree, my tree	Mrtav ja biću život živi
and even if I die I still shall be alive.	Živ na dnu mora
Alive, alone in the bedrock of the sea,	Na morskoj pučini nevidljiv
invisible, in the boundless sea,	I ma šta crna mašta zlog boga učini
Against evil lord's any ill-will	živ sam živ
I, still alive, shall live on[10]	

Victory against evil—in the heavens or on the earth—is thematized as typically Manichean, but its stage is set in the landscape claimed as personal possession: my valley, my crane, my tree. The practice of situating Manichean symbolism within Bosnian geography is consistent throughout *Stone Sleeper.* The trope of defiance plays a central role in the application of dualist cosmology to the situation on the ground, whereby defiance actually becomes a function of Bosnian geography and history. As discussed in chapter one, this idea did not originate with Dizdar; it is a commonplace in the Bosnian cultural imagination, often presented as an essential feature of its in-betweenness. But in-betweenness is not even. Because history never repeats itself verbatim, the modalities of historical experience must be refashioned regardless of the world's seeming circularity. In linking defiance as a social response of Bosnians to the cosmic duality, Dizdar underscores the teaching that the cosmos is replete with tension and thus the binaries can never be fully resolved. Life is experienced through ongoing historical and cosmic contradictions that affect everyone, and it is the answerability of individual deeds, to put it in Bakhtin's language, that ensures the survival of the collective. The poem "Wedding," for example, captures well the perpetuity of contraries set as a post-mortem reflection on the passage of time:

With my death my world has died	Smrću mojom umro je i moj svijet
An age-old darkness	U prazne oči
Occupies	Mrak se
My empty	Pradavni
Eyes.	Naseli
With my death my world has died	Smrću mojom umro je i moj svijet
But the world's world	Ali svijet svijeta
Will not be pushed	Neće da se
Aside.	Raseli
Memory's white tape	Sada kroz sudbinske tišine
Pierces the armour of darkness	Bijeli trak sjećanja
Between the silences	Probija oklop
Of fate.	Tmine
And through that strange pane	Kroz čudno okno tog prozora
A deep new	Rodi se neko novo
Eye is	Duboko
Born.	Oko
And on my skyline I see the dawn	Pa vidim na svom obzorju
Rise from	Kako se iz ničeg
Nothing	Podiže opet
Again	Zora

To be born again, to assert oneself as the maker of historical conditions rather than a passive recipient or mute sleeper, is the volition of memory, whose markers are propped in nature as well as culture. Defiance in this poem amounts to giving voice to the soil that has decomposed the flesh of the dead and adopted their sensory abilities. Witnesses to cyclical time, the earth and its dead move from the micro-cosmos ("my world") to the macro-cosmos ("the world's world"), allowing memory to persist from within and without. Defiance thus becomes a collective enterprise of nature and culture, a matter of their mnemonic cooperation against defeat. Dizdar here not only creates a territorial framework for historical events but also politicizes nature so as to align Bosnia's deathscape with its natural landscape.

These forms of poetic rendition and production of myth in poetry shed a different light on Barthes's argument that poetry and myth are mutually exclusive endeavors. Arguing that poetry cancels out myth insofar as it "assassinates" its tendency to turn human creativity to ideological ends, Barthes deems their roles irreconcilable: "Whereas myth aims at ultra-signification, at the amplification of a primary system," he writes, "poetry tries to recover an infra-signification, a pre-semiological state of language."[11] The inauthenticity of myth and the authenticity of poetry set them apart as contrary modes of signification: Myth manipulates language so as to present itself as a factual system, while poetry penetrates language so as to get to the facts of things.[12] In *Stone Sleeper*, however, the two modes—myth and poetry—interrelate in an attempt to add texture to historical findings and, at the same time, legitimize popular imagination in scholarly discourse.

How Does the Subterranean Speak?
Disclosure and Mimesis as Poetic Acts

Because neither the collection nor the motivations propelling it happened *ex nihilo,* an analysis of *Stone Sleeper* makes most sense if one goes back to the time before the poetry came to life. With several trends and genres converging in its pages, *Stone Sleeper* testifies to the interpretive eclecticism invoked by Dizdar's encounter with the medieval tombstones. Though potentially multidirectional, the analysis here springs out of the interface between the external and internal loci of Dizdar's work: the unmediated presence of the medieval tombstone in his creative imagination, and the scholarly and folkloric material that frames his interpretation of it. The gift of voice given to a stone image through poetry is a dialogic moment of disclosure of interpretive possibilities lying between the politics and poetics of nationhood. Disclosure, an act variably applicable to every work of art, refers here to the moment that turns a tombstone, the mute object of Dizdar's curiosity, into the speaking subject. The voice is excavated from earth through stone to poetry.

Disclosure, then, is the outcome of a process that has a dual beginning, at least—in historiography as well as autobiography. Dizdar's frequent excursions to Radmilja, one of the best preserved medieval cemeteries located

at the outskirts of his hometown Stolac in Herzegovina, seem to be etched
on his psyche as numinous moments of self-affirmation. He explains:

> For hours I have stood among the stećci of this land, in their cemeteries
> scattered at the feet of the ancient forests. Various symbols—the sun, twin-
> ing plants, outstretched human hand—have entered into me from the huge
> stone tombs. At night I have been assailed by notes scribbled in the margins
> of ancient books, whose lines scream question after question about the
> apocalypse. Then the sleeper beneath the stone comes to me. His lips open,
> limestone-pale, and his dumb tongue speaks again. In him I recognize my-
> self, but I still do not know if I am on the way to unveiling his secret.[13]

The feeling of awe experienced in the presence of a stećak is intertwined
with a sense of estrangement. Revelation is juxtaposed to mystification;
movement, visual and auditory, is juxtaposed to stillness. But the sensation is not paralysis; it is akin to what Michael Fischer terms "ethnic anxiety," that is, a feeling of uncertainty generated by the sense of loss of
cultural rootedness.[14] Dizdar expresses this anxiety as an experiential and
intellectual challenge that, if met, can recuperate the meaning of the lapidary text and initiate a dialogue with the stone sleeper in whom Dizdar
"recognizes himself." The urge to resolve the mystery of the stone is thus
mimetic and self-referential, albeit not in the Cartesian sense of transcendental self-confirmation but in historically specific, dialogical connection
with the cultural roots. "Ethnic anxiety," Michael Fischer suggests, "is re-
lieved by establishing continuity with the past where previously there was
breach, silence."[15] With Dizdar's efforts to establish continuity, the immobility of a stone image is now transformed into a movement through poetic space. The subterranean subject is stirred but never uprooted from his
bedrock, from his land.

As already suggested, Dizdar's approach to the stećak does not silence the
existing discourse about it. His understanding of the medieval phenomenon
is mediated by its construction in the colonial and later communist discourse on Bosnia, as well as folkloric imagination. He draws upon both
modes of knowledge, blurring the line between the instigators and the re-
cipients of records. In this respect, Dizdar's poetry is a form of postcolonial
protest insofar as it modifies the detached scholarly initiative around the
stećak with empathetic folklore, but without ever succumbing to the limitations of either. Although Dizdar's poetic act is deeply embedded in the colonial findings—since he too is a product of their circumstances—it is within
these parameters, which had actively and discursively shaped his knowledge
of medieval Bosnian history, that he creates space for a new subject location.

Intimating it lyrically in *Stone Sleeper,* Dizdar lets this new subject location complicate the relationship between the authentic and inauthentic, subject and object, colonizer and colonized. The living and the dead are brought into the controversies of scholarly findings and localized folk values. They meet in the political interface between testimonial and inferential, subjective and objective, past and present. This act of poetic resistance to colonial appropriation of the stećak, and to the stećak's fragmentation in popular lore, pays homage to all authors and readers—past and contemporary, apocryphal and real—of funerary images and epitaphs.

In the poetic medium, the ambiguity surrounding knowledge of the stećak is never fully resolved. The veil is never completely lifted. Even after Dizdar's effort to know the stećak, it eludes Dizdar as much as it bestows on him a sense of rooted comfort. The process of writing becomes at once external and internal, personal and public. The medieval mystery is objectified on "the brink of primeval forests" and "the margins of ancient manuscripts," and the quest for it gains a spiritual dimension, at least at the rhetorical level. In Islamic mystical tradition, for example, the metaphor of unveiling so as to "know thyself" emphasizes that the mystic traveler is caught up in a perpetual paradox of movement: The more she or he ascends toward the summits of "Truth," the more deeply she or he descends into the self. In the Sufi tradition, the ability of the mystic to encounter "Truth" is predicated on his or her ability to remove the veils (*kashf*) from the inner self, as per the Qur'anic verse 41:53, "And We shall show you Our signs on the horizons and in yourselves—do you not see?" The link with absolute meaning is achieved through a descent, step by step, into the inner self that embodies the workings of the universe.

The theistic principle that propels the mystic's journey in Islamic tradition is, in *Stone Sleeper,* replaced by an ethical and political commitment to cultural memory. Dizdar's imperative is to capture the vibrations of the lost world by tracing the genealogy of Bosnian national culture, as an antidote to the fractures caused by imperial intrusions. His inner self, negotiated in relation to the collective self, forces him to seek unity for himself and his collective. The "I" is archetypal insofar as it compresses the multivocality of the event into the unity of the national pedagogy. The individual "I" retains its integrity but also expands in association with the *communitas* with which it culturally and historically bonds. The feeling of individual displacement is always counteracted by the feeling of cultural placement. Dizdar's poem "A Text about a Spring" expresses that convergence of outbound and inbound forces of selfhood in the following way:

I dissolved	Rastvorio sam se
And streamed	I potekao
Streamwards	Potocima
Riverwards	Rijekama
Seawards	Morima
Now here I am	Sada sam tu
Now here I am	Sada sam tu
Without myself	Bez sebe
Bitter	Gorak
How can I go back	Kako svom izvoru
To whence I sprang?	De se vratim?

Return, then, like Dizdar's ritualistic return to the Radmilja cemetery, happens also in the poetic text. *Stone Sleeper* is that recuperative text. In Bogomil teachings, return is a primordial aspiration by the fallen angels who long to be taken back to the heavenly realm:

The earth is sown with a deathly seed	Zemlja je smrtnim sjemenom posijana
But death is no end for death indeed	Ali smrt nije kraj Jer smrti zapravo i nema
Is not and has no end for death is just a path	I nema kraja Smrću je samo obasjana
To rise from the nest to the skies with the blest	Staza uspona od gnijezda do zvijezda

If death is just a path, the graveyard is its point of departure, the space that arrests but also liberates life. *Stone Sleeper,* in turn, is a framework in which the deceased, condemned to silence, speak again as members of "our" lot. Their values, once deferred, are reawakened and reflected on through the mirror of history. In eliciting, to rephrase Stanley Fish, a specific "community of interpreters,"[16] Dizdar enables his poetry to counteract the loss of memory and turn the burial ground into a site of remembrance. The still images are incitements to action. But since actions happen in history, their meaning can never be fully fixed; rather, their meaning must be sought in the context of our times. As the aphoristic poem "Hand" puts it: "This hand tells you to stand, and think of your own hands" (Ova ruka kaže ti da staneš i zamisliš se nad svojim rukama).

The stone hand neither explains the course of its deeds nor does it dictate it to the living one. Instead, it demands self-reflexivity—"return"—that blocks out mechanical replication and appeals to interaction. Propelled by a mimetic impulse, one hand ("this hand") becomes the mirror for the other ("your own hands"). Michael Taussig suggests that mimesis is both a faculty, activated in human behavior in response to the outside world, and now a practice of modernity reliant on the machines of replication and representation of otherness. Mimesis can therefore not be separated from history because it is through contact with the outside world that the faculty is exercised. Taking a cue from Walter Benjamin's observation that "the gift of seeing resemblances is nothing other than a rudiment of the powerful compulsion in former times to become and behave like something else," Taussig suggests that the compulsion to imitate and duplicate the other must rely on historical tools.[17] In Dizdar's case, mimesis grows out of conviction that the two historical subjects, facing each other in physical proximity but through ontological as well as political distance, ought to meet in the poetic space where layers of separation are not erased but perforated. His tools are history and mythology. It is through these perforations that common language can be found and a dialogue induced. The process is therefore not one of mechanical duplication but of the search for common cultural traits and actions which, in Dizdar's view, are incised in the historical experience of the Bosnian people. The identification of a shared condition turns the medieval alterity— frozen in time and amassed as a stone sanctuary—into an interactive configuration of the self. Dizdar's treatment of medieval deathscapes as ethnographic material, embedded in the land and buttressed through folklore and scholarship, culminates in the returning of the self to its cultural roots. His poetry is thus not a simple imitation of lapidary text: It is a medium that replaces the stillness of the medieval gaze with a voice negating the solitude of death. In the poem "the garland," he says:

And whosoever will see let his eyes be unlocked	Pa neka otvori oči kto hoće da vidi
And whosoever will hear let his ears be unblocked	Neka otvori uši kto hoće sada da čuje
Let one eye spy and scry the coast and cliffs all round	Jednim okom nek odmjeri i žali i hridi oko nas
Let one eye seek inside him till his voice be found	Drugim nek zadje u sebe duboko da nadje svoj glas
For the time is at hand	Jer je vrijeme blizu

The process of return is one of recuperation that allows Dizdar and his readership to relieve the sense of "ethnic anxiety." In literary terms, too, recuperation is a formal process that allows the reading of one text through another. It is contingent on the act of doubling, where the original is at once effaced and made accessible through the mediation of another text. Jonathan Culler warns that recuperation manipulates the quality and nature of signification by making the intermediary texts say only what we want to hear, not the reality of the original. Recuperation then functions as a form of closure, whereby the meaning is produced as a form of displacement from the original to the intermediary.[18] Yet in *Stone Sleeper* the structuralist principle of recuperation comes about as the process of disclosure, not closure. Partly thanks to the poetic genre in which no word and every word can be final, and partly due to his intertextual efforts, Dizdar stretches the elasticity of interpretation at every creative contact with the funerary text, assigning it a unique pedagogy in the Bosnian cultural imagination. The pedagogy is *disclosed*, as it were, not *imposed*.

INTERNAL ORGANIZATION AND
THEMATIC MOVEMENTS OF *STONE SLEEPER*

The coming to life of *Stone Sleeper* was a long and arduous process that can be traced back to the early stages of Dizdar's career. Before their final publication in 1966, a number of poems had appeared in Dizdar's previous collections and/or literary journals. For example, the poem "Gorchin" was first published in 1956, a full ten years before the appearance of *Stone Sleeper,* with a footnote announcing a new cycle entitled "Sleeper under the Stone." Similarly, the poem "Lullaby" was first published in 1953, while "A Text about a Spring" and "A Text about the Eyes" are found, albeit under different titles, in the 1960 poetry collection. "The Swan Girl" and "The Languished" were first published in Dizdar's 1963 poetry collection *Knees for a Madonna* (that also included the second appearance of the poem "Gorchin"). Finally, the poem "A Text about the Five" had originally been composed during World War II, and, because of its politically sensitive content and his activism in the resistance movement, Dizdar had written it in Arabic script as a strategy of self-protection.[19] This poem, incidentally, is one of the rare contemporary Alhamiado compositions, a genre that combines Slavic language and Arabic script and that enjoyed quite some popularity among Bosnian Muslim poets in Ottoman times.

Enes Duraković, the acclaimed Bosnian critic of Dizdar's work, suggests that *Stone Sleeper* should be seen as a product of several streams of poetic creativity that can be found in earlier collections but that joined forces in this final collection of his career. But 1966 did not mark an end to the making of this collection: A second revised edition appeared in 1970 and yet a third in 1973, two years after Dizdar's death.[20] To quite a considerable degree, differences among the three editions indicate that the ideas spinning out of the ongoing dialogue and gaze between Dizdar and the medieval subjects never brought about complete disclosure. To put it in Dizdar's own language, the modifications of the text attest that the veil of mystery has never been fully lifted. Identity remains in the process of figuration, without the fantasy that it could ever be complete.

Overall, then, *Stone Sleeper* underwent several structural revisions and internal modifications between the time of its conception and the final version. Ironically, the third edition is not the most comprehensive because the changes undertaken between 1966 and 1973 were not simple additions in composition but complex reorderings of individual poems, including a number of exclusions and abridgments of the originals. These compositional modifications did not affect the critical reception of the book. On the contrary, *Stone Sleeper* maintained its popularity in all its versions, but it is the third edition, despite other interventions, that has been accepted as definitive. The cumulative effect of these interventions is well summarized by Enes Duraković:

> *Stone Sleeper* amasses and assimilates the totality of Mak Dizdar's poetic experience. In fact, *Stone Sleeper* follows the path of his creativity and poetic destiny, points to the diversity and wealth of his enterprise, and highlights it as a unique and powerful synthesis. Everything that had informed the mood and quality of Dizdar's poetry over a thirty-five-year-long career appeared anew in *Stone Sleeper* with a new aesthetic maturity and clarity, and ridden of the weak and unrefined ingredients.[21]

In terms of its composition, the third edition contains three out of the four original cycles: "A Word on Man," "A Word on Land/Earth," and "A Word on Heaven/Sky." The fourth cycle, "A Word on the Word," is removed from the final edition, thus erasing what initially could have been the poet's conscious identification of four textual locations on which Bosnian culture and nationhood can be imagined and experienced. The fourth cycle posits "language" not just as a mode of communication but as a determinant that both desensitizes the process of self-figuration and rejuvenates it by virtue of introducing new phonetic, semantic, and syntactic possibilities to be placed into and taken out of medieval Bosnian. Whereas in the first two editions language is treated as the subject in its own right, not just a mode of communication, the third edition reassigns it a primarily instrumental value. In this study, however, all four textual locations are considered, as they form the analytical framework through which *Stone Sleeper*'s themes, motifs, and ideas about medieval Bosnian culture can be addressed, and their allegorical functions explored.

In the third edition, two autonomous poems, "Roads" and "Message," function as the prologue and epilogue to the main body: "Roads," suitably, suggests the paths into the collection, whereas "Message" provides the reader with an exit, an ending that encapsulates both the moral and philosophical overtones of the collection. Their demarcating presence draws attention to the issue of thematic coherence: If poetry collections are generally not concerned with linear progression and narrative structure, what cohesion should one expect when crossing such textual thresholds in and out of *Stone Sleeper*? An answer may lie in Dizdar's decision to intertwine fiction and truth, transcendence and immanence, spirituality and politics. As a way of balancing these seemingly opposite platforms, the internal/poetic and the external/scholarly, "Roads" and "Message" sharpen the reader's ability to dislocate the "sleeper" from his subterranean domain and situate him into the cultural imagination. "Roads" thus sets the tone and mood of the collection by identifying the historical moment from which the subterranean subject speaks. It draws attention to the struggles—political and theological—against the assimilationist Other:

You've decreed me not to be cost what may	Ti si nakanio da mene nema i pod svaku cijenu
Weeping with grief and joy	Ideš prema meni i u jurišu
You charge me down	Smijući se i plačući
You cleanse and destroy	Pred sobom
Everything in	Sve čistiš
Your way	I ništiš

This opening stanza evokes an atmosphere of suspense on the eve of complete destruction. The destruction is not an act of God, but an act of those who claim to be emissaries of God against the vanquished people of Bosnia. The cause-effect is clear, as it stems out of the particular theology of self-righteousness. Power relations between the speaking "I" and "you" of the poem are ostensible. A similar tone is perpetuated in "Message" as well, but there the perpetrator takes a more identifiable form. Referred to as the armed northerner in the first stanza, he epitomizes the bankruptcy of ethical values that happens when religion joins forces with political power:

You'll come one day at the head of an armoured column from the North	Doći ćeš jednog dana na čelu oklopnika sa sjevera
And reduce my city to rubble	I srušiti do temelja moj grad
Smugly saying	Blažen u sebi
To yourself	Veleći

Now it is razed	Uništen je on sad
And razed	I uništena je
Its	Nevjerna
Faithless	Njegova
Faith	Vjera

Significantly, the "you" and the "I" in both "Roads" and "Messages" are historically framed: The speaking voice of the poem belongs to the Bosnian *krstjan* (Christian, but primarily the follower of the Bosnian Church) labeled as heretical and targeted for obliteration in the crusades of 1203 and 1459. The "you" is the powerful, determined, and merciless ecclesiastical Other, set out to eradicate a community of people because of their heterodoxy. In both poems Dizdar speaks from within history, not allowing his poetic voice to slip away from the course of events that turned medieval Bosnia into a site of destruction. The tone is brusque and noisy, but also bitter and spiteful. The immanence of invasion is clear as the crusaders, driven by their sanctimonious and military disposition, zero in on the enclosed space of Bosnia. Loss and death are a reality that can neither be delayed nor deterred. In "Message":

And secret and sly as a Western spy	Pa tajno ćeš kao vješt uhoda sa zapada
You'll burn my home to the ground	Moje žilište sažeći
Till all	Do samog dna
Fall	I pada
And then you'll say these dark words	I reći ćeš onda svoje tamne riječi
This nest is done for now	Sada je ovo gnijezdo već gotovo
This cursed cur	Crknut će taj pas pseći
Is slain	Od samih
With pain	Jada

But as the stormy entry into the land of the Bogomils portends destruction, it also signals, at a metaphorical plane, the crossing of the book's threshold. The power of words pierces its first page, mimicking the medieval conquest. Yet, life in the enclosed space about to be ravished seems unwilling to accept defeat. It challenges the self-assurance of the Other. In this place, no truth about human fate, other than its uncertainty, is upheld. Defiance fractures the intrusive proclamations of defeat and loss ("and you'll laugh you'll roar that I am no more"), negating the fact that inevitability equals finality ("But by a miracle I will still be dreaming here on earth"). Thus, in both poems the fragility of human life is challenged by the belief in its endurance, while the claims to truth, theological and political, are affronted by an appeal to difference and ambiguity. The power relations between the conqueror and the conquered are inverted, and the survival of the latter is made into a strategy of resistance:

You've decided to root me out at any price	Ti si nakanio da me pod svaku cijenu uništiš
But nowhere will you find	Ali nikako da nadješ
The real road	Istinski put
To me (. . .)	Do mene (. . .)
Your path to me poor though I be	Ti misliš da je tvoja putanja do ubogog mene
Seems sure and tried	Veoma sigurna i česna
In your sight	Ona
A path that comes	Što dolazi
From left	S lijeva
Or	Ili
Right	Zdesna
You fool yourself I can be found	Zavaravaš se stalno da do mene treba ići
By setting your course	Smjerovima sličnim
For north	Sa sjevera
Or	Ili
South	Juga
But that's not all	Ali to nije sve

And in "Message":

But then you'll be amazed	I čudit ćeš se potom kad čuješ kako
To hear me walking through	Ponovno koračam
The city again	Tih po gradu
Quietly stalking you	Opet te
Again	Želeći

In the past decade, the poem "Message," still uncompleted at Dizdar's death, regained much popularity for its alleged prophetic quality: The image of a society under attack evoked uncanny analogies with the 1992–1995 siege of Bosnian cities, leading to Dizdar's characterization as a visionary "who best conveys the common fear about the destruction of Bosnia and its people."[22] Indeed, to many Bosnians this is not a historical coincidence; as if imprinted in their national destiny, the image of Bosnia's perpetual strife against domination and assimilation, so poignantly encapsulated by Dizdar's poems, is deeply etched in the collective memory.

A Word on Man

In the first cycle, "A Word on Man," Dizdar focuses not on the scriptural basis of the dualist teaching but on anthropological concerns: Human beings are fallen angels whose souls, tormented by bodily incarceration (*inclusi in corpore*), aspire to be released. Their life thus centers around the desire to be free. As suggested before, according to Manichean teachings, the binary opposition of body and soul as captivity and freedom is a manifestation of the primordial conflict between evil and good. Prompted to reconcile the particularity of their conduct with the universality of their existence, human beings are caught up in the struggle with forces that are at odds with their aspiration to be free. But does the primordial conflict deter, rather than encourage, historical intervention? Here is where Dizdar's own dualist tendencies are put to the test: Can he exorcise life from the cycle of cosmic predetermination and treat dualism as a historical pattern to be swayed, broken, and perhaps reversed by human agency? Against the Manichean *allegory* of good and evil, which is heuristically attributed to colonial narratives of their civilizations' superiority, Dizdar starts with *historical* Manicheanism that, he believed, produced the funerary text that contained pleas against cultural amnesia. He does not develop his poetic fantasy around a simple reversal of roles, of victims becoming victors and victors victims with the stroke of his pen. Yet, unless the fixed polarity between the victim and the victimizer is destabilized, resistance cannot happen except as the manifestation of cosmic will unaffected by historical struggle. Thus, in an effort to remove the theistic predetermination to continue speaking from within the Manichean system of values, Dizdar reinforces the atmosphere of ambiguity that compels every individual to self-criticism. He makes a mnemonic effort to represent indisputable religious facts as never fully within the purview of human cognition. Dealing with the strategy of resistance, he focuses away from the macrocosmic field of tension between evil and good and turns to the self as the prime locus of the struggle to shake off the rhetoric of certainty about the world. While this may appear as an inappropriately individualistic approach to medieval culture, the I's eye is foregrounded but never fully separated from the divine eye/I. The middle stanza of "Roads" evokes this relocation of Manichean categories from metaphysical perpetuity to human activity in a way that, it is worth noting, resembles the Qur'anic teaching on personal strife. The poem reads:

You don't know that in your life	Jer najmanje znaš da u svome žiću
The one true war	Najteža rvanja su
The hardest strife	I ratovi pravi
Is at your very core	U samome biću

Indeed, a highly sociological ambience dominates the "A Word on Man" cycle. Shortest in terms of its composition, the cycle consists of five poems. Ordered numerically as five aphorisms, the poems follow a spiral sequence, zeroing in on the message that the conflict between captivity and freedom is the dialectical principle of life, and that it is up to every individual/collective to accommodate it. The stylistic organization of the five poems resembles five concentric circles, in which the largest one mimics God's eye/I and the smallest matches the mind's eye/I. In the first poem the dualist aporia is presented as intrinsic to human life and thus unencumbered by human intervention. Gradually that changes, and in the last poem cosmic determinism is inscribed as the individual challenge within which life gains value only in reference to human action. In shifting emphasis from the essential to the existential, the theological dimension of the aporia raised in the first poem cascades into a series of social questions about the condition of human life. The "First" poem reads:

Born in a body barred in with veins	Satvoren u tijelu zatvoren u koži
Dreaming that seven heavens descend	Sanjaš da se nebo vrati i umnoži
Barred in a heart bound into brains	Zatvoren u mozak zarobljen u srce
Dreaming the sun in dark without end	U toj tamnoj jami vječno sanjaš sunce
Bound in your skin ground into bones	Zarobljen u meso zdrobljen u te kosti
Where is the bridge	Prostor taj do neba
To heaven's thrones?	Kako da premosti?

The visual contrasting of human anatomy as a viscous mass to the sun as a smooth and perennial source of light—the circular grouping of the poems—echoes medieval imagery. The intermeshing of bones, blood, and flesh ("bound into brains," "barred in a heart," "ground into bones") intensifies the feeling of discomfort, despite its organic (and organized) quality, while alluding to the perseverance of sensuous experiences within the tomb. The tomb, the ultimate symbol of life's finality, is represented as an extension of imprisonment. Dizdar here collapses the common assumptions about the separation between life and death: In moving from living flesh to mute stone without a visible rupture in the quality of experience, he unites people in a cause, not in ontological location. The cause—liberation from captivity—thus extends beyond the visible horizons of one's life and persists as the axis around which participants in culture—both those who live and those who once lived—can bind. Movement and action are necessary even when people are not free. The "Fifth" poem expresses this message quite well:

In this kolo of sorrow not leader not led	U tom kolu bola ni potonj ni prvi
You're a tavern of carrion a maggots' bed	Igrište si strvi i ročište crvi
Robbed from its body the tomb acts alone	Zaplijenjen od tijela greb za sebe djela
But when will this body Be an act of its own?	Kad će tijelo samo da Postane djelo?

In the "Second" and "Third" poems the Bogomil teaching of the bodily encasement—*inclusi in corpore*—feeds into the memory of spiritual freedom. The impulse to break away is, in effect, a desire to return to this primordial memory. The body is both the experiential site of oppression and its multifaceted symbol. In fact, moving from the cosmic to the political, and eventually personal, in response to the social and cultural conditions of poverty reflects the multifarious effects of oppression. Colonial presence features quite prominently in this process: After all, what is colonialism but "incorporation" of the faceless, powerless subject by a higher force into a framework whose workings, distant and imposing, leave him only with his body as the witness to injustice, and with a dream of salvation? The closing lines of the "Second" poem poignantly link the exile from good fortune with the loss of homeland:

Cast out of heaven you thirst wine and bread	Otrgnut od neba žudiš hljeba vina
When will your home Be your homeland instead?	Al u domu tvome Kad će domovina?

A Word on Heaven/Sky

An extension of the first one, the "A Word on Heaven/Sky" cycle turns the reader's attention to the interplay between culture and the persistence of memory, collective and individual, in nature. In Manichean cosmology, *zemlja*, in the double entendre of earth and land, and *nebo*, of heaven and sky, are elemental and ethical opposites. While the earth/land harbors captivity, the sky/heaven reflects the positive force and salvation. It is a space that seems out of time, that shelters memories and preserves hopes, and it is contrasted to the dark temporality of the material world. It stands for freedom and affirmation of the "self" against earthly mortality and decay.

But "sky" is also a text through which medieval Bosnians learned about the cosmic order. The sky's transcendental plane brings together human aspirations to be free of historical and geographical limitations, in that it inspires their creative impulse. The sky imprints Bosnian Bogomils' experiences of the natural order as well as their memories of historical time.

Epistemologically, however, the earth and the sky are not very different. Overlooking the land, and life as it passes from one generation to another, the sky acquires anthropomorphic qualities. Like the earth, as suggested earlier and discussed in more detail later on, the sky oversees the passage of time and records human experience of the world. Yet in spite of its seeming immunity to spatial and temporal limits, the sky too succumbs to the dualist cycle. The overshadowing of its blueness in the nocturnal cycle does not signal heavenly demise. Heavenly light and darkness alternate visibly to the human eye, confirming over and over again the Bogomil belief that duplicity governs all creation. The infusion of the sky's vastness with specific mythological allusions opens to a set of associations between nature and culture. By analogy, the death of an individual does not put an end to the collective: Culture and common values continue being shaped within and outside the limelight of history, in mediums that are both material (stone) and immaterial (sky, memory).

Probing thus the relation between the temporality of human life as captured in stone imagery and the infiniteness of time as exemplified by nature, the cycle "A Word on Heaven/Sky" alerts us that the natural world is susceptible to cultural shaping. This is where lapidary motifs of nature become animated through poetry. Remarkably eclectic and nonlinear in terms of its composition, the 27 poems that constitute the cycle form an uneven cluster of aphoristic rhymes, free verse poems, narrative segments, rhymed prose, and folk lyrics. Unlike the first cycle that addresses human captivity and perpetuates an atmosphere of entrapment of the soul, the second cycle liberates human beings by empowering their imagination with creative impulse. The clarity of biblical fusion between divine creation and human expression yields to a more uneven relationship between the experience of the natural world and its representation in stone. The artisan, poet, community, and nature all join forces in the production of meaning. Here Dizdar foregrounds the different links in the creative chain, starting with nature and ending with culture. In between stand common people and artisans, scholars and poets, myth and history. The cycle thus bursts with fragmented images of life that are neither metaphysically nor visually static since they depend on such disparate cognitive endeavors. This exuberant atmosphere, constructed from the stećak's imagery, is recycled back into nature, transforming the Bogomil tension between mortality and immortality into a series of incomplete comments about culture. This kind of poetic ecology enriches the already complex link between nature and culture insofar as it diversifies the signification of the stećak's imagery. The transformation of limestone into tombstone, and tombstone into text, allows Dizdar to explore these multiple yet historically mediated associations between nature and culture. Consider, for example, the following two poetic animations of nature: The first one focuses on the lunar and the latter on the hunt motif, both of which commonly occur on the stećak. The first poem is entitled "Moon":

From the thick dark of a weary day the delicate	Iz guste tame dana na umoru iznikao je
young face of a moon appeared above our heads	ponad naših glava mlad i nježan lik mjeseca
Now he sails the whole wide reach of his sky	Sada plovi cijelom širinom svoga neba
waking those who have lost themselves	budeć iz snenosti one koji su sebe izgubili
Before he tires of his shining journey	Prije no što se umori na tom sjajnom putovanju
before his waxing falls out of step	i prije nego što u svom rašćenju izgubi korak
(before he's swathed on every side in white and silver hair)	(i dobije okolo svih svojih strana bijelu i srebrenu kosu)
Carve his sign in the soft white of a millstone	Ureži njegov znak u mekoj bjelini miljevine
so you may absorb as faithfully as can be	kako bi mogao što vjernije upiti u sebe sliku
The image of your infinite pain and hope	Svoje neizrecive boli i nade

Following the orbit of the moon from its birth out of the vestiges of the fading day, through its passage along the infinite sky, to its anchoring in the funerary artifact, the poem submits the two constructs—nature and culture—to an intense interplay. The nocturnal idyll depicting the luminous tranquility of the new moon turns into a statement on the bleakness of the human condition. But their encounter yields to the dualist myth that the moon is a vessel that delivers the dead to heavenly peace. The cultural reproduction of nature—the sky/moon motif carved in limestone—brings together belief and historical condition: Against a life of deprivation and poverty, the moon is the cyclical reminder of a better future. In fact, the lunar movement within the poem follows the conventional rite-of-passage sequence: the original separation of the moon from its place of birthing, the liminal time of its "shining journey" as if without purpose or end, and its capture in the limestone where the moon is invested with a new symbolic purpose. Although the rite of passage is a pattern delineating sacred space and time in the ritual life of a community, the poem above successfully integrates nature into that social cycle, facilitating a fusion of the two constructs. The moon is appropriated by art as a reminder that salvation is facilitated by the lunar disc that trespasses the sky on a nightly basis. The effort to enact the Bogomil ethos through this celestial movement points to the psychological importance of finding solace in nature against suffering and mortality. The stećak thus functions as the social medium that ascribes to culture a role in nature—and, conversely, to nature in culture.

A similar treatment is applied to frequent lapidary representations of hunting which, art historians tell us, suggest two interpretive possibilities: literal, whereby the hunt reveals the social status of the deceased by being depicted as his favorite pastime; and allegorical, as it conjures the Bogomil myth of the chase of the soul by the horsemen of the netherworld. Dizdar's "A Text about a Hunt" toys with both readings, blurring the distinction between the realistic and metaphorical, subject and object, hunter and prey. Consequently, the reader is encouraged to keep in mind both interpretations and to reflect on how art and language can transcend their own limitations. The poem opens with an idyllic portrayal of a pristine forest where a gushing spring creates the image of water flowing out of the page and out of time, in an unceasing movement that has neither beginning nor end:

An underground water wakes
    from deepest sleep breaks free
and streams through a clear and
    glorious dawn
towards a distant river
towards a weary
sea
	Neka se podzemna voda budi u
	    jasnom sjajnom ozoru
	iz svog dubokog sna i teče nekoj
	
	dalekoj rijeci nekom
	umornom
	moru

This outbound, linear movement of the water is intercepted by other sets of movements in the second, third, and fourth stanzas, each assuming, spontaneously, a different direction but each clearly choreographed by an invisible author. The atmosphere is one of forest traffic: A fawn is looking for the water spring, a doe is searching for its offspring, a stag is following the doe. The segments of action, while still idyllic, disrupt the water's cosmic tranquility and create suspense. The reader, as a hidden voyeur, becomes the broker of that atmosphere of tension in which danger lurks from afar. Indeed, the following stanza robs the forest imagery of its transcendental purity as the hunter disrupts the scenic frame and charges toward the prey:

A tall horseman masters seething
   spaces of unrest
Handsome Dumb with deep desire Blind
without a sound he tramps behind
the baying and howling of hounds
panting thirsty straining for the
   blood of future
battlegrounds

Jedan konjik velik osvaja vrele
   prostore nespokoja
Lijep Slijep od velje želje Nijem

Bez glasa on gazi za lavežom pasa
Što urla što žedno diše i
kidiše u krv budućeg

rozboja

Again, we cannot decide if Dizdar treats the hunt motif as figurative, descriptive, or both. A closer reading suggests that he toys with both levels of meaning, since the imagery of pursuit as he lays it out suggests figurative and descriptive processes of signification. Furthermore, concurrent references to all episodes—the spring, the animals, and the hunter—reveal the simultaneity of all time-lines. While every subject in the poem is both the observer and the observed, there is a sense that one voyeuristic presence is beyond everybody's field of vision. The location of the invisible onlooker, physical and epistemological, propels swift and erudite connections between the sequence of events, enabling narrative shifts from one frame to another. While the voyeuristic presence is in theological terms applicable only to God, in literature (especially poetry), the author commonly assumes the impersonal role of the objective teller. Here, however, uncertainty about the mode of signification—literal or metaphorical—makes identification of the unknown omniscient ever so difficult, although his authority is made unequivocal:

I see it all in a second in this day's
   sun
As if with a glance
Of a hand

Vidim sve to u jednom trenu u
   suncu ovog dana
Kao na dogledu
dlana

In what follows, the authoritative voyeuristic "I" shatters the initial idyll with a series of dramatic disclaimers about the seeming predetermination of the forest commotion:

I know that starveling sparkling
   spring will never enter its distant delta
its gentle shelter I know that
   source
will never caress its pebble of pure
   quartz

Znam da nikada onaj gladni
   harni vrutak neće ući

u daleko ono ušće u svoj krotki
   kutak
da nikada zagrliti neće svoj čisti
bjelutak

The restive doe will never hear the tiny cry that greets her trails her tails her through the cover will never hear the bleats of mother No more will the stag climb the cliff and never again will he bell his reply to the green cry of the green rain Nor will the tall horseman hunts- man splendid in his battledress amid the cavalcade and all its show ever loose that battle arrow from his bended bow	Košuta brižna više nikada neće čuti onaj mali glas što pred njom ide što prati je kroz vlati što nikad neće više reći mati Na stijenu onu propeti ljeljen neće se nikada više na onaj zelen zov one zelene kiše odazvati Ni konjik tragač velik u sjajnom bojnom odijelu usred sjajne tragačke svite nikad odapeti neće iz sulice vite onu ubojnu strijelu

So, who is it that speaks here with so much confidence? Who can offer such macro-visions of every movement in nature? With the different planes of signification at hand, the hierarchy of authority descends from God's heavenly eye to the poet's creative "I," then to the hunter, and, finally, is pinned down to the "I" of the lapidary artisan. Through prolepsis, the mason alerts us to his memory of things seen and experienced, and now shaped by his art. The forest idyll is thus turned into a plot of his lapidary choreography that laid out the physical world with the strokes of the chisel:

For in that single instant that split second when rapt in self all were hunters and utterly alone I Grubac the hewer did hunt these hunters down threads unseen them I writ with humble wit them I truly drew in the height in the white of this stone	Jer u tom jednom jedinom trenu u tom magnovenju kad sobom obuzeti bjehu goniči svi i sasvim sami Te strašne lovce ulovih u nev- idime konce ja kovač Grubač i vjerno upisah i smjerno narisah u ove vele u bijele u kâmi

The world of nature is posited as the construct of the artisan's imagination. It is mediated through cultural artifact, and even further in the poetic composition. The filtering of the natural world through several modalities underscores, once again, Dizdar's complex understanding of culture as being inseparable from nature. The initial atmosphere of the divinely predestined motion of the natural order is now reworked as the medieval experience and representation of nature. Funerary representations of the natural world, Dizdar seems to suggest, are valuable not for their appeal to the universal, trans-historical quality of nature but, quite to the contrary, for their ability to relate the natural world to cultural conditions. Even in the seemingly unmitigated images of wilderness the cultural filters cannot be ignored: They replace destiny with history and align the external world with the cultural imagination. Divine creation is thereby made relevant only as serial cultural re-creation.

A Word on Earth/Land

Identity in space is identified here as the central concern of Dizdar's poetry, one that will be treated at length in the following chapter. In attaching Bosnian nationhood to land, Dizdar opened a dynamic dialogue with the issue of spatial belonging, which also implied negating the tripartite division of Bosnia. Medieval Bosnia, the land clearly demarcated as an independent political entity before the imperial conquests, was a home to Bosnians—not Serbs, Croats, and Muslims as the national categories would later have it. Returning Bosnian land to Bosnians of all confessions implies removing the discursive content that informs modern political constructions of Bosnia and replacing it with something more immediate, spatially more continuous, and culturally more integrative.

To this end, Dizdar's focus on the mountainous countryside of Bosnia-Herzegovina away from the clamorous modernity of urban space grounds nation-narration in the simplicity and "authenticity" of an unconquered homeland. This space amplifies the voice of the individual, echoing it through a seemingly unbound void. Human intervention in the natural space is concretized only through the deathscape. A sense of aesthetic harmony is rather compelling, melting away the demarcation line between human-made gravesites and the land in which they rest. This is a common poetic strategy; as Elisabeth Helsinger argues, rural life and national life are often made to appear as wholly natural.[23] However, Dizdar's aim is not to recreate a rustic idyll in order to exalt folk spirit. His impulse is medievalist, not folklorist. Thus, although the voice of the dead does not dissolve into the polyphony of urban voices and choices, remaining singularly clear, its place in society at large is imbued with the existential dilemmas of a society on the brink of destruction. Alarmed by the fear of oblivion that naturalization may entail, culturally more than physically, the individual and the local are allegorized at once as the collective and the universal, absorbing in itself the totality of a culture and history. In "A Text about Time," from the second cycle, Dizdar says:

Long have I lain here before thee	Davno ti sam legao
And after thee	I dugo ti mi je
Long shall I lie	Ležati
Long	Davno
Have the grasses my bones	Da trava mi kosti
Long	Davno
have the worms my flesh	Da crvi mi meso
Long	Davno
Have I gain a thousand names	Da stekoh tisuću imena
Long	Davno
Have I forgot my name	Da zaboravih svoje ime
Long have I lain here before thee	Davno ti sam legao
and after thee	I dugo ti mi je
Long shall I lie	Ležati

Despite the relatively small circumference of the physical space of which Dizdar writes, its importance is measured by the antiquity of its gravesites. The temporal coordinates in the above poem firmly lodge the dead into the deep layers of Bosnian soil and authenticate it for past, present, and future generations. The subterranean entity dwells as a witness to the naturalization of culture by the landscape. He guarantees its continuity and reminds the posterity of its complex attachment to the land.

The cycle "A Word on Earth/Land" reveals that necessary double-entendre in which politics and space converge: Like the Bosnian word *nebo* that can mean either sky or heaven, *zemlja* is both land in the political sense, and earth, soil, in the geological sense. The importance of *zemlja* is therefore conceived in multiple terms—economic, agricultural, political, and psychological. This cycle of poems clearly reflects Dizdar's consideration for the implicit and explicit aspects of the attachment between the land and its people. Although not all these poems are built around the land motif, all are staged on this land. Consisting of 22 poems, the cycle tells stories about the people who passed and lived in the land. The imagery varies, from domesticity to perilous journeys and campaigns, from boastful declarations of wealth to pitiful laments on poverty, from lyrical reflections on fragrant flora to exasperated cries over the barren soil. Every stride of the wild beast, every prance of the horse, every bud, every footstep, and every grave conjure up the medieval landscape as cultural property to be reclaimed and reinstated by the historical subject against claims of denial. In "Lilies":

And while you're quietly walking	I kada tiho izmedju procvalih cv-jetova
Between the blossoming	Zamišljen tako
Flowers	Prolaziš
Perhaps like me you'll think of those	Možda kao i ja pomisliš na one koji su
Who've quietly walked here	Prije tebe ovuda tiho
Before you	Prolazili

A Word on the Word

The last thematic cycle further centralizes the issue of cultural continuity, this time through language. As mentioned earlier, however, the cycle is in a way experimental, appearing in the second but not the third edition of *Stone Sleeper*. Given its limited existence, the cycle is introduced here as an aspect of Dizdar's larger concern with the aesthetics of language on the one hand and, on the other, with language as the marker of national culture. This is not to say that linguistic interplay between modern and medieval idiom is not probed in other parts of the book. On the contrary, it is present throughout, but in this cycle it is both the medium and the object of poetic reflections. The cycle consists of 16 "words," identified numerically from "First" to "Sixteenth," each evoking the generative power of language while acknowledging its contingency on the larger cultural context. The word *slovo*, which in modern Bosnian means "letter," was used in medieval Bosnian in the sense of "word." The word and the letter thus form the fabric of the same complex, fusing the oral and scriptural dimensions of Bosnian language. Insofar as *Stone Sleeper* embodies the coming together of script and word, every *slovo* represents a form of doubling in which the stone speaker speaks while the poet writes. This doubling connects the two modes of communication—oral and written—and also warrants a form of semantic recycling in which words cease to be used in their original form. Every *slovo*, by sheer virtue of being declared, textually or verbally, confirms the vitality of linguistic culture but also betrays its limitations. As "Fourteenth" enunciates:

The greatest of all is the word foretold	Najveće je slovo što se samo sluti
The deepest of all is the word untold	Najdublje je ono što u nama ćuti[24]

Stone Sleeper's interplay between the spoken and the unspoken takes a cue from the stećak's epitaphs. The paradox inherent in the epitaph of both announcing and denying death, of disrupting as well as perpetuating mortal silence, shapes Dizdar's attitude toward poetry writing. The unmasking of funerary meaning comes in uneven bursts of luminosity and enigma, at times self-representational and at others descriptive, which necessitates that poetic language be deemed unstable and vulnerable as much as concentrated and precise. Part of that interplay is in Dizdar's lexical experiments: Through reviving medieval Bosnian idiom, Dizdar also introduces new phonemes, coins new words, and probes new syntax so as to enrich the lexical texture of his poems. These experiments draw on Dizdar's intertextual imagination insofar as he reaches out to folk poetry, aphorisms, liturgy, and other available sources in an effort to conjure up the flavor of medieval idiom. The doubling of speech—the original and the neological—adds a new sense of continuity between modern and medieval linguistic culture, highlighting the necessity to produce meaning contextually rather than intrinsically. As Karen Mills-Courts rightly points out, poetry must be situated between the presentational and representational workings of language. The interweaving of presence and absence, analogous to the epitaphic gesture, situates poetic speech "between the desire to present the thing itself and the knowledge that language can only stand in place of that thing."[25] The ambiguous state renders poetic speech as much ghostly as incarnative, and this quality, at least in Dizdar's observation of funerary text, is ascribable to language in general. The poem *"bbbb,"* inspired by what looks like funerary graffiti, points out to its ambiguity that allows us to have faith in language but robs us of the ability to count on its semantic durability:

Words are everything and words
    are nothing at all
(And even these that I utter
Dust is already choking with its pall
And sweeping into the road
The gutter
And the dust falls more and more
For
Words wither and age the instant
    they're stated
And are ignored
By the rabble in the street
By the thirsty faces
At the seminary
Door)
But a new word is what we're waiting for

Riječi su zapravo sve i riječi upravo nisu ništa
(Pa i na one ovdje izrečene
Prašina je već gusta pala
I odvela ih na kolovoze
Do kala
I prašina ta još veće pada
Jer
Mada kazane tek sada

One u hipu postaju uvele i stare
I za njih više ne mare ništa
Ni gomile sa ulica
Ni žedna lica
Sjemeništa)
Ali se čeka nova riječ

In the interplay between speech and silence, however, the ethical dimension appears as important as the aesthetic or semantic. Silence exists not just as a mode of communication, but as a catalyst intimating a psychological response, an ethical commitment, or a pattern of behavior. All too convinced that unsaying may be as powerful as saying, Dizdar's message conveys the pedagogical and political importance of keeping silent. "Lullaby," a poem excluded from the third edition of *Stone Sleeper*, expresses it in the following way:

In life you must be wise and discreet	U životu treba mudro da šutiš
And when you speak	Al riječ kad rekneš
Let your word be laden as any truth	Neka bude teška kao svaka istina
Let it be worthy of mankind	Neka bude rečena za čovjeka[26]

Silence can thus be a form of linguistic empowerment, just as speech is. The two modes of communication nurture each other and ensure that language is understood in its wider sense—as a dynamic system kept in constant tension, as Martin Buber would argue, by its speakers' experience of self and the world around them.[27] Expectedly, however, Dizdar configures this as a dualist tension, so that linguistic continuity is understood in its exoteric and esoteric manifestations that alternate and thus bear witness to the cyclical motion of the world.

This dualist conception of language also extends into the political arena, in which the existence of a Bosnian language has been contested despite evidence of its historical existence. As discussed before, in the age of national awakening among South Slavs, the dominance of Serbian and Croatian paradigms suppressed the category "Bosnian" from all national nomenclatures. This ideologically propelled denial of Bosnian historical continuity in the national narratives of Serbia and Croatia has encompassed linguistic autonomy too. Ironically, when the linguistic reformer Vuk Karadžić codified the national language of South Slavs, he based it on the dialect in Herzegovina, which, he argued, was the purest of Serbian dialects. The fact that the region that inspired Karadžić's linguistic research (though he never visited it!) lies barely a hundred miles from Dizdar's birthplace, which contains some of the best preserved funerary examples of medieval Bosnian script, is a political irony that ought not be overlooked. Karadžić's search for pure folk expression that could achieve linguistic unity for South Slavs was disrupted, over a century later, by Dizdar's poetic reanimation of a language whose preservation in manuscripts and funerary inscriptions testifies to the vigor of medieval literacy.

In fact, his effort undermines the claim to the region's folk purity. In what amounts to an act of resistance against the institutional amnesia of the Yugoslav academe, Dizdar's poetry asserts the language's literary integrity in medieval times, in contrast to the national nostalgia for folk spirit. In his poetic intervention, it is not just the history of orality but the history of literacy that legitimizes the national culture.

The texture of this language, while not completely distinct from the one that served as the basis for canonical language, nevertheless demonstrates a different kind of cultural expressivity. Here Dizdar goes further to mimic medieval expressions in his use of modern words and phrases. To the uninformed reader, these neologisms appear fully authentic, not like a mimetic experiment in the phonetic and lexical patterns of the medieval idiom. But there is no intention to deceive the reader; on the contrary, linguistic play is but another strategy of reconnection that enriches Bosnian folk and literate culture by redirecting it toward the source from which all expressions, modern and medieval, derive their etymologies.

This, of course, does not challenge the established notion of low literacy rates in medieval ages: As medievalists argue, it is quite likely that the presence of literary tendencies could not eschew the overwhelming oral tradition but found a way of coexisting with it. This is especially noticeable in oral-formulaic writings—of which funerary inscriptions can be said to form a part—since the authors of such texts were aiming them at an audience familiar enough with formulaic rhetoric to interpret such texts accordingly.[28] Significant in the case of medieval Bosnia is the employment of four different alphabets, usually in response to liturgical practices. The presence of the three churches—Catholic, Orthodox, and local Bosnian—occasioned the usage of Latin, Cyrillic, Greek, and Glagolitic scripts in accordance with confessional, and ensuing regional, criteria.[29] The Glagolitic script, used in Bosnia most commonly by the *krstjani*, was also associated with Dalmatian Catholics, and some claim that its pervasiveness was a decisive factor in the shaping of Croatian national culture.[30] In Bosnia, on the other hand, Glagolitic by and large faded away due to two central factors: First, it was eschewed by the increasingly common Cyrillic script from the early thirteenth century onward, when the psalter tradition, apocryphal stories, and many other Church- as well as non-Church-related writings started appearing predominantly in Cyrillic (albeit with regular textual interventions in Glagolitic). Second, and more decisive for sealing the fate of Glagolitic, was the advent of Ottoman imperial culture that rapidly absorbed local converts to Islam. The disappearance of the Bosnian Church following the Ottoman consolidation was instrumental in the demise of the Glagolitic script on which the Church had relied all along.[31] Hence, contemporary

Bosnian literary culture is decisively severed from its Glagolitic precursor, and much of the medieval idiom remains alien as well. Yet the importance of reviving some of its elements amounts to instituting the pedagogical dimension of nationhood where the performative is not sustainable. The poetic intervention authenticates the medieval language, whereby *Stone Sleeper* is conceived at once as the original and translation; the poems in ostensibly autochthonous idiom (albeit not written in Glagolitic script), are accompanied at the end of the collection by a glossary of terms explicating the grammar, syntax, and semantics of the lost idiom. But the glossary has the opposite effect: In highlighting the differences it also reinforces common threads, tracks the etymology of expressions common in contemporary slang, establishes a sense of continuity between words. This effort of the collection to translate itself while mimicking the original at once demarcates and bridges the space between medieval and contemporary linguistic cultures. It is here, then, that the split between Bhabha's pedagogical and performative, object and subject, becomes most visible: the former, in an effort to understand the latter, maintains it in a temporal elsewhere. It preserves its integrity by association, not analogy, with the language of contemporary readership. The pedagogy, then, lies in accepting similitude, not parity, as a road to unity and continuity. Again in "Wedding":

With my death my world has died	Smrću mojom umro je i moj svijet
But the world's world	Ali svijet svijeta
Will not be pushed aside	Neće da se raseli

Linguistic culture is thus always in the process of becoming. As the semiology of deathscape continuously evolves, the understanding of the funerary text must be built around anthropological concerns as much as its constitutive scriptural or visual elements. The poem "*bbbb*" repeatedly conveys the message that the semantic flux requires the production of meaning to be contingent on the context of one's time:

As if on wild waters some words swiftly come and still more swiftly go	Kao niz brzu vodu nekada riječi dodju brzo i još brže odu
Some patiently wait for the moment they dream	Ima ih koje dugo čekaju svoj sanjani čas
Some recklessly rush to let off steam	Ima ih što bezglavo jure svoju tjeskobu
Anywhere and any day	Na bilo kakav dan i bilo kakvu slobodu

A word only becomes a word	Riječ je tek tada riječ ako
When its meaning becomes a	
feeling	Za nju i čulo steknemo
And the greatest may	Najgolemija je nekada ona
Be the word we do	Koju i ne
Not say	Reknemo
The self-same word	Jedna te ista riječ
When it enters the chest	Nije ipak ista
Is a different word	Kada ulazi u
When it is	I izlazi iz
Expressed	Ulišta

LAPIDARY IMAGERY AND EPITAPHS
IN POETIC RENDITION

The transition from funerary silence to poetic utterance intertwines two central texts of lapidary art: images and epitaphs. Treated as complementary, the two form the basis of *Stone Sleeper*'s compositions. Although there is a sufficient number of formulaic images and inscriptions to attest to a considerable degree of uniformity in lapidary aesthetics, it is through their different combinations, based on historical interpretation, folklore, and the poet's imagination, that the texture of Bosnian medieval culture is woven. Because of the lack of consensus, scholarly or cultural, on the meaning of most funerary motifs, *Stone Sleeper* probes several relational modes between image and text in an effort to test out the nature of their reception by both medieval and modern audiences. With no master key into the stećak puzzle in hand, then, Dizdar situates *Stone Sleeper* between scholarly research and folk tradition, advocating that the meaning of lapidary art be established in a conscious and complicit predilection for poetic rendition of the two modes. When combined, folk legends bring common folk into the scholarly enterprise and enrich its vocabulary with talismanic knowledge and local relationship with the stećak gravesites. Conversely, scholarly findings validate folk legends by creating objective grounds, as it were, to enhance their connection with Bosnian culture at large.

Since, according to Dizdar, visual and written texts reinforce each other's meaning and establish a link between cosmology and history, almost every one of his poems draws on the universal and local, channeling the production of meaning through both frames of reference. Words and images are considered as having parity. This features as the organizing principle of Dizdar's poetry: Instead of epic narrations of medieval history or grand narratives of primordial nationhood, Dizdar focuses on verbal and visual fragments so as to conjure the episodes in individual lives that make up, through their beliefs and practices, an indissoluble unity of Bosnian culture. Describing neither lofty births nor chivalrous deaths, naming no heroes or villains, and giving no hope of immortality, each poetic fragment reconstructs an aspect of dualist cosmography and the realm of the (un)known. *Stone Sleeper* thus comes to the reader in a staccato presentation of individual voices and fluid images, and not as an orchestrated symphony of formulaic messages and immutable symbols.

The assumption that there is linguistic and pictorial parity between the two lapidary texts prompts Dizdar to treat them as if they were emblematic art. Didactic engravings composed of visual and scriptural signs, the emblems are based on the premise "that the image and the word—the "body" and the "soul" of the emblem—join to create a total effect richer than that of either component alone, that the two parts are commensurate and reinforcing."[32] While Egyptian hieroglyphics may constitute proto-emblemic art reflecting complex epistemological connections between word and image, the emblem became popular in Renaissance Europe and especially among Jesuit educators in the seventeenth century. Maturing thus through the biblical exegetical tradition as well as the methods of the classical *ars memorativa,* the emblem demands that its meaning be produced by treating visual memory as a prescriptive narrative. Such engravings that bring together image and word force the mind to focus continuously on both modes of representation. As Gilman suggests, "In Jakobson's terms, the relationship between word and image is, potentially, at once metonymic and metaphoric: metonymic in that the two complete each other sequentially and as parts of a whole; metaphoric in that each translates into the other's medium. Ideally, image melts into speech, speech crystallizes in the immediacy of the image."[33]

Of course, Dizdar's treatment of the stećak is neither formally nor substantially typical of emblematic genre. The lapidary texts do not compromise Dizdar's poetic freedom as he does not present them as a didactic imperative. He does not fix a particular image to a particular inscription, and as such, does not think of their relationship as conclusive. Although the stećak, like the emblem engravings, juxtaposes the image and the word, their mutual dependence is not explicated. Yet *Stone Sleeper* does channel the production of meaning by unifying word and image, connecting stone and poetry in such a way that image and text become transported and arranged as if they were emblematically connected. Expanding as it were the emblematic *ut pictura poesis* ("poetry as image") equation, *Stone Sleeper* proposes the *in poesis pictura* mode whereby the poetic language maintains the iconicity of the stećak while animating the range of its associations. Without poetry, the two texts remain disconnected in the historical imagination of modern Bosnians despite their juxtaposition on the stone. Through poetry, they interlace, generating a sense of consonance and assonance between medieval and modern Bosnian culture. As a bonus, most poems also achieve acoustic beauty through this same principle. For example, consider the "*kolo*" motif: a circular dance traditional to the region, the *kolo* is depicted on many stećaks. As Benac puts it, "we feel the most powerful rhythm in the representations of the *kolo:* the figures move in measure, the feet beat out the time; we almost seem to hear the muffled note of the *tambura,* a kind of mandoline, or of the shepherd's pipe, accompanying these dancers graven in stone."[34] In Solovyev's interpretation, on the other hand, the *kolo* is a sacral motif associated with Bogomil soteriology.[35] In Dizdar, both interpretations are present; the stone *kolo* is set in motion, and the rustic atmosphere is captured as the rhythm of life on earth, a routine leading to liberation. This is where the Bogomil soteriology enters: Human beings, originally angels expelled from Heaven, are imprisoned in bodies and forced to wait until the Last Judgment before their soul can be released to heaven:

Hand in hand	Ruka do ruke
bound in a bond	luka do luke
Hand on hand	Ruka u ruci
salt on a wound	muka u muci
Earth pulls down heavy	Zemlja priteže
heaven is high	nebo visoko
Were I a falcon	O da sam ptica
then I would fly	da sam soko

The poem thus mirrors the rhythmical movement of the round dance while intimating the common human destiny as reflected by the intertwining of hands and the sharing of misfortune (the fourth line, "*muka u muci*" in the original, literally means "misery in misery"). But another spatial reference, the up-down in addition to around, extrapolates the dualist tension between the earth and the sky, freedom and captivity. The poem is laden with religious symbolism, folklore, and political message. There is a flow of meaning, one into another, in the same rhythmical way in which stone dancers seemingly perform their act.

    Another worthy example of the conflation between image and word is the poem "*bbbb,*" inspired by an enigmatic alphabetical repetition of the letter "b" found on one stećak. Whatever its historical explanation, the inscription motivated the making of one of the longest and most textured compositions of the anthology, consisting of 14 stanzas/narrative segments originally presented as 14 separate poems. Whereas the poem does not iconically represent the visual motif, it nevertheless responds to its spatial ordering by virtue of juxtaposing related themes in an open-ended way, the way that the letters "b" seem to be sequenced on the stone. Spanning different ideas yet playing with aposiopesis in most of them, the poem challenges the reader to think about the notions of language, creation, and representation without pairing the lines in any definite way. In that sense the poem fosters a tension between different forms of expression between word and image, from sensory and mental configurations of the world, to motion and stasis:

A word is the image of a world we see and do not see	Riječ je slika svega onoga što okolo sebe vidimo i ne vidimo
Some words we acclaim but some give us shame	Riječima se nekim divimo a nekih se riječi opet stidimo
Some words come to stay and some hide away	One su se nastanile u nama i one su pobjegle od nas
Words all have their colours and smells	On imaju svoj miris i boju
Some words have a tongue	One su nemušte ili
And some	Imaju
Are dumb	Glas

The poem speaks clearly about ambiguity, giving a sense that what one sees on the stone—bbbb—is laden with hidden meanings waiting to unroll. The onus is placed on expanding the interpretive possibilities rather than treating the sequence of *slovos* (letters/words) as just the sum of its parts:

And so I'm still not sure	Je ne znam još uvijek dakle kako
What my word to Thee must be	Da oslovim Tebe
Hence I have only my poor	Pa ostah stoga na svome hudome
B and B	Be i Be
B and	Be i
B	Be
(Lord	(Bože
Forgive me	Oprosti mi
That I only arrived	Što sam tek došao
Back where I'd started so hope-ful-hearted)	Tamo odakle sam pun nade i pošao)

In many ways, then, *Stone Sleeper* treats lapidary imagery as signs that lend themselves to different modes of signification. In semiotic terms, these modes can be assessed in accordance with Charles S. Pierce's triad classification of signs into icons, indices, and symbols.[36] According to Pierce, the icon relies on the similitude between sign and object (signifier and signified) insofar as it denotes the visual qualities of the object it refers to. For example, a diagram is a form of iconic depiction, deliberately simplified and unambiguous, and comprehended because of a resemblance between the signifier as the signified. The index, on the other hand, establishes a metonymic relationship, either in terms of causality (illness→fever) or contiguity (smoke→fire). It points to, rather than resembles, a connection between the signifier and the signified. Finally, unlike the iconic reliance on similitude and the indexical on pointing, the symbol depends on a convention between the signifier and the signified. In that sense, the symbol is more of an arbitrary sign, demanding a culturally habitual association with the object or concept it signifies. That the crescent moon and the sun are "dwelling places of the souls of the righteous before their entrance into Paradise," is, according to Alexandar Solovyev, an ancient Manichean and Pauline doctrine that came to be deeply rooted in the Bosnian religious imagination.[37] This, then, is neither a matter of similitude nor indexical pointing, but of a convention produced and sustained in specific historical circumstances.

While the complexity of semiotic analysis varies between linguistic and extra-linguistic signs, its application to funerary art can shed some new light on the directions to which the interpretation of any given image could be taken. Drawing on a composite source of information, Dizdar's reading of the visual motifs suggests various iconic, indexical, and symbolic interpretations. But the meaning cannot be simply produced: It relies on leaps of poetic imagination in which intertextuality plays a pivotal role. Mitchell argues that "the world may not depend upon consciousness, but images in/of the world clearly do. An image cannot be seen as image without a paradoxical trick of consciousness, and ability to see something as 'there' and 'not there' at the same time."[38] Dizdar's poetic interpretations of the stećak motifs reveal his own "trick of consciousness," manifested as a skill to activate a set of static images into movement with the help of any of the three types of signification. The poem "The Rightwise" is a fine example of such blending: Here, Bosnian folk tradition that refers to the dead lying under the stećak as "good people" meets the Sufi concept of the "perfect man" (al–insān al–kāmil) on the one hand, and, on the other, the local belief in the stećak's healing powers. Although this particular poem embraces all three possibilities, one and the same motif can signify different things in different poems of the collection. The common hand motif, for example, is at times interpreted as denoting just that—the hands of the deceased:

I bore these hands like two banners	Kroz kamen živi nosih ruke dvije
through fields of living stone	kao dva znamena

| But now in the stone's heart these tired hands are living on alone | Sad ruke ove trudne žive u srcu tog kamena |

Elsewhere, the hands are treated as imperative pointers, in a metonymic sense, to the ethical questions about human deeds: "This hand tells you to stand / and think of your own hands." In yet a third version, the hand is suggestive of the bridge between the earthly and heavenly realms. Writes Dizdar in his Notes to *Stone Sleeper*: "The hand motif, especially that of a hand turned toward the sky, is very common. If combined with celestial symbols of sun, moon, and stars, it stands for worship because celestial bodies were deemed to be vessels transporting the soul of the Krstjani to the hereafter." Buttressed by religious culture, the symbol is modeled in the act of "reaching out," in an upward trajectory, aiming to put in line different realities, earthly and heavenly, and give them a sense of common purpose. This reading is based on the thesis championed by Alexander Solovyev that the man with the outstretched arms "denotes the deceased who draws closer to Jesus Christ by taking the form of the Cross."[39] Here is Dizdar's rendering of the symbol:

| With hand raised high to the endless sky To the mighty signs around me I say this day My daily words braided from the grave Which halted me in this aching move To magnify the pain on the way To Him | S podignutom rukom do beskraja neba Znamenjim veljim oko sebe velim Sva nasušna slova spletena od greba Što me zaustavi u kretanju bonom Bol da pojača na putu Ka onom |

Other motifs too are expanded in their signifying potential: Animal and floral representation, celestial bodies, and various inanimate objects continue to surprise us as rich and fluid signifiers. While the repetition of these motifs indicates the breadth of their reception in medieval times, the sensibility of the modern viewer is hardly animated without the guidance of scholarly or folk opinion. As historical conditions removed the conventional relationship between the signifier and the signified, Dizdar's lyrics tried to recapture it by appealing to historical and mythological detail. As suggested earlier, Solovyev's study is the most prominent source explaining Dizdar's advocacy of Bogomil dualist mythology. Of the different aspects of this mythology, the tension between the transcendence and the transience of life seems to capture Dizdar's attention as the underlying didactic of lapidary art. Human beings are thus caught in between two opposite movements: On the one hand, as fallen angels, their memory of the heavenly realm evokes an urge to be liberated from the shackles of earthly existence. On the other hand, the demands of everyday life pull them away from heavenly repose and bind them into a corporeal prison of which the grave is the most unwavering testimony. The quest, then, is not so much to capture or challenge the truth about either realm, but to resist captivity, metaphysical and physical, by finding solace in the memory of a life of freedom that once was and again must be. Memory is at once the resonance of the past (life before the expulsion), and the apocalyptic projection of the future (a comfort zone after this life). And now, thanks to visual memory, the interface between the transcendental and transient dimensions of life acquires richer meanings, while defiance becomes the unifying ethos of past, present, and future participants in political and religious culture.

To that end, the reading of imagery opens up to the issue of belonging, not in any partisan sense to a particular teaching or institution, but to a more comprehensive framework in which the land and history form inextricable aspects of both scholarly and mythological allusions. Whatever happens on/in an image is a reflection of both the belief system and cultural praxis. Therefore, Dizdar's play with different dimensions is not a question of inconsistency; rather, it is grounded in the viewpoint that archeological material and popular lore can aid each other in deciphering the meaning of funerary motifs. If the meaning of the common shield motif, for example, was recognizable to the medieval audience thanks to the presence of immediate or mediated clues, the modern audience can be guided into this meaning in a similar fashion—that is, by relying on external guidelines found in historical or popular sources. It is thus a function of convention whether the shield is taken as "the wondrous shield of salvation" (in *"bbbb")* in the biblical sense (Psalm 18:35), or a heraldic icon as in "A Text about a Shield":

To shield me I sought me a good shield	Poiskah štit dobri da štiti me
But I cast it away for now I wield The good shield	Bacih ga potom dobrog jer Tišti me

Whatever the case, its seems important to acknowledge that the meaning of imagery, while probably unambiguous to the medieval viewer, can only be suggested, through poetic agency, to the modern viewer. The act of interpretation is therefore Dizdar's act of reaching out to the ancestors without superimposing his expectations on their commemorative sensibilities.

The epitaphs, on the other hand, are narrative abstractions that evoke vignettes of personal experience, thereby grounding cosmology in a local context. Their ostensible purpose is to carry on where life does not. Life is sustained as memory of which the epitaph is a visual reminder and a narrative cue. Epitaphs counteract the propensity to forget. Through them, personal stories persevere as textual abstractions even after the body perishes and the individual is no more. Dizdar's detailed examination of the stećak epitaphs suggests that two main attitudes, at times mutually exclusive and at others intertwined, seem to govern the epitaphic compositions: One provides poetic or prosaic details about the location, the name of the dead, sometimes the name of the family member who erects the stećak, and, albeit rarely, of the *dijak* who carves it. The other one is more philosophical, as it expresses profound emotions or thoughts about life and death, the mystery and inevitability of death in contrast to the unpredictable nature of life.[40] The dual intent conforms well to what Erwin Panofsky identifies as the "prospective" or anticipatory, and the "retrospective" or commemorative movements in funerary art, whose mutual balance varies in different philosophical and historical contexts. The biographical iconography, for example, is typically commemorative because it conveys facts and stories from one's life, unlike mythic representations that reveal a belief that the deceased has now passed into a new world whose quality is didactically expressed in stone. Although the two modes can be mutually exclusive, Panofsky suggests that their simultaneous assertion usually beckons a "panoramic vision" whereby the life on earth prefigures a life in the next.[41] Panofsky's analysis in this case is based on Greek sarcophagi, and given the multiplicity of eschatological paths one can follow in the Greek cosmos, iconography allows for a more individualistic link between worldly and otherworldly existence. In monotheistic cultures the choice is understandably more limited; in stećak imagery the same path is signified, regardless of the funerary signifier. This explains the frequency of formulaic epitaphs that state the basic recognition that death is a different reality, inevitable but mysterious. Its universality points to the insignificance of worldly status and wealth, and many epitaphs in medieval Bosnia cynically reflect how disrobing, literally and figuratively, death must be. For example, the epitaph of Ivan Maršić of the fifteenth century Hum region—rendered in *Stone Sleeper* as "A Text about a Leaving"—reads: "In this world I lived long, for eighty-eight years, and now I lie pennyless." Another epitaph found in the same region states: "Here lies Dragoj, left with nothing—in the end."[42]

Whereas the standardization of epitaphic language of the stećak suggests that death in medieval Bosnia was at least partly perceived as an equalizer of confessional and social differences, the presence of textual variations points to the impulse to be remembered as an individual in one's own right. This tension between cultural uniformity and subjective memory is enacted throughout *Stone Sleeper* with the effect of blurring the lines of differentiation between the collective and the particular or the experiential and the philosophical. Highly effective in that sense is his usage of direct speech and reported speech whereby the poetic "I" both merges and departs from the epitaphic "I" in an effort to foster cultural unity amidst individual differences.

In that sense, the interplay between the commemorative and anticipatory remains crucial for Dizdar's rendition of epitaphs. Some of the formulaic epitaphs, such as *"a se leži"* (here lies) or *"a se neka se zna"* (let it be known), are preserved, although most of the poems rework the phraseology into a more personalized reflection on the past and future life. In most of the poems, the epitaphic gist to be remembered after death is honored, but poetic remembrance is induced in a multidirectional way: The posterity, prompted by the pervasiveness of medieval deathscape, are reminded that they too will become what the sleepers are now. Many poems hint that remembrance is a weapon against our own vanishing in the squalls of amnesia. Equally important, however, is the persistence of memory in space, in the landscape and among our kin and kind. The two routes through which culture perpetuates itself predicate each other: Unless we are bonded in a mnemonic trajectory with our forbears, our cultural kinship is rendered inconsequential. In Dizdar's poetry, the epitaphs fulfill the function of establishing and/or making visible the cultural links in space and time. For example, the first stanza of the poem "Gorchin" introduces us to a soldier, apparently lost to a battle against a foreign intruder, through the epitaph rendered from his tombstone. What remains of Gorchin's life story is a gnomic inscription—introduced authentically with *"a se leži"* (here lies)—that testifies to the mortality of his body but suggests the immortality of his hope:

Here lyeth	Ase leži
Gorchin soldier	Vojnik Gorčin
In owen earthe	U zemlji svojoj
In straungers	Na baštini
Herytaunce	Tuždi

The name Gorchin is therefore both personal and impersonal. It travels along the road of history, reappearing in one generation after another. With it, the culture establishes a genealogical tree, allowing itself to expand and move in different directions without losing its roots, in landscape or in history. Likewise, memory recovered from epigraphic details is culturally referential insofar as it relies on the voice of the living to align it with the passage of time. Significantly, then, Dizdar avoids the danger of cleansing the medieval voice from the impurity of history and the subjectivity of the ear that hears it. While his poetry presents the sleeper with a chance to speak, it does not, in and of itself, replicate his authentic voice or lead to his complete disclosure; instead, the two voices intertwine and negotiate boundaries without either hushing or overtaking each other. Vigilantly dialogic, they appear, to borrow Homi Bhabha's phrase, as "almost the same but not quite."[43] Therefore, mutual disclosure, partial as it is, becomes the function of mimesis carried out as a conversation between the dead and the living. It attends to the urgency of the self-reflection that Dizdar so explicitly undergoes when facing the stone residences of his medieval ancestors. Distilling his creative imagination through lapidary text, Dizdar does not remove himself from the experiential plane of the message but offers to it a mediated, hybridized empathy by virtue of expanding it. The "I" always appears ambiguous, both poetically intrusive and textually authentic, demanding that the poem be treated in toto as an epitaph. "A Text about Wealth" reveals well the compelling interface between the imagination and the stone object:

To no man never did I telle	Nikada nikom ne rekoh
How I my welth did gayne	Kako stekoh blaga
Now let it be knowne	Sada neka se zna
That then	Da tagda u ruke vraga
Into the Divils hands I fell	Stigoh
That thorough him	Da s njega
I for my welth was slayne	Zbog blaga da pogiboh

We do not know which of the above narrative fragments (if any) stem from the original epitaph: Does the original center on the acquisition of wealth, its loss, or death by slaying? In his study Dizdar lists a fifteenth-century epitaph that reads: "Here lies Juraj on his cross. May it be known to all, how I, Juraj Ivanović, gained wealth, and for wealth did I die."[44] Whether indeed this epitaph served as inspiration for "A Text about Wealth" seems less relevant than the fact that its narrative expansion is consistent with Bogomil teachings: Material power is a diabolic affair bound to be punished. "A Text about Time," on the other hand, is more explicit regarding the epitaphic source: The opening lines of the poem are borrowed from a fourteenth-century epitaph commemorating Stipko Radosalić of Premilovo: "My lord, long have I lain, and long shall I lie." The rest of the poem, however, is the product of the poet's imagining of a body deposited into the land and sentenced to dwell therein for eternity. As the body merges with the soil, the possession over landscape is asserted as irrevocable reality. Similarly, the poem "A Text about Hope" takes inspiration from the fourteenth to fifteenth century epitaph on the tombstone of Vrsan Kosarić that says, "Here writes Vrsan Kosarić, a prisoner who has no joy." Dizdar turns it into:

And here is written	A ovo pisa
A prisonner which rejoyceth not	Sužanj koji se ne raduje
May he be the last prisoner	Nek bude potoni sužanj
Whom hope forgot	Što izgubio nadu je

Poetic addenda can thus work in chronological or thematic terms—and Dizdar rarely gives a clue—but they never fall outside the realm of Bogomil allusion. This is, for Dizdar, a strategy of authentication: The life of the deceased, if told, must be placed in context of his or her system of values. The poetic "I" and the epitaphic "I" can merge at any given juncture. Occasionally they fuse, turning into an inclusive "we" that crosses historical time and appears as a declaration of shared values. What would otherwise remain external to the observer's eye now melts into the same cultural space. Because the epitaphs in Dizdar's texts are not deterministic, their main value lies in an ability to restore polyphony; each and every epitaph has a story to tell but no story can be told without the poet's mediating role. In that sense, the poet not only seeks continuity with the experiences of the past; he also delimits the culture of which he speaks. The voice of the sleeper, doubled by Dizdar, is self-referential both in individualistic and cultural terms. It is configured both through space—in the land in which it rests—and through time—in the memory of the living. Land and history are locked in producing the meaning of the past which is then disclosed, epitaph by epitaph, image by image, through poetry. "A Text on a Watershed" is an excellent illustration of such horizontal/cultural and vertical/historical fusion as inspired by funerary art:

Pardon me	Oprostite me
that I pray that ye	što ipak vas molju
and my brethren my fellows my betters	i bratiju i družinu i gospodu
do come to my door do visit me	do vratiju mojih da dojdu da me pohodu
	molju i kume i prije i strine i nevjeste
that I pray that godmother motherlaw aunt and bride	da me ne minu već da me kad
do speak my name keep me in mind pass at times by my side	pominu da me se kad sjete
for once I was the same as ye	jer ja sam bil kako vi sada jeste
and as I am so shall ye be	a vi ćete biti kako sada jesam ja

The interplay between these different forms of discourse in *Stone Sleeper* is highly effective. More than a simple poetic exercise, they are a strategy of reconnection, of erasing the gap in cultural memory. Based on epitaphic information, the names of places and people are historically and culturally specific, giving a sense of intense familiarity with the background context. Direct and indirect speech overlap, allowing the reader to be drawn into the poem's double vocality. Then again, there is a subtle alienating dimension in the rhythmic and linguistic quality of the verse as well, which signals the importance of discursive and stylistic intermingling in creating an atmosphere of authenticity. Suggestive of intricate personal destinies before the finality they capture, the epitaphs never paralyze the poetic imagination. In that sense, Dizdar, who through this kind of double vocality expands the epitaphic vignettes into historical narratives, turns the physical absence of the deceased into a haunting allegorical presence of soliloquies.

Frontispiece 4: A cross shaped Stećak, Radmilja Cemetery. Photo by András Riedlmayer.

CHAPTER FOUR

MAPPING THE BOSNIAN IDENTITY

SACRED SPACE, ROOTEDNESS, AND CONTINUITY IN *STONE SLEEPER*

As suggested in the previous chapters, the originality of Dizdar's *Stone Sleeper* lies in the poetic transformation of the medieval burial ground into the cradle of national culture. Marginalized as spaces of death and forgetting, the stećak cemeteries are assigned by *Stone Sleeper* a new role in the collective memory of contemporary Bosnians. The stećak's taciturn presence, seemingly impervious to the passage of time, also turns attention to the land in which the tomb is anchored. In animating stone inscriptions as ancestral voices, *Stone Sleeper* establishes the importance of cultural genealogy and continuity in territorial terms. Brought together in the poetic text, the two components—geography and nationhood—refashion the sentiments of belonging and introduce a new possibility for contemporary Bosnians to appraise the cemetery as the sacred ground of their national culture.

Why this emphasis on the link between nationhood and geography? The answer to this question, as suggested in the first chapter, should be sought in the specific circumstances that enveloped the political culture of Bosnia-Herzegovina in the twentieth century—especially during the socialist era, when the territorial component of the Bosnian people's national taxonomy officially lost currency. At a more general level, of course, the issue of territoriality features prominently in the process of self-definition and self-determination in societies at large. In the formation of national communities, some scholars argue, "Territory is so inextricably linked to national identity that it cannot be separated out. Neither the identity, or consciousness, shared by members of a nation nor the physical territory of the nation itself can be viewed in isolation."[1] Indeed, while geography is neither a key dimension of identity nor its determinant, it is one of the most important categories through which nationhood can be explored and articulated. It both grounds a sense of national selfhood and gives it a framework through which a continuous shaping of identity can "take place." Narration is key to that process, since it reveals the modes and conditions of a people's communal relationship with the land. Whether literary or political, narratives allow the land to be told and retold, at times as a continuous tabula rasa, in accordance with the evolving concerns of national selfhood, thanks to the seeming immobility of national space. Even when competing nationalities lay claim on the same territory, the contested narratives rarely lose their pedagogical force for the community they target. Within such narrative productions, specific locations feature as focal narrative points. As John Agnew suggests, the significance of these places is defined through their physical characteristics (locale), the meaning given to them in the national narrative (sense of place), and their position in the overall territorial setting of the nation (location).[2]

In the case of Bosnia-Herzegovina, as suggested earlier, it is important to historicize the territorial question: In contrast to other republics in the former Yugoslav federation, territoriality was a conspicuously absent category of national self-definition. As Bosnia never attained the status of a national republic, its population was partitioned along nonspatial, ethnoconfessional lines into Serbs, Croats, and Muslims/Bosniacs. Reduced to regional consciousness, Bosnian territorial identity never attained discursive weight in the national self-definition. Instead, the Serbian and Croat identities were spatially redirected to Serbia and Croatia, while the Muslim, on the other hand, was aspatialized (or, in some views, had to be redirected to Turkey). The ideological evacuation of the Bosnian people from Bosnian land, especially in the case of Muslims, made the land a nonfunctional category of belonging. Consequently, the material vestiges of Bosnian historical culture, including the stećak, became little more than landmarks of curiosity. This political dislocation of national culture from land was a reality that was partly compensated by the fostering of a dual sentiment of belonging among most Bosnians: a merely "regional" sense (Bosnian) and a recognizably "national" one (Serb, Croat, Muslim).

Against such dissonance, Dizdar attempts to fuse the regional and the national by assigning to the stećak a distinct topographic relevance, and making it both consanguine and contiguous with contemporary Bosnian identity. Through the stećak, the two dimensions of identity—nationhood and region—were placed in an interactive space where the boundaries of common history and culture were more clearly demarcated. As Dizdar relocated the map of the imagined Bosnian community, the land and the material objects scattered over it were symbolically returned to the people of Bosnia. Through his treatment of the stećak as ancestral abode, Dizdar allocated a more fundamental function to the land in the national imagination. Imbued with a new significance as the sacred site of national birthing, the stećak became the material marker of territorial expression of nationhood—and, in its seemingly embedded permanence, an ever-flowing fountain of knowledge about the deepest layers of Bosnian identity and culture. To be Bosnian, *Stone Sleeper* suggests, implies sensing the roots of culture in the local soil, the *ius soli,* and ascertaining its continuity within the sacred ground of medieval Bosnia. Sacred space, cultural rootedness, and continuity emerged as three interlaced tropes around which the sense of territorial belonging in *Stone Sleeper* came to life.

OF IDENTITY AND SACRED SPACE

The consecration of land in *Stone Sleeper* happens inductively, through the consecration of the stećak. Although cemeteries are treated by most religious cultures as sacred sites in that they mark eschatological transition from one world to another and provide space for ritual and spiritual connection between them,[3] Dizdar's consecration of the stećak takes on a literary impulse through which both ritual and spiritual sensibilities are evoked. For Dizdar, "remembering" the medieval dead is neither an act of mourning nor a soteriological assertion, but a process of self-configuration in reference to the land where the medieval dead rest. The process is initiated only when the dead and the living are confirmed in their lineal association and the land is reclaimed as national possession. The fact that the medieval landscape does not otherwise play a role in the formation of Bosnian national identity signals that the historical imagination has not established a symbolically consistent and rhetorically persuasive attitude toward Bosnian medieval history. Dizdar's intervention is therefore remedial in that it supplies contemporary culture with some of the most persuasive metaphors for the territorial formation and continuity of Bosnian nationhood. It is also potentially contested, insofar as the expression of the relationship with the stećak cemetery is neither ubiquitous nor fully shared by all Bosnians, despite the fact that the poet aims to reach out to all of them. Finally, it is testimonial since it posits the messages on the stećak as silent reminders that the dead are here to stay, coexisting with us regardless of our loss of memory. The poetic consecration counteracts the mortal silence: Speaking *for* the dead is therefore an act of speaking *to* them. The sanctification of space marks the reclamation of land, as if through the rite of passage enunciated in *"the gate"*:

If the gate of the word is just a dream a fairy tale	Ako su vrata iz riječi samo san ako su samo gatka bajana
Still I will not leave this door	Ja ipak neću više da se s vrata vratim
Here I want to live once more	Ja opet hoću tamo da snim
This supreme	Tu slatku
Dream	Gatku

What are the modes of treating the stećak as sacred ground? To begin with, As Jamie Scott points out, any discussion of sacred space ought to refer at least to at least some aspects of Mircea Eliade's work, despite the severity of objections to many of his conclusions.[4] In his broad-ranging studies of religion, Eliade has suggested that the notion of "sacred"—conceptualized as something evoking awe, out-of-the-ordinary emotions and/or values—manifests itself in a variety of temporal and spatial possibilities. Terming these manifestations "hierophanies,"[5] Eliade argues that hierophanies should be understood in a semantically open-ended way, both in reference to space and time. As regards space, hierophany can manifest itself in any locale, natural or constructed—stone, tree, building—that brackets off the location, both psychologically and ontologically, as "privileged." In Eliade's view, "Even for the most frankly nonreligious man, all these places still retain an exceptional, unique quality; they are the 'holy places' of his private universe, as if it were in such spots that he has received that revelation of a reality other than that in which he participates through his ordinary life."[6] Sacred space is a microcosm in that it replicates the cosmogonical process of the organization of life and the centering of human consciousness on numinous powers. Sacred space opposes profane space: In contrast to the latter's homogeneity and neutrality, it establishes and demarcates the qualitative border between different modalities of experience, pointing out to the layering of space in vertical terms according to specific cosmological hierarchies.[7]

Before any consideration of the heuristic merits of Eliade's spatial hierophany in reference to *Stone Sleeper,* it needs to be emphasized that Eliade has recently been criticized for essentializing the bifurcation of sacred and profane and dissociating them from other discourses that can shape the notion of sanctity. For example, his argument that sacred and profane are intrinsically polar modes of being in the world has raised many eye-brows among those who take an increasingly multidisciplinary approach to religious phenomena. Some of the main points of criticism relate to Eliade's disregard of the effects of historical forces on the construction of space, and of the frequent treatments of space as at once sacred and pro-fane. Indeed, the assumption that space exists as either holy or lay, mean-ingful or meaningless, organized or chaotic, implies that there exists in every religious tradition a stable and exclusive set of values that govern its followers' understanding of their environment. In fact, as most recent studies indicate, the line of separation between sacred and profane is not only variable across different religions but within any given religion as well, according to denominational, gender, pietistic, and other sensibilities that make up its system.[8]

Yet, despite these critical objections to Eliade's binary understanding of the world, his insights can still be valued for shedding light on the variety of processes through which space can be deemed holy. In fact, his ideas exude more elasticity and subtlety when articulated in definition of the term "spatial hierophany" rather than "sacred space" per se. The latter term evokes a sense of static locale continuously actualizing spiritual potentials. Sacred space is where numinosity occurs and recurs independently of human presence.[9] In contrast, Eliade seems to allow the term "spatial hi-erophany" to be defined in a more dynamic and less essentialist way as the *act* of spatial manifesting of the numinous, rather than numinosity per se. Thus, unlike his discussion of sacred space as the *outcome* of a process, Eli-ade introduces "hierophany" as the actual process. Hierophany appears as contingent, since it is ascribed rather than inherent, and as induced and sustained according to a variety of experiential criteria. Eliade himself uses the term "constructed" when speaking of the act of consecration,[10] and al-though he places the initial agency in divine rather than human action, he contends that it is the ritual and spiritual attitude of an individual or a community that sustains the quality of any given hierophany.[11]

Accordingly, Eliade draws attention to different techniques that can be adopted for consecrating a territory, each of which points to the social ten-dency to organize space as a cosmos that provides human beings with an orientation for their actions and visions. At the experiential level, then, the consecration of space need not be a function of any institutionally pre-scribed act. Further, a hierophany need not have commemorative and spir-itual value for the community at large, nor does it need to deploy explicit markers to highlight its sanctity. Spatial hierophany is primarily an experi-ential process that has implications for the administration of space. Since hierophany stands against profanity, its numinosity is induced independ-ently of any consensus on spiritual symbolism. In fact, the markers of spatial hierophany may be as much individual as communal, and as much meditatively personal as ritually public. Consequently, a hierophany is not always to be equated with a theophany. As Jamie Scott points out, "From an Eliadean standpoint, not only such overtly religious sites as Stonehenge or Salisbury Cathedral, Mecca or Mount Fuji, but even such secular domains as James Joyce's Dublin or the stadium facilities of any modern major sporting franchise may fruitfully be interpreted as sacred space, insofar as each in its own way works as a site of individual and collective efforts to exercise a ritual sensibility."[12]

So while Eliade does not offer satisfactory examples of the tension that may emerge from the historical and cultural situatedness of any given hierophany, he rightfully subjects hierophany to experiential relativism. Hierophany, he proposes, "is a fitting term, because it does not imply anything further; it expresses no more than is implicit in its etymological content, i.e., that *something sacred shows itself to us*."[13] A hierophany, then, can be examined as a construction rather than a given, and its durability is predicated on outward, relational criteria rather than intrinsic and invisible qualities. The act of sanctification points to an important paradox in human communication with space: The space is confirmed as numinous through the crossing of an invisible line, not exclusively but inclusively, beyond which two or more systems of meaning converge. The implosion of different realities in a particular site opens them both to symbolic reconfigurations while providing them with topographic solidity.

It is in this moment of convergence of different realities that the poetic consecration of the stećak takes place. Enabling the nostalgia toward the stećak—and Eliade speaks of a profound nostalgia to live in the cosmos as it was in the beginning[14]—to interact with the life around it, Dizdar diminishes the dissonance between the actual and imaginary roles of the stećak in contemporary Bosnian culture. Initially, the psychological and aesthetic impressions that the stećak had made on the young Dizdar enhanced their lines of separation despite the geographical proximity of the two cultural spaces. Random but potent, Dizdar's intuition that the stećak bears an extraordinary cultural importance repeatedly prompted him to ritual visitations that galvanized his sense of cultural connectedness with the dead. Rather than faceless targets of mourning, the dead entered Dizdar's life as charismatic voices. The zone of mortal silence thus became a hierophanic zone of multivocality as Dizdar integrated in his poetry different interpretations of the stećak, all of which featured in the awakening of national sentiments. While these interpretations never risked disturbing the stećak from its resting ground, they did agitate Dizdar's world with sensations and questions that were to be resolved only by marshalling the stećak for the administration of cultural space. In poetry, the process is necessarily two-directional: The stone sleeper speaks and is spoken to. Historical time and mythic time intersect. Meaning is induced as much as it is produced. Memory is recovered as much as it is invented. In such interlacing, the stećak functions as a spatial hierophany, for, to paraphrase an Eliadean conclusion, it becomes apprehensible in the measure in which it reveals itself.[15] As Dizdar writes in "Recognition": "For in the deepest depths of death/ the colors will be clearer then."

The process, of course, is neither as spontaneous nor epiphanic as it may appear at first. The challenge of recovering the meaning of the stećak by allowing it to speak, both as it once was and as it became, required navigating through the different stages of the stećak's history and tying them into a coherent yet complex narrative chain. The stećak could not have been claimed as a cultural possession capable of balancing the cultural discord without a careful consideration of the history and memory that nourish it. While Dizdar understood that the burial ground once existed as sacred ground, the circumstances of that solemn history remained essentially alien. Of course, feeling moved by someone else's solemnity is not uncommon at sacred sites, especially in multiconfessional societies: A non-Christian entering Christian sacred ground (as was in fact the case with Dizdar) will often be affected by crossing of a threshold to a place where other people's sacred communion takes place. The self and the other, while differentiated by the criteria of participation, can nevertheless experience a form of bonding evoked by the frame of reference. This is where, perhaps, Erving Goffman's theory of frames can be considered: "I assume," Goffman writes, "that definitions of a situation are built up in accordance with principles of organization which govern events—at least social ones—and our subjective involvement in them."[16] Identifying the primary frameworks that allow individuals to locate, perceive, identify, and label "a seemingly infinite number of concrete occurrences" within a social structure,[17] Goffman discusses the importance of social criteria that provide a background understanding for events. These primary frameworks control the acceptance and understanding of social values in any given event or concept: The participants and observers in a social context accept the rules that govern the juxtaposition of their different roles and frameworks.

By analogy, encounters with someone else's sacred place can elicit recognition, or an act of social acceptance, of the place's sacral function, even when the spiritual dimension of experience is absent. While the clarity of the line that separates the emic and etic domains is maintained at the level of membership and symbolic meaning, the blurring of that line can occur at other levels of experience: aesthetic, political, intellectual, and other dimensions of cultural praxis. Furthermore, the sacred, while not universally accepted, can be descriptively associated with a particular location and thus sustained in a mediated way through literature, visual arts, and other forms of representation. Sanctity thus implies more than spiritual quality. In Dizdar's case, however, the ritual movement in and out of the frame of medieval cemeteries created a tension between the insider's and outsider's symbolic representations. Overwhelmed by the stećak's mysterious presence in the outskirts of his town, Dizdar sustained and nourished his fascination with the stećak in its "natural habitat" through repeated visitations to the Radmilja cemetery. The unmediated experience evolved into a fascination with the stećak as depicted in historical records and preserved through folk practices. Therefore, the initial ritual patterning of life around the stećak did not gain a paradigmatic significance, either for Dizdar or for the community. The disconnection with the medieval sacrality was far too extreme. Instead, Dizdar translated the symbolic density of the cemetery that had accrued through personal experience into a *poietic akt*—that, as an answerable, public, and productive effort, created a bond of kinship with the dead, placing them at the center of his national imaginings. As a reaction to the stasis of the memorial stone, the act of writing became a symbolic commemoration of the dead, and the reading of poetry a ritual invocation of questions about the continuity of Bosnian national culture in space and time. Poetry administers the stećak; the stećak, in turn, administers the land. At the literary level, Dizdar's comfortable and extensive deployment of religious metaphors, drawn from mystical as well as scriptural sources, draws on the Bogomil sanctification of the stećak. At the political level, confirmation of the forgotten medieval sanctity as a modern cultural space enabled Dizdar to pull the broken strings that dangled loose in the national imagination. On the one hand, then, Dizdar's journey is horizontal and linear, involving the juxtaposition of different historical contexts in the same geographic zone: a medieval cemetery on the outskirts of a modern town. On the other hand, that journey is imaginary, in that the horizontal crossing of the threshold between urban and suburban space necessitates a multidirectional leap of fancy and hope that the other space can articulate some deep-lying answers about Bosnian historical culture.

Important to note, then, is the multiple consecration of the stećak. Initially, it was sanctified by medieval religious culture as the site/rite of passage into a better life. Because of the disappearance of the religious culture that had created the stećak, its sanctity lost the original eschatological underpinning and was instead sustained by folk culture, which maintained continuity between the living and the dead through its mythological repertory and healing rituals. Finally, Dizdar's *Stone Sleeper*, productive and *poietic* in intent, allocated to the stećak a new symbolic value that, drawing on the stećak's cultural history, appeared germane for the construction of contemporary Bosnian identity. Thanks to this cumulative process of Dizdar's enterprise, the stećak does not just occupy the landscape; it gives it meaning and wholeness. Treated as a source of cultural energy, the stećak both sets off and renews national sensibilities. Consequential for the collective memory and the sentiments of belonging, this cumulative sanctity is weighed through the stećak's axial location as an ancestral abode, its both centering and regenerating implications for Bosnian culture, and its physical commitment to the land. In "Krajina: Ending":

Look a shoot is sprouting from the white stone	Iz onog bijelog kama eno niče klica
Sprouting from an ancient hand a dark face	Iz neke davne ruke iz nekog tamnog lica
From it a white flower has painfully budded and grown	Niče i raste u neko bolno bijelo cvijeće
And from its hidden nest a bird has already flown	Već ptica iz svog skrivenog gnijezda sliječe
Into the lonely ring of someone's gleaming dream	U skrovit krug nečijih samotnih svijetlih sanja

As these verses suggest, then, while the stećak as a memorial stone testifies to death, it also chronicles continuity of life by depicting, both textually and visually, the vibrant landscape in which it is lodged. Dizdar's emphasis on the stećak's connection to nature greatly reinforces the link between land and culture. As the poetry sets stone images in motion in an effort to disclose the stećak's records of Bosnia, the link between the landscape and Bosnian nationhood becomes more axiomatic for the collective memory. Dizdar's frequent appeal to the familiar geography in *Stone Sleeper*— Bosnia's rivers, towns, and mountains—ascertains recognition of the topographic outline of the poetic setting. On the other, the treatment of different elements of landscape as *topoi* (as in "A Text about a Spring," "A Text on a Watershed," *"the vine and its branches")* illustrates an intense intertwining of real and figurative associations between nationhood and landscape. As the natural world in which the stećak rests takes part in this complex symbolism, nature becomes sacred nature, and space, sacred space. Their sacredness, of course, is contingent, having come out of a particular reading of land as embodying the fundamental purpose of uniting the community and its lore. In the context of Dizdar's effort to conceive nationhood in terms of territorial continuity, remembering the medieval dead takes on a genealogical direction with clear geographical implications. Therefore, the depth of national culture could be measured spatially only if the space could be said to provide the community with re-generative symbolism. This, of course, would not imply the restatement of the meaning the land may have once "possessed," but enhances its relevance through the commemorative acts of poetry reading and/or stećak visitations. In "Wedding":

I'm dead	Mrtav sam
Dead	Mrtav
But with my death	Ali sa smrću mojom
The world	Nije umro i
Did not	Svijet
Die	Opet se u nekim očima
Once again the gleam	Svjetlost
In an eye	Zanavjek
Fades	Gasi
For good	U nekim mekim
In another soft eye	Tek počinju
The dream	Da plamte
Is just beginning	Snovi
To blaze	Pa preko visokih brana
And over the high levees	Preko zabrana
Over the nays	Preko
Over the graves	Grobnog
And their	Kamena
Stones	Preko kostiju što sve jače
Over the bones	Svijetle
That glow	U tami
In the dark	Gorom i dolom
Like ever brighter lights	Kićeni
High and low	Svatovi
Elaborate	
Wedding rites	

As the poem enunciates, the stećak is not isolated from the landscape in which it lies: The stone, while axial in the poetic imagination, belongs to land and nature, where it witnesses renewal and continuity. In her study on eighteenth-century English ruin poems, Anne Janowitz highlights the importance of "naturalizing the ruin," that is, the blending of the ruin into the natural environment with the intent of promoting "a feeling for, rather than an assertion of, the permanence of the nation."[18] The naturalization of the stećak as sacred ground bears implications on the ontology of the landscape itself: While the stećak stands as the axis of the land where it rests, it shares its numinous quality with this land. Like the stećak, the landscape is symbolically animated by virtue of its sheltering the stećak in a stable and durable environment. Not only does the stećak embody tangible markers of the depth (roots) and breadth (scope) of national culture, it also helps direct, in its silent but decisive way, the modes of interaction with the present. In *"the garland,"* the necessity of that interaction is clear:

And whosoever will see let his eyes be unlocked	Pa neka otvori oči kto hoće da vidi
And whosoever will hear let his ears be unblocked	Neka otvori uši kto hoće sad da čuje
Let one eye spy and scry the coast and cliffs all around	Jednim okom neko odmjeri i žali i hridi oko nas
Let one eye seek inside him till his voice be found	Drugim nek zadje u sebe duboko da nadje svoj glas
For the time is at hand	Jer vrijeme je blizu

Interaction, urgent as it is (since "time is at hand"), is articulated as a process of self-disclosure: unlocking the eyes, unblocking the ears, excavating the voice. This inbound and outbound process necessitates a sentient engagement with the environment ("spy and scry the coast and cliffs all around") as a strategy of contextualization. In many ways, the stanza recounts the complexity of Dizdar's engagement with the stećak *in* the landscape, not the stećak of the museum or tourist catalogues. Its fixed presence in the Bosnian terrain ensures that it is safeguarded as well as assimilated by nature, and never aborted by it. Whereas, as Janowitz points out, the interplay between poetic thematization of land and national territorial assertion is quite common in romantic poetry, Dizdar's emphasis on the territorial pedagogy of the stećak replaces celebratory depictions of transhistorical harmony between nation and nature with deliberate ambivalence. Human beings are naturally both forgetful and attentive. If left to naturalization, the stećak may be conserved physically but will be forgotten culturally. As "A Text about Time" suggests, naturalization carries the danger of transforming the stećak's idyllic repose in land into the agony of amnesia:

Long have I lain here before thee	Davno ti sam legao
And after thee	I dugo ti mi je
Long shall I lie	Ležati
Long	Davno
Have the grasses my bones	Da trava mi kosti
Long	Davno
Have the worms my flesh	Da crvi mi meso
Long	Davno

Have I gained a thousand names	Da stekoh tisuću imena
Long	Davno
Have I forgot my name	Da zaboravih svoje ime
Long have I lain here before thee	Davno ti sam legao
and after thee	I dugo ti mi je
Long shall I lie	Ležati

The return to the land is accordingly thematized as a mystic's return to the self in order to formulate a new attitude toward the landscape. The sacred space of the stećak is not theophanic in the Eliadean sense but reflexive in a pedagogic sense. It does not descend on the participants from a divine source since it does not draw a vertical hierarchy of cosmic meaning. Instead, it implies a horizontal spilling over of the stećak's pedagogy into other spatial manifestations of Bosnian culture, complicating the versions of national belonging that have been officially accepted. Because of that horizontal trajectory, the stećak's symbolism is most effectively understood when viewed in its larger geographical setting. Consider, for example, the poem "Madderfield," which takes its name after a small cemetery containing a number of richly decorated stećaks. It announces that a solution to the disjunctive national selfhood of the Bosnian people, its causes and effects, can be found only in reference to the land and its lore:

Past time's thorns and switches	Kroz kupinje crno kroz drače vre-
past wizards and witches	mena kroz vražije kroz vrače
Our hands are still here but we still	Ruke su još tu al još ne ruko-
haven't clasped each other's	vasmo
hands	
We're still not free of their sorcery	Od opčinjenosti još se ne izlije-
	čismo
For we've still not found a cure	Jer lijeka još ne nadjosmo
Except this ancient lore	Osim one stare molitve
Except this curse this prayer	Osim one stare kletve
Except from river to river	Osim
From Drina to Ukrina and Sava	Od Drine do Ukrine i Save od
from Una and Sana to Rama	Une i Sana do Rame i Neretve
and Neretva	

Once the collective gaze turns toward the land and its lore, the old world can help shape the contours of the new one. The stećak stands, testimonially, between the ancient lore and its (forgetful) modern beholder. The reference to the hands in the above poem is a reminder of spatial presence ("our hands are still *here*") and a need for its validation (our hands need to be clasped). Important here is the role attributed to the rivers of

Bosnia. Listed by name in the last line, they appear like arteries by way of which life spreads through the landscape, connecting the community with its history and lore. As the waters give sustenance to the land, irrigating its soil and renewing its riches, they participate in the dissemination of knowledge about the ancient lore, enable the flow of culture across the land, and mark its geographical scope. "The river," Wyman Herendeen argues, "is coextensive with history, unfolding as history itself does, and sharing the cultural consciousness of each successive age. It is not only the present, but also the future. . . . The river, in geography and as an image, takes on the characteristics of culture of which it is a part."[19] This astute observation is especially relevant here if we remember that the name of the land itself—Bosnia—is taken from one of its major rivers. Bosnian nature, as manifested in the arteries of its flowing waters, becomes the agent of cultural circulation as well, complementing the stećak's immobile presence. The stećak is a transitional object in this sense as well, in that it is culturally manufactured but naturally preserved by an environment in which land and society form a dynamic unit, as enunciated in "Wedding":

Because these swallows are swooping	Jer pravo od travničke Lašve
Across all her rivers from Swift water	Pa preko Rame i Neretve
Lašva	Do travunjske Lastve
Over the Rama and Neretva	Lete te laste
To Lastva the Swallow	Na Lastovo
Above blue Lastovo	Plavo
Isle of Swallows	Samo ptice kamne ove ptice amo
Only stone-birds these birds here	Sve kroz puzavice
Forever keeping	čuvaju vječno
Through the creeping ivy	Čuvaju vjerno
Faithfully keeping	Toplinu rukavice
The warmth of a mossy glove	Od mahovine

With an Eliadean resonance, Nigel Pennick notes that the main quality of sacred space is its immediacy: "The creation of sanctity," he says, "is more than the mere acknowledgment or reproduction of some specific perception of a place. It is a unique presentation of its inner qualities that does not act as an intermediate filter, interpretation, and representation. Rather, nothing comes between: there is total transparency."[20] In the case of the stećak, however, the in-betweenness is necessary, since the loss of transparency occurred in the course of different occupations of Bosnia, which makes its elevation to the realm of timeless sanctity impossible as much as undesirable. It is only through poetry that the hierophanic mode

is re-animated and the stećak's transparency partly retrieved. Without poetry, the stećak remains eclipsed from its interaction with land and the national imagination. Poetry is a mode of sanctification of the stećak in the
landscape as well as an affirmation of territorial belonging. In a reverse
analogy, just as the cemetery, once upon a time, signified collective hope
that each buried individual would experience continuity and redemption,
the poetry now signifies the hope of an individual that the collective can
affirm that continuity and redemption. Only through poetry can the
grammatical tense used to describe the historical condition of the stećak
be replaced by uninterrupted poetic time in which the stećak's symbolism, even if amorphous and broken, becomes an integral marker of Bosnian culture.

Dizdar's construction of the stećak as a site of dense but fragmented
meaning, replete with questions and answers that are both eclipsed and
partial, bestows on it a mediating role between different dimensions of
Bosnian cultural history. Not only does the stećak bear witness to the unknown but also, like the mirror in the poem, it bears witness to the
known—specifically, the landscape and the people, dead and alive, who
inhabit it. This mediating role of the stećak, understandably, calls back
the notion of liminality as discussed in the first chapter in reference to
Bosnia's geography. As a common feature of literature, Bosnia's topographic function as a border zone, at once conjoining and separating civilizations, cultures, religions, and communities, is said to have shaped
not only the psychology of belonging but also the ethics of nonconformity. The derivative tropes of resistance and defiance have featured
prominently in reference to the historical and cultural formation of
modern Bosnia-Herzegovina. In defining the stećak as the focal point for
national imaginings, Dizdar integrates the prevailing rhetoric of territorial belonging, in all its geographic and metageographic connotations,
into the images of the stećak. In this sense, the memorial stone as Dizdar
constructs it condenses a much more centered representation of Bosnia's
liminality than any of its other topographic and literary depictions. The
construction is playfully ironic: Situated on the fringes (of forests, villages, and manuscripts) of the marginal Bosnia, the stećak provides
Bosnia with a frame that not only encompasses it but also enhances its
in-betweenness. Bosnia's liminality is thus defined and confirmed by the
stećaks that lie along its edges. However, in Dizdar's reading, the double
marginalization is not only a function of political geography: The
stećak's location is determined by the interplay of cultural, natural, and
psychological factors. Dizdar's stećak therefore mediates between several
building blocks of national selfhood: geography and cosmography, nature and culture, history and myth, memory and forgetting, mortality

and immortality, textuality and orality. Its sanctity lies in the interface of these different possibilities, their continuous tension, and a symbolic openness to preserve and express territorially bounded values to which all Bosnians, regardless of the national dissonance among them, can relate. The stećak anchors Bosnian in-betweenness and enhances its sanctity. It is the micro-version of the Bogomil cosmos and of Bosnian metageography.

Consequently, then, several factors feature in the poetic consecration of the medieval cemetery: the stećak's intimation of order and meaning despite its relentless silence; its tangibility as the site of memory; its record of historical culture; and its enhancement of territorial representations of Bosnia. Dizdar's repeated crossings into its zone are ritual moments that try to make and maintain a convergence of the two worlds to which Dizdar commits his sense of belonging. Because the distance in time and space collapses during these visitations—as they commonly do in visitation and pilgrimage rituals[21]—a new possibility emerges to treat the medieval cemeteries as the organizing principle of cultural identity and practice. But as long as these different meanings are allowed to shape Dizdar's knowledge of the stećak, sanctity cannot be thought of as transparency; on the contrary, the stećak cemeteries are a zone of high voltage, where different epistemological currents meet and create a charismatic brew of poetic possibilities, some based on history, others on fantasy. Only an interlacing of these different interpretations can lead to a new, integrated future in which neither the past nor the present can exist independently from each other. In the poem "Rain," for example, Dizdar coins the word *odkameniti* ('unstone') as a cultural response to a torrential downpour (of signs and meanings), that, like the river, symbolizes the bounty and vigor of nature and culture, while it gains a spiritual dimension of cleansing. Almost as an act of collective ablution, the act of "unstoning" under the rain amounts to taking on new challenges of rejuvenating the self in the land. This self is inevitably Janus-faced: it must look back at the past, and into the land, in order to move toward the future. The message, expressed by the poem's voice as both a spiritual and moral necessity, is also sensuous, built around distinct spatial metaphors of physical cleansing, discovery, land, and rites of passage:

We need to learn again	Trebalo bi opet naučiti
to listen to the rain the rain	da slušamo kako dažd pada pada
We need to unstone ourselves	Trebalo bi se odkameniti
and eyes straight to walk	i poći bez osvrtanja kroz kapiju grada
unwavering through the city gate	Trebalo bi ponovo pronaći

We need to uncover the lost paths

that pass through the blond
grass...
We need to wash ourselves anew
and dream in clean drops of
dawn dew...
We need to meet our own hearts
again
that fled so long ago
We need to unstone ourselves

and eyes straight to walk
unwavering through this stone
city's stone gate
We need to wish with all our
might
and listen all night

to the rain the rain the righteous
rain

izgubljene staze od one plave
trave...
Trebalo bi u obilju bilja

zagrliti panične makove i mrave
Trebalo bi se iznova umiti

i sniti u jasnim kapima ozorne
rose...
Trebalo bi onesvijestiti se
u tamnim vlasima neke travne
kose
Trebalo bi načas stati
sa suncem svojim i sjenkom svo-
jom stasati
Trebalo be se konačno sastati

sa već davno odbjeglim vlastitim
srcem
Trebalo bi se odkameniti
i proći bez osvrtanja kroz ka-
menu kapiju ovog kamenog
grada
Trebalo bi htjeti
i svu noć bdjeti slušajući kako
dažd pravedni pada pada pada

Finally, worthy of note in the process of poetic sanctification is Dizdar's claim to territorial rights as a form of testimony on behalf of both the dead and the living. Because the claim is expressed in literary rather than legal terms—despite the fact that dead bodies can and do constitute forensic evidence—the contention has been avoided, and in fact reconciled, by the poet's appeal to cultural sensibilities rather than overtly political agendas. Political discourse is therefore never explicitly challenged, thanks to Dizdar's focus on the stećak as a cultural icon that pre-dates the "sacred" time of any of the official Bosnian nationalities. On the other hand, by virtue of its involvement in Bosnian literary practice at large, the political discourse is implicated in Dizdar's construction of the spatial sacredness of and around the stećak. Whereas it is Dizdar who, like a ventriloquist, disrupts ancestral silence, it is the reader of Dizdar's verse who validates and reiterates that disruption. That there is a durable pedagogical and critical dimension to this process can be observed in the nature of the response to Dizdar's work, shortly after—as well as decades after—the publication of Stone Sleeper in 1966, especially among advocates of Bosnian cultural pluralism. Rusmir Mahmutćehajić, in the Afterword to the 1999 bilingual edition of *Stone Sleeper*, makes the following observation:

> *Stone Sleeper* was first published in an age of deliberate deafness to sacred science and sacred art—an age which thought it had put 'superstitions about the unseen' behind it once and for all. But its author's intense meditation on the signs carved on the *stećci* and penned in the few surviving medieval Bosnian manuscripts enabled him to descend into the innermost depths of language and return with the speech of eternity. For this speech has never been entirely silenced: it has welled up in all those who, down the ages, have borne witness to the nature of their own being and to their belief in the signs they see in the world around them.[22]

Resonating a critical attitude toward the agnosticism of the former Yugoslavia, Mahmutćehajić's statement highlights the political repositioning of Dizdar's readership toward the past as much as the ongoing fascination with the possibilities that the reading of *Stone Sleeper* can evoke. Dizdar's consecration of the stećak is an ontological claim about the sanctity of land; the continuous validation of that claim through the process of reading, despite the change of political climate, reveals the ongoing need to territorialize cultural identity. As Stanley Fish points out, "Within a [interpretive] community, a standard of right (and wrong) can always be invoked against the background of a prior understanding as to what counts as fact, what is hearable as an argument, what will be recognized as a purpose, and so on."[23] Dizdar's incitement to his readers toward such recognition and understanding dates to his nostalgic returns to the stećak—and also to his sanctification of the stećak and its environs as the symbols and sites of territorial belonging. The final goal is to return to the cultural roots, lodged in the local soil but forgotten by the people.

ROOTEDNESS AND TERRITORIAL BELONGING

"We need the past," David Lowenthal writes, "to cope with present landscapes. We selectively perceive what we are accustomed to seeing: Features and patterns in the landscape make sense to us because we share history with them. Every object, every grouping, every view is intelligible because we are already familiar with it, through our own past and through tales heard, books read, pictures viewed. We see things simultaneously as they are and as we viewed them before; previous experience suffuses all present perception."[24] The complexity of such visions was accentuated in Dizdar's work once he constructed the stećak as an interactive "feature in landscape"

that both contained answers and demanded questions. To the extent that
Dizdar experienced the stone sleeper as a mystery that haunted him even
outside the sleeper's frame, he sustained a psychology of tension between
how he viewed the stećak in his youth and what he read into it as he wrote
poetry. The desire to possess the mystery of the stećak and to be possessed
by it formed the ongoing tension of the symbolic space. Sacredness, as suggested, is not conceived as divine dispensation—as it would have been in
the medieval rituals of burial and mourning[25]—but as a reflexive effort of
self-discovery akin to a spiritual/mystical journey to the soul. "In him [stone
sleeper] I recognize myself," Dizdar writes, "yet I am still not certain that I
can ever remove the veil from this mystery." "A Text about a Text" encapsulates well the uncertainties evoked by the medieval legacy and the reflexive
implications of the search for its meaning. Inspired by the inverted, right-
to-left inscriptions, the poem "A Text about a Text" speaks about the process
of interpretation; the initial silence caused by the confrontation with the
unknown is broken by attempts to engage with the text. The puzzle is tack-
led by five sages and unraveled, paradoxically, only as the hermeneutic chain
closes down on it. The more questions that are asked and the more interpretations that are made possible, the more trapping is the puzzle. The mirror is brought in to cast back the textual order and to reflect the correct
alphabetic ordering of the puzzle. In the end, however, reflection leads to
deflection: The meaning is shifted from the text to the reader, in a cathartic
moment of self-recognition:

The fifth with clenched fists/	A peti od nas iz čvrstih pesti/
and trembling fingers tries to hold	i drhtavih prsti
This mirror of clear redeeming grace	Ogledalo spasonosno i jasno
But it slips	Nehotice na tle pusti
To the	Prepoznavši u tome trenu u njemu
	Izgubljeno
Floor	Svoje
For in it that instant he recognises	Davno
His own	Lice
Ancient	
Forgotten	
Face	

But, contrary to the poem's message, Dizdar never gives a sense that the
self-reflection was ever complete. And it cannot be: Individual identity,
like the collective identity of the nation, is always changing. In fact, the effort to perceive the self as always evolving necessitated the treatment of
the stećak as at once familiar and unfamiliar, eerily ambiguous like the

Freudian space of the uncanny—*heimlich* and *unheimlich*. The simultaneous feeling of connection and amputation from the medieval ancestor reflects, on the one hand, the anxiety of preserving the stećak as a cultural nest, and on the other, the stećak's genealogical implications. Such an ambivalent sensation can be described, as suggested in the previous chapter, in terms of Michael Fischer's notion of "ethnic anxiety"—that is, experiencing the awareness of the self because of severance from the cultural past. Relieving ethnic anxiety, Fischer argues, is possible by producing a self-conscious text that inscribes, from the author's position, certain norms associated with that past—even though, he aptly notes, such reflexive, autobiographic narratives are inevitably ironic in nature since history never works the same way twice.[26] In fact, the merit of such narratives lies precisely in their explicitly fictive tendency to use "fragments or incompleteness to force the reader to make connections," and, even more effectively, "to activate in the reader a desire for *communitas* with others, while preserving rather than effacing differences."[27]

Because, for Fischer, establishing rootedness is self-referential in ethical and psychological terms, he does not develop his argument about spatial rootedness in any deterministic way. In fact, the ethnic autobiographies he discusses are authored by immigrants to the United States who define their identity partly though the sense of spatial uprootedness from their national cultures. This would not be applicable to Dizdar's circumstance: Dizdar's sense of uprootedness involves a sense of historical discontinuity from the medieval landscape without the malady of his own displacement, which makes his effort to relieve "ethnic anxiety" in spatial terms so much more ironic. There is no physical distance between Dizdar's world and the world of the medieval dead; on the contrary, the cemeteries he frequents are in the precincts of his town, so the only sense of distance is culturally induced. Yet their boundary is clear. Dizdar's dilemma thus relates to the question of being in continuous physical proximity to a de-familiarized location, of sensing its historical and cultural weight while feeling severed from it. In the interface of such dissonant experiences of his birthplace, Dizdar concludes that the medieval dead must be granted the same territorial rights as the living, and must be integrated into the same value system as his. Or should that be the other way around? Rootedness is therefore an attestation of territorial continuity in its historical, lineal, and cultural ramifications, not just a process of nostalgic bonding with the ancestors on the *ius soli*. It is also a geological mode of relating to the "features and patterns in landscape," that is, its historical and cultural layers that constitute Bosnian cultural selfhood in such an uneven, or textured, way. The deeper the sense of rootedness, the more tangible the relationship with the physical vestiges of the different histories of landscape. In other words, the community as Dizdar sees it is continuous, just as land is continuous. The community is land-bound, and the land is community-bound. In "Lilies," the depth of Bosnian history is appropriately measured in relation to the actual occupancy of the land:

White lilies bloom in hill and coomb	U polju i u gori bijeli krinovi procvali
In forest and field lilies seem to be talking	Po polju I gori kao da krin kao da nešto zbori
In hill and valley every lily	Po gori i dolu svaki krin
Seems to be burning	Kao da gori
And while you're quietly walking	I kad tiho izmedju procvalih cvjetova
Between the blossoming	Zamišljen tako prolaziš
Flowers	Možda kao i ja pomisliš na one koji su
Perhaps like me you'll think of those	Prije tebe ovuda tiho
Who've quietly walked here	Prolazili
Before you	Izmedju procvalih bijelih cvjetova
Between	Pitajući se isto tako kao i ti
These flowers blossoming white	Šta li su ovi bijeli
Wondering just like you	Krinovi
What they might be	Da li su to nečiji klikovi
Whether they might be cries	Ili krikovi
Of delight	Znaci onih koji su nekad prolazili
Or fright	I u bespućima ovim beznadno
Signs of those who passed here once	Gazili
Callously trampling	U potrazi za bijelim cvijećem
This trackless land	
Of ours	
In search of white flowers	

As the lily's perennial blossom signals the continuity of Bosnian culture, its snow-white presence also evokes questions about collective memory. The land, like the stećak, is elusive. In its soil, the flower is embedded like the footprints of its people, but the memory, collective and individual, is torn and fragmentary. The renewal of nature both reveals and obscures the material vestiges of history, both confirms and negates the memory of previous landscapes. A useful insight into such processes is the geographer Yi-Fu Tuan's differentiation between "rootedness" and "a sense of place." In his view, to experience rootedness is to know place primordially, without concern for "the flow of time."[28] The spatial coordinates deployed to assign meaning to location do not play a major role because the place is buried deeply in the human psyche and is experienced without concern for historical time. The Jungian overtone of such a definition of rootedness is contrasted with the intellectual effort to achieve a "sense of place," which implies a conscious act of constructing space according to one's multifarious relationship with it. In order to achieve a sense of place, Tuan proposes, one must be essentially distanced from the place, viewing it with an eagle eye and never losing sight of its historical or physical coordinates. In the context of territorial nation-narration, the "sense of place" is what John Agnew associates with the meaning ascribed to a locale in order to make it relevant for identity formation in a more public and modular way, rather than personal and analytical.[29] The exchange between individual and collective production of a place's meaning is neither harmonious nor continuous, but, as Dizdar's case illustrates, both agencies can initiate and maintain narrative authority over that production. The role of agency, therefore, need not be in effacing the uneven acquisition of a "sense of place" but in allowing the place to be kept alive in the historical imagination.

Dizdar's poetic agency is deliberately ambivalent between a sense of place and of rootedness. In treating the stećak as a puzzle, as a site in which meaning is as elusive as it is solid, Dizdar enables the production of spatial hierophany in and around the stećak. The emphasis on the process rather than the product is consistent with Eliade's interest in hierophany as an *act* of manifesting, rather than as the manifestation per se. The consecration of medieval deathscape therefore happens as the two cultural zones—the sleeper's and the poet's—are referred to each other in a poetic search for rootedness in that primordial sense, and in a scholarly and voyeuristic recognition of its importance for Bosnia's historical culture. The quest to find answers takes place, first, through asking questions about the broken links in the lineage of culture; and, second, by investigating the historical and geographic layers that make up, cumulatively, the cultural identity. The poem "Rain" quoted above appeals to the collective participation in the search for selfhood; it encourages readers to animate memories of the past and assign a new meaning to it. The appeal takes the form of a ritual renewal whereby a new spatial link between the individual and community is established as an effort of "unstoning," turning out of stone, which implies a more vibrant and engrossing relationship to history and land than what has existed before. The memorial stone, contradictory to its signification of fatality, becomes the nodular point in the landscape through which the meaning of nationhood is reinvigorated. In a comparably sensuous and lyrical way, the poem "Apple Blossom" bridges gaps in collective memory by focusing on the regenerative processes in the landscape:

Snowflakes are falling ever thicker and blacker like sins In a life that's nearing its end So will we still have eyes When the apple tree in the garden puts forth its first white blossom?	Snjegovi postaju sve dublji i crnji kao grijesi U životu koji se bliži svom kraju Hoćemo li još uvijek imati oči Kada jabuka u vrtu pusti prvi bijeli cvijet?

The apple tree takes on, as a synecdoche, the role of the territorial marker of collective memory. The whiteness, of both the snow and the blossom, is perhaps indistinguishable in the aesthetic impression, but its meaning is differentiated. Reaching behind the white veil and recovering the vision of those who looked at the same tree in the past is a way of establishing a connection. In light of Dizdar's frequent deployment of the language of mysticism—unveiling, awakening, returning, mirroring, even unstoning—it becomes obvious why establishing rootedness and connections with a place is repeatedly expressed as a reflexive process of recognition, in a way comparable to the mystic's search for the divine kernel, which is—at least, in Islamic mysticism—believed to lie stored in the innermost fibers of our body. Dizdar here walks a thin line between exoteric and esoteric idioms, thriving on their interface and allowing them to evoke both spiritual and aesthetic associations. The new territorial self-awareness is therefore multidirectional, drawing on a rich subtext, not only the salient political choreography. "You know nothing about this road-map of mine!" is a warning issued in "Roads" to those who cross over Bosnia in an attempt to subjugate it. As the poem "Roads" continues,

Your path to me poor though I be Seems sure and tried In your sight A path that comes From left Or Right You fool yourself I can be found	Ti misliš da je tvoja putanja do ubogog mene Veoma sigurna i česna Ona što dolazi S lijeva Ili Zdesna Zavaravaš se stalno da do mene treba Ići
By setting your course For north Or South	Smjerovima sličnim Sa sjevera Ili Juga

As the poem creates the atmosphere of a multidirectional offensive against Bosnian space, the determination of the intruder to redraw the map of Bosnia, to bring chaos into the nature of things, is counteracted by the Bosnian people's determination to maintain the inner calm. The inner order stands against outer disorder. Guntram Herb argues that nationalism tends to transform the land into holy ground, especially when under threat: "The soil is soaked with the blood of national heroes, the mountains are sacred, the rivers carry the national soul. Much like the places and icons of religious worship, the reified landscape becomes the altar of the nation and invokes supreme loyalty,"[30] as in, in Dizdar's case, "Message" to the occupier:

But therefore after me	Al ostat će zato posije mene
On the first stone cairn	Na prvoj kamenoj gromači
A message of flowers will still remain	Iz nekih dobrih
In blossoming strands	I bolnih ruka
From good and	Procvala
Bloody	Cvjetna
Hands	Poruka

More than he emphasizes sacred blood and soil, however, Dizdar reinforces the image of renewal as a moral imperative, since it is through renewal, nested in the tombstones of Bosnia, that cultural continuity takes place. As a poetic theme, then, the renewal speaks the language of land, but also of religion and genealogy.

"VINE AND ITS BRANCHES"

One of the central themes in *Stone Sleeper* is the recognition that the world goes on even in post-mortem absence. Most poignantly told when presented as stone sleepers' dilemma, the idea of stillness in and against movement is often referred back to the stećak's fixed poise in the midst of historical change. As Dizdar reaches out to the stećak for both literary and political reasons, the question of the stećak's relevance in territorial identification turns attention to the question of continuity between the medieval sleepers and their contemporary keepers. For example, the poem "With Hand Raised High," which takes inspiration from the common lapidary motif of a man holding up a grotesquely large hand as if signaling the passerby to stop, articulates the dilemma of being eternally present in stone amidst the flux of life:

Stop	Stani
I say	Velim suncu
To the sun which burns my brow	Što tjeme mi prži
To the earth which grips me tight	Velim zemlji čvrsto što me drži
To the day as it slips away	Velim danu što opet odlazi
To the old serpent with his flickering tongue	Velim zmiji drevnoj što okolo plazi
I say	Velim
To the aged bard	Pametaru
Whenever he visits my hands	Što gori i plamti
And flames still burst from his glowing embers	Kad pohodom čestim ka rukama mojim
Whenever he thinks me and remembers	Još uvijek me misli i uvijek se pamti
I say	Velim
But nothing	A ništa . . .
Stops	. . .
Only my scream	Samo je moj krik
Is as solid as this stone of mine as steady and firm	Čvrst kao ovaj moj kamen postojan i stalan

As the dead observer registers change, the link between geography and history is enhanced. The land, occupied by the dead and the living, alerts us to the question of continuity. Its importance or lack thereof becomes a matter of national volition. In affirming its importance, Dizdar's approach to land, from a comparative standpoint, parallels complex narratives that imagine nations as bounded by particular space but also give them a sense of movement and continuity within that space. Hence, one of the most important dimensions of territory is that it allows culture to evolve in reference to its past and present manifestations and shapers. Poetry about land is therefore poetry about cultural continuity, and Dizdar's construction of continuity takes on several forms, all of which return to land as their prime referent.

In addressing the complexity of this effort, it seems useful to recall some of the theoretical literature on national images of continuity and the immortality of culture. Benedict Anderson's work readily comes to mind: In his seminal study *Imagined Communities,* Anderson speaks of the centrality of "ghostly imaginings" in narratives of national identity. The cultural roots of national projects, Anderson argues, are clearly concerned with death, though not death in any personal sense but, quite to the contrary, the anonymous death of unknown martyrs.[31] Drawing a parallel between religious rhetoric and national rhetoric in reference to the "style" in which communities are imagined, Anderson argues that neither religion nor nation is an ideology (though, one might add, both can be exploited for such purposes), and both necessitate narrative uniformity and ritual sensibilities. As regards the subject of death, however, Anderson underlines the pitfalls of nationalism in not being able to provide a satisfactory eschatological account of post-mortem continuity. Monuments to heroic but anonymous soldiers seem to be the best that national rhetoricians can muster. Consequently, Anderson argues, national discourse borrows from the realm of religion and dynasty, the two models it supercedes, using their rhetoric of immortality and redemption in an attempt to create a sense of national continuity against fatality and loss. Secularly construed, these ideas are customarily processed through multiple genres of creative expression and in a particular written language, which, at both the aesthetic and the ideological levels, tighten the links between "fraternity, power, and time."[32] Sacredness is maintained as the organizing principle of national communities, even if not conceived in terms of divine associations. This can be most clearly observed in the context of territorial identification. According to Anderson, the metaphors of cosmic time, order, divine dispensation, and sacred speech feature as the foundation-stones of national rhetoric. The form that was appropriated from their three constructs—sacred language, divine rulership, and sacred time—began to decline in the eighteenth century, when these metaphors lost their original religious value and became secularized in the national imagination.

While the power of rhetoric imported from previously dominant or monopolizing discourses is one of the most relevant testimonies to the evolving and contextual nature of national identities, Anderson's emphasis on the paradigmatic role of religious metaphors in national rhetoric has lent itself to criticism. As his insights into great world religions centralizes the macro-cosmological order of things, they eclipse the importance of other structures, including nuclear family or communal bonds, as well as the emergence of problematic and ironic identities that can decenter any national narrative. As far as the centrality of micro-structures for the attitude toward death is concerned, some scholars argue that quite often such structures offer the primary referent for questions and answers about life, at times modifying, if not subverting, religious teachings. An insightful objection to Anderson's thesis that nationalism relies on religion to account for death, Gopal Balakrishnan's thesis argues that it is family, not religion, that invariably ensures a sense of continuity and connectivity. How is it that nationalists still call on the people to sacrifice their lives in the name of the nation, yet do not promise immortality? Balakrishnan criticizes Anderson for not being able to answer that question mainly because, in his view, Anderson fails to pursue associations between nation and family lineage, despite initial interest. He suggests that Anderson's thesis would have been more convincing had the analogy between nuclear kinship and nation been better explored. After all, Balakrishnan argues, "If there is an anthropologically invariant desire to overcome death through artifacts which evoke social continuity, it is surely the family and not religion which more universally fulfils this role."[33] Nation behaves like extended family: It allows all of its members, who may be of different religious or ideological persuasions, to care for a common future. This suggests, then, that neither the dead nor their world need to be nameless, unknown, or ghostly in an impersonal sense when incorporated into the genealogical tree of a national culture. In fact, as the controversies arising around cemeteries suggest, there often exists a tension between the memory of the anonymous dead and the memory of specific persons from among them.[34] Because remembering a person requires remembering at least some of her or his biographical details, the right to difference and individuality in post-mortem identity construction undermines the rhetoric of clarity and singularity of the national memories of anonymous heroes. Jay Winter, for example, discusses, quite poignantly, the ways in which the "anonymous heroes" of World War I return in cultural memory as specific persons. Questioning their family and neighbors about the purpose of their death,[35] they intertwine their family ties with the grand, national cause, treating the family as a synecdoche for nation.

Along with, or between, family and religion, however, stands sacred kingship. Although Anderson does not explore in much detail the presence of sacred kingship in national language, he introduces this category as another general precursor to national discussions on immortality. In many ways, his initial analogy to family, which Balakrishnan detects, melts into a discussion on religious rhetoric, eclipsing the synergetic quality of sacred kingship. In many ancient cultures, from Mesopotamia to Mesoamerica, sacred kingship interlaces the cosmic order with family structure: emulating blood ties by appealing to the parental role of the divinely appointed ruler, the king stands as the intermediary between heaven and earth. Through his divine appointment, the king aligns his society with gods, and through different rituals his line of descent from the divine source is repeatedly confirmed.[36] The emphasis on vertical continuity through sacred rituals, as well as on horizontal ties among the members of society, with both trajectories bounded by specific place, ensures a sense of unity and continuity. Although, admittedly, Anderson does not treat in detail the modus operandi of such structures in the national rhetoric on continuity, his analysis aptly detects the proclivity of national imagination to view itself as unbroken, nonperishable, and secured in the lineal trajectory, that is common in such religious systems. In fact, even the monotheistic traditions that Anderson has in mind maintain, to varying degrees, familial metaphors that were inherited from their Near Eastern predecessors; Christianity's concepts of the Kingdom of Heaven and Earth and of divine lordship are examples. In that sense, religious and family metaphors in national rhetoric are not as incompatible as Balakrishnan suggests.[37] Their association in ancient systems of belief is what scholars of religion refer to as "national religions," that is, religious structures based on the idea of common lineage on holy ground, into which members are born and out of which they cannot convert.

In *Stone Sleeper*, for example, Dizdar also draws on the language of the dynastic realm in order to supply the reader's imagination with claims, more political than literary, on national space. As he reflects on both cosmological and social hierarchies, he looks at the members of the community as both creatures of the dualist cosmos and creators of a specific social space. Everyone inhabiting the space is entangled in the network of social and cosmic relations, participating, in an unbroken way, in the shaping of Bosnian territory. The religious language infuses the language of legal rights with a sense of purpose; the latter sprinkles the former with irony. The poem "A Text about Blessing" is replete with a ceremonial but jocose bestowal of honor and fortune on the society, as represented by its different offices. The cosmic order, starting from divine to royal throne, from nobility to common folk, is carefully preserved as each class is hyperbolized in its merit and function, private and public, and each is intrinsically connected to those who come before and after. The poem starts with:

Blessed be every governance from whatever hand	Velika čast svakoj vlasti što stiže nam bilo ma od koga
Blessed be our King and every lordling of this Bosnian land	Čast kralju našem i svoj vlasteli rusaga bosanskog
Blessed be the King's father and our dear Queen Mother	Čast neka je kralju otcu i kraljici majci
Blessed be his royal offspring and every royal brother	Čast blagorodnoj djeci kraljevskoj i blagorodnoj kraljevskoj bratiji
Blessed be the King's blood brothers and their brotherly battalions	Čast pobratima njihovim i svoj bratojskoj satniji

The poem then moves on to list, in a cascading yet ostensibly punctilious manner, the royal progeny, their subjects and objects, as well as those who can be added to the society by virtue of their association with the scribe:

And from this high table of bless- ings may some morsels remain for me still— So I may bless beside all the rest our headman and squire And all these blessings may be shared With shrewdness And skill	Sa velikog stola časti neka i meni na kraju ostane nešta— Čast velika da skažem kmetima i kmetićima i ostalim svima Kako podjela te časti bi Mudra i Vješta

Throughout the poem, however, there is a burlesque interlacing of status, fortune, and merit, delivered in an oratorical tone typical of medieval festivities that seems more befitting of opulent kingdoms than the humble Bosnian state. The atmosphere is carnivalesque, integrative but not necessarily subversive. Yet the final two lines add a pinch of political sarcasm by appealing to the ethics of participation in the same scroll of life. The worldly title becomes practically necessary but metaphysically irrelevant; and the tension between the two, played out as part of the complex Bosnian lineage, functions as a reminder of the continuous interplay between sanctity and profanity.

Somewhat similar though more royally focused is the poem "Strife," in which the historical conditions of Bosnia are presented as the main concern of all its kings and potentates. United in struggle against foreign dominion—Greek, Hungarian, Turkish—the great men of Bosnia die heroic deaths, one after another, defending the cause "of their lord." But we know nothing more of the lord and his cause. A thin line separates irony and solemnity in each of these biographical characterizations. The last few verses, which speak of a principled dedication of all Bosnian monarchs to an unnamed transcendental cause, immerses the entire glory to the medieval kingdom in existential paradox, dotted with paronomastic allusions on the fierce dynasty of *vuk* (the wolf):

And this is how their pedigree
Is later recounted to run:
Vukas before his death sired
   Vukan his son
And Vukan sired Vukoman
And Vukoman then
And so it went on down the line
Right until the present time
All in the service most loyal
Of their lord
	A potom potomstvo ovo
	Prema predanju starom ide ovako:
	Po smrti Vukas svojoj rodi sina
	   Vukana
	I Vukan onda jedne godi rodi
	Vukomana
	Vukoman poslije
	I sve tako redom
	Do današnjeg
	Dana

Although the stanza is playfully genealogical, it is not conceived as a precise enumeration of descent from medieval times to the present, but as a poetic affirmation of the chain of patrilineal royalty based on the funerary record. In addition, however, one can detect poetic modes around which consanguinity is achieved, especially the one that bears distinct and irrevocable implications for territorial identification.

Like kingship, religion and family permeate *Stone Sleeper*, and they too speak the language of land. Because they appear as interconnected modes, their presence reflects Dizdar's approach to the past as textured with characters and social relations that, in the spaces of death, inevitably lose their worldly value but maintain their allegorical one. The most obvious mode in creating a sense of cultural continuity is the deployment of religious language. As discussed on several occasions, Bogomil eschatological tension between mortality and immortality is purportedly engraved in the lapidary imagery, and inscribed in the epitaphs, in accordance with the belief system of medieval Bosnians. The poem "Death" is the most obvious example of the religious confirmation of immortality as recorded in the national stone:

The earth is sown with a deathly seed	Zemlja je smrtnim sjemenom posijana
But death is no end For death indeed	Ali smrt nije kraj Jer smrti zapravo i nema
Is not and has no end For death is just a path	I nema kraja Smrću je samo obasjana
To rise from the nest to the skies with the blest	Staza uspona od gnijezda do zvijezda

Since Bogomilism has been commonly interpreted as a simplified form of Christianity and in some ways a precursor to Bosnian Islam, speaking from within the Bogomil system of belief relies on teachings familiar to all existing Bosnian religious/national communities. In other words, appealing to Bogomilism does not generate an epistemological chasm between the poet and his reader. In fact, as the modern reader learns more about the belief system of the ancestors, she or he also reflects on its continuing presence in contemporary culture. Continuity is thus created at this pedagogical level as well, insofar as Bogomil themes transcend their historical framework without completely losing their symbolic currency and, significantly, without undermining the reader's authority on the subject. The deployment of religious language draws on Dizdar's extensive knowledge of Western religions, and he generously borrows from them without jeopardizing the integrity of his Bogomil focus. Biblical references (in "Rain,"

"Radmilja," "Prayer," "*vine and its branches*"); Christian hagiography and heresiography ("*sun Christ,*" "*the garland,*" "Madderfield"); and Sufi and Qur'anic, even quasi-Kabbalistic, influences ("The Rightwise," "*bbbb,*" "Roads"); all shape the poetic construction of transcendental and historical Bosnia.

However, Bogomil religious teaching is not just a theme in *Stone Sleeper*, it is also developed into a trope. As a trope, it allows the questions of belonging to be asked and answered in reference to the dualist cosmological scheme. References to hopes of a better life, to this life as impermanent and deceptive, and to the ultimate victory of good over evil, are recurrent motifs in *Stone Sleeper* that draw on the Bogomil ethos. This trope is also topographically referential in that it provides a persuasive reinforcement of Bosnia's place on the world map. This takes us back to the metageographical representation of Bosnia as a fringe, the space in between dominant spaces. The Bogomil rejection of certitude and immutability fosters a spirit of rebelliousness against the claimants of theological or political omnipotence. In its secular rendering, then, Bogomil teachings allude to the spirit of defiance and uprightness characteristic of Bosnian culture in all its historical manifestations. In the two—the Bogomil theological challenge to the singularity of truth, and the Bosnian historical resistance to cultural assimilation—Dizdar dissociates the motif of defiance from its customary association with Slavic (and other!) mentality, turning it into a stable and regenerative myth of Bosnian culture. Defiance, too, is thus a form of continuity, and its territorial implications are best expressed in "A Text about a Land." In this poem, to the questions of the where and when of Bosnia, the answer centers on the ethos of land:

Forgive me there once was a land sir called Bosnia	Bosna da prostiš jedna zemlja imade
A fasting a frosty a	I posna i bosa da prostiš
Footsore a drossy a	I hladna i gladna
Land forgive me	I k tomu još da prostiš
That wakes from sleep sir	Prkosna
With a	Od
Defiant sneer	Sna

Such religious metaphors also permeate the language of genealogy and dynastic lineage. Consecrating both, spiritual allusions allow the lineage to be conceived as both symbolic and genetic. This cosmic unity of the Bosnian family is enhanced by the convergence of religious and familial metaphors grounded in the land. "The House in Mile," for example, speaks of the home of the *djed*—the grandfather—evoking scenes of domesticity and harmony in and around the family property. But "*djed*" is also the title given to the elder of the Bosnian Church. Because the latter were not organized around institutional hierarchies, the elder maintained a sense of communal and lineal relations in spiritual life. The poem thus gradually moves between the nuclear and the universal, from home to homeland, allowing these categories to develop with a full range of associations. There is a subtle interplay between a legal assertion of ownership over land and its generous offering to all passers-by:

Our Grandfathers' House was built to last	Djedovska tu hiža bi stvorena
So its strength would stand fast	Krepča da krepost
In our	U srcima
Hearts	Ostane
So let its doors stay open wide	Pa neka je zato vazda otvorena
For welcome guests and passers-by	Za doste drage
And all whose hearts are	I velikane
Grand	Srčane
For all good people beneath the sky	Za sve pod nebom dobre ljude
And all who live in Bosnia's	I za sve dobre
Land	Bošnjane

The poem goes on, at great length, extending hospitality to people of different persuasions and beliefs, vocations and locations, desires and aspirations, all united in goodness and righteousness despite their visible differences. Historical references to dualist martyrs across Southern Europe (Dalmatia, Provence, Lombardy, and so on) draw attention to the concept of brotherhood as expressed in kin, cause, faith, and ethos, again revealing Dizdar's application of mystical language to the exoteric and esoteric planes of life. The celebratory welcome of the plethora of human destinies is accompanied by the following warning:

But if someone in selfish pride	A ako li kto ta vrata kreposti
Should suddenly slam	U sebeljublju svom
The doors of our	Nenadno
Citadel	Zatvori
Let our Grandfathers' House be dashed to the ground	Neka se hiža djedovska do temelja
And let it be smashed	Sori i sruši
In my	U mojoj
Soul	Duši

This statement alerts us to the recurring message in *Stone Sleeper:* Unless guarded in its uprightness, home—in Bosnia—cannot and should not be saved.

Another common poetic theme around which lineal ties are established is based on the lapidary motif of vines. Interpreted as having the mainly decorative value of a frame for human or symbolic representations, the vine motif is especially common in the "Herzegovina school" of lapidary art. A vine frequently appears as a poetic motif in *Stone Sleeper* as well. As Francis Jones explains, Dizdar's deployment of the motif carries a symbolic value that can best be appreciated in reference to the biblical allusion in John XV:1–4, "I am the true vine, and my Father is the husbandman / Every branch that beareth not the fruit he taketh away: and every branch that beareth fruit, he purgeth it, that it may bring forth more fruit." In fact, in the poem *"vine and its branches,"* the biblical image of renewal as a divine commandment places emphasis on the fertility and continuity that conjoins the heavenly and earthly realms:

Present here is He	Ovdje je prisutan onaj
Who said for verily it is writ	Koji po vjernom očitovanju reče
I am the true vine and my Father	Az esam loza ostinia a otac moj
is the husbandman and Every	moj je vinogradar
branch in me	
That beareth not fruit I shall take	I vsaku rozgu na meni a ploda ne
away	da ja ću odsjeći
But that the field wax fat the fruit	Al onu koja rada da polje bude
be sweeter the root be deeper	bolje
The branch that beareth	Da sladi dar i plod veći
I shall purge	Čistim

At another level, however, it is to be noted that *loza* is the Bosnian word for lineal descent, so its presence in poetry also symbolizes abundance and renewal in terms of ancestral continuity. When read in this triple entendre of the vine as an agricultural/geographic, spiritual, and lineal asset, the verses that refer to the vine become even more symbolically charged, as in the final lines of the same poem: *"I descend toward Him / down the line / of this white / vine."* In this sense, the catastrophic invasion anticipated in "Message" becomes ever so pertinent when the assault on the vineyard is interpreted as an assault on the totality of culture:

A meddler from the South disguised as a peddler	Sa juga lukav robac prerušen kao trgovac
You'll hack my vineyard back to the root	Vinograd ćeš moj doj žile sasjeći

So that beneath my poor feet	Pod nogama ubogim da
There'll be less shade	Bude manje hlada
And deeper	I ponor
Chasms	Veći

As the danger of hacking the vine signals the danger of cultural extrication, the importance of safeguarding the roots of vineyards becomes an imperative. Roots are thought of in geographical terms, but also in genealogical and, as suggested by religious language, spiritual terms. Yet despite such rich naturalist representations of lineage, fundamental to Dizdar's search for genealogical representations are stone inscriptions. Nature and culture interlace again. As argued in the previous chapter, the visual imagery of the stećak upon which Dizdar bases his mythographic reflections on post-mortem continuity is supplemented, in a balanced and persuasive way, with epitaphs that record the mundane struggles and, occasionally, petty concerns of medieval Bosnians. Because graveyards inevitably eclipse horizontal connections, the biographical information, as marked by epitaphs, is incomplete and partial. Life is therefore much more than a sum of the epitaphs. To go behind the epitaphs means to transcend the tangible marks of history and to imagine communal associations that are neither assumed nor engraved in stone. In "A Word about a Son" a mother laments both the loss of her son and the pithiness of stone inscriptions, which speak not and hear not, yet anchor the memory of her lost son. The poem allows her to invite the reader to go beyond the stone silence, to listen to her elegiac narration of her son's life, as if that will make her loss more bearable:

I would hold silent like a stone	Šutjela bih kao kamen
Woe's me I am not stone	ali kamen jadna nisam
And so forgive me that I speak	Oprostite zato slovu
This word that will become stone[38]	koje će se skameniti

In this sense, although constituting the basis of Dizdar's search for cultural selfhood, the rootedness that is established in the stećak's space of death discloses myriad threads in the fabric of national culture. The narratives of pollution and taboo usually associated with the space of death enable the treatment of the stećak as cultural text, which, in contrast to the shrines of saints or the mausoleums of heroes, does not glorify death. Death is accepted as both impurity, threat, and an innocuous warning against solitude. The stone epitaphs thus testify to loss and confirm fatality. Wisely, Dizdar does not enshrine that past, nor does he yield it to poetic catharsis. Loss is not redeemed; it is only demystified. The balance between lofty and abject events in a person's life, oscillations between compassion and animosity, responsibility of thought and irresponsibility of action, the vicissitudes of emotion and reason, are all captured on the epitaphs and translated into poetry. The roots are disparate. Truthful to the cosmological duality of medieval Bogomilism, Dizdar consciously engages the reader in cultural self-critique, not self-exaltation, while nesting the roots into Bosnian soil. In "Third" of the "Word on Man" cycle, the stone images capture the lowly struggle for survival of human beings who are torn between the desire for spiritual salvation and the cruel realities of the world:

Barred in with bones woven in flesh	Zatvoren u meso zarobljen u kosti
Soon will your bones poke through this mesh	Pa će tvoje kosti tvoje meso bosti
Cast out of heaven you crave wine and bread	Otrgnut od neba želiš hljeba vina
Stone and smoke's all you get instead	Kamena i dima samo ima svima
I see your one hand but where is the other	Od te ruke dvije tvoja jedna nije
Was it lifted To kill its brother?	Jedna drugu ko da Hoće da pobije?

The hint of fratricide in the above poem, of corruption and loss in "A Text about a Leaving," of betrayal and disappointment in "A Text about Hope" and "Unwilling Warrior," of deception in "A Text about Wealth," and so on, all echo the sentiments of acceptance of individuality within collectivity, of the many facets of selfhood and its complex fashioning. The breadth of historical experience implies that cultural roots can also harbor disenchanting, painful, even shameful dimensions. The epitaphic memory, fragmentary that it is, is thus a poignant testimony to the diversity of cultural experience. The merit of the epitaphs lies not in a uniformity of biographic record, but in their ability to chronicle a variety of experiences through a culturally cohesive form of funerary inscriptions. "Lilies" appropriately asks if the voices from the past are cries of delight or fright. "Unwilling Warrior" laments that "glory and praise vanished in bloody days," while "A Text about Wealth" admits a personal failure to succumb to the allures of material wealth. The epitaphs record different kinds of stories, some sad and lowly, others merry and noble. Yet all beg for remembrance. Memory is therefore a form of salvation. The call for acceptance is articulated throughout the collection, including in "Madderfield":

May all the foul and fair may all
the poxy and pure
Share this wine to the dregs share
this bread to the crumbs
As killers and killed share their
fraternal tombs
For this song must be heard to the
very last word
Or corruption will be our daily
bread
While we live and while we are
dead
And by our frowning faces may
we not be judged
On our way to love we trudged . . .
For now

We've stopped for the first time

On our way
Knowing it's time to look time in
the eyes
Time to admit we've waited in
vain for word and deed to meet
(And let it be said in the end with
the right measure in our voices

That if our cries didn't rise to the
depths of the skies
At least our shrieking was in
keeping)

Za dan taj nek lipte rane vijeka
nek kipte rijeke srdite ljubavi
Kroz tumuše i tmače neka sve jače
moćni mačevi
Neka svi lijepi neka svi dobri svi
ružni i gubavi
Do mrvice podijele ovo vino ove
hljebove
Kao što ubice i žrtve podijeliše
bratski ove grebove
Jer treba do kraja čuti ovaj plač i
ovu pjesan
Da nas ne nahrani trulež

Da nas ne sahrani plijesan
Ne sudite nas po tom što nam je
zamračeno lice
Na putu ka ljubavi to gazimo kroz
smetove i vijavice . . .
Na ovom putu
Sada smo prvi put zastali

Znajući da je vrijeme da vremenu
pogledamo u oči
Vrijeme je da priznamo kako smo
sastanak riječi i djela uzalud
čekali
(Na kraju valja i ovo reći s pravom
mjerom u izrazu i glasu-
Ako nam glas i nje stigao duboko
do neba
Vrisnuli smo bar
Kako treba)

National genealogy, then, is re-established only as the lives of individuals recorded in epitaphs are looked upon as illustrations of life in a struggling community. The ancestors are therefore neither glorious nor transparent in *Stone Sleeper;* they are abstruse and full of contradictions, just as the living are. In a "Text about Wealth," for example, the end is anything but lofty:

To no man never did I telle
How I my welth did gayne
Now let it be knowne
That then

Nikada nikom ne rokoh
Kako stekoh blaga
Sada neka se zna
Da taga u ruke vraga

Into the Divils hands I felle	Stigoh
That through him	Da s njega
I for my welth was slayne	Zbog blaga da pogiboh

These lines suggest that there is always something disturbing about the way in which the dead are deposited, mourned, and then remembered. Their location on the outskirts of villages and towns is a sign of that unease. "The expulsion of the dead beyond the boundary of the village," Michel Ragon writes, "preceded in fact the expulsion of the dead from our everyday life."[39] On the subject of cultural roots in such shadowy zones, Michel Foucault warns against the dangers of glorifying roots in the spaces of loss. According to Foucault, the ability to accept the past in its ambivalent developments and implications is the redeeming quality resulting from genealogical enterprise. In a provocative analysis of Nietzsche's *The Genealogy of Morals*, Foucault argues that genealogy, for all its meticulous and documentary value, does not align itself with history but to the search for origins. It is the concept of "origin" that assumes the presence of essential qualities, frozen in time and thus incorruptible by the vicissitudes of existential forms. Because the quest for origins essentializes inception as something sheltered from the flux of time, the possibility of penetration into, and disclosure of, the kernel of truth defines and informs that quest. The myth of origin gains validity across time, and is not to be questioned or altered, only discovered. But in postulating that there is an unadulterated truth in the genesis of things, the search for origin runs against positive knowledge and therefore threatens to refute itself: "The origin," suggest Foucault, "lies at a place of inevitable loss."[40] On the other hand, the genealogical enterprise appeals to history so as to dismantle the misconception of a beginning as derived from a lofty, inviolable source in favor of an understanding that what lies behind any beginning is much more derisive, erroneous, and often incoherent.[41] As opposed to "roots," genealogy concerns itself with "emergence." It teaches that the organizing principle of "emergence" is a series of accidents, which are neither fixed nor secured, neither simultaneous nor symmetric, in any cohesive sense. Moreover, "emergence" is never singular but always happens in the interstices of a struggle for domination between two parties.[42] In that sense, while the search for origins singularizes truth, deeming it inviolable, genealogy underscores its uneven texture and demands "the decisive cutting of the roots, the rejection of traditional attitudes of reverence, its liberation of man by presenting him with other origins than those in which he prefers to see himself."[43]

Establishing connections persuasively draws attention to the multiplicity of sources and voices that currently make up the collective self. Dizdar never denies that multiplicity, but he does not simplify it either. Instead, he posits it as a historical legacy and, as such, as a collective responsibility. The responsibility primarily calls for digging through the layers of cultural expressions in an effort to reach to the roots. This is an act of self-acceptance in history, not a myth of national glory. In that sense, even though Foucault repeats the warning against looking for "roots," cultural roots as Dizdar creates them are not inviolable in their contents but are inviolable in their location. The impulse to preserve culture is an urge to face historical reality, to secure cultural roots in the landscape, since the self ought to be accepted in all its complex entanglements. After all, as the ritual of return implies a return to the cemeteries, the memory of the past is inevitably the memory of wars, losses, and failures. Even if its medieval dead are not heroes, they can, in the final analysis, be considered martyrs: As Dizdar reminds us in the closing pages of *Stone Sleeper*, "[medieval] Bosnia was doomed to dream of justice, to work for justice, to await justice, but never to experience justice."[44]

In many ways, then, *Stone Sleeper's* oscillation between micro-cosmic and macro-cosmic realms, between particularity and generality, constitutes an interface between Anderson's emphasis on the religious and monarchical influences on the national rhetoric of immortality and Balakrishnan's anthropological focus on family as the main narrative glue in the construction of nationhood. But, although reliant on their language, Dizdar avoids establishing the sanctity of national experience in the Bogomil myth or in ancestral glory, but in the biographical detail of stone sleepers whose naturalized presence infuses the land with rich symbols of renewal and continuity. The images chiseled in the whiteness of limestone—images of sprouts and blossoms, irrigating rivers, animated gestures, revealed fragments of personal lives, and social diversity—enable the sites of death to reawaken as the sites of vibrant life and diverse medieval lifestyle. Consequently, although charted as sacred ground through which the medieval voice invokes spiritual and ritual sensibilities of contemporary Bosnian readership, the stećak is made into a site of ambivalence. On the one hand, its marginal location in contemporary space has an ironic resonance, being a common trope of Bosnia's in-betweenness. On the other hand, fixed in the landscape, the stećak bears witness to the *ius soli*, the ancestral right to land, exposing the displacement of the current national cultures from their own land.

This is consistent with the view that territorial belonging, for all its importance in nation-narration, often assumes different forms and meanings, reflecting rhetorical vicissitudes of nation-construction. "Territory," Herb argues, "clarifies national identity by sharpening more ambiguous cultural and ethnic markers."[45] Although common territory ranks high on any list of national projects, territory need not be seen in any homogeneous way.[46] In the case of Bosnia, its absence from national projects was symptomatic of a political, rather than cultural and social, incongruity, since the land has been inhabited and valued for its bountiful gifts to history and culture. For Dizdar, the reclamation of land counterbalances its absence from national formation. Even so, land in *Stone Sleeper* is explicitly poeticized, and only implicitly politicized. While the poetic focus reflects the significance Dizdar assigns to the continuity and consanguinity of national culture in geographic terms, it does not suggest a removal, only a deepening, of the existing rhetorical bonds with the land.

Benedict Anderson shows that some European nations, as of the first half of the nineteenth century, have seen themselves as "awakening from sleep," that is, establishing memories of ancestral glory by appealing to vernacular language and folklore as if "'rediscovering' something deep-down but always known."[47] At first glance, Dizdar's *Stone Sleeper* corresponds to such efforts. Vernacular language, folklore, ancestors, and myth feature prominently in his poetic animation of the medieval stillness. However, Dizdar's main effort is to align the nationalities of Bosnia with the medieval abode. The question "When will your home be your homeland again," poignantly posed in the poem "Kolo," has found an answer: when reading Mak's poetry.

Appendix

Translating Spiritual Space-Time

Recreating *Kameni Spavač* in English

Francis R. Jones

Any act of literary translation does more than reshape an original ("source") text into a "target" text in another language: It also mediates between source and target writer, source and target reader, source and target culture. In this essay I describe how, as the English translator of *Kameni spavač*, I attempted to reshape and mediate Dizdar's world in the light of my own relationships with Bosnia, with Dizdar's text, and with my mother tongue.

Borderlands

Let me start by charting the outer lines of these relationships. In the late 1970s I, a young Englishman with an accent from a Yorkshire industrial town and a Cambridge degree in Serbo-Croat, was a postgraduate student of poetry in Sarajevo. There, I became spellbound by Dizdar's numinous verse. But *why* did Dizdar seize me so? The answer parallels that to another question: Why study in Sarajevo, rather than the bigger centers of Belgrade or Zagreb? Some things cannot be explained that easily, especially now that history's seismic shifts have savagely, irrevocably changed the physical and cultural landscape of what once was Yugoslavia, and my feelings toward it. I have tried to write out these feelings elsewhere.[1] Here, suffice it to say this: What attracted me both to Bosnia and to Dizdar was an intense and heady beauty, but also a sense that I was in the borderlands, the marches of my world until then. What I glimpsed was indeed beautiful—the serene yellow leaves of an autumn lime tree in a mosque courtyard, for instance, or a unique poetry whose rhythm and images had the rush of strong *rakija*. But the beauty had a double—edged frisson: History lay close to the surface, and wisdom, even then, had often been bought at a terrible cost.

Whatever—I resolved to translate *Kameni spavač* into *Stone Sleeper*. Mounting my own expeditions into the shadowy worlds Dizdar had travelled, mapped, and so intensely felt, I spent many days in Sarajevo's National Library, reading Bosnian, Serbian, and Croatian verse, heretical and antiheretical tracts, and tomes of nineteenth-century folklore. But the book took 20 years to complete. Still only a novice translator, I found that reproducing Dizdar's dazzling form was initially beyond me: indeed, the course of my apprenticeship can be traced through the pages of the final work. And without a publisher or a living poet pressing me to find one, *Stone Sleeper* was a slow-burning, private passion. A bilingual edition finally appeared in Sarajevo in 1999, but *Stone Sleeper* has not yet been published in an English-speaking country.

WHAT THE TRANSLATOR DOES: MODELS OF TRANSLATION

Before starting the analysis proper, it is worth referring to the translation-theory assumptions on which it is based. The work of the literary translator can be viewed from various standpoints. One is the familiar, faithful, free cline, which might be better described as a cline oriented between source text and target text respectively. Here, I see the literary translator as looking both ways—as a demiurge whom the source writer has entrusted to create a new world, but who rebels against the source writer at the translator's own peril. The translator as Sataniel, perhaps.

Another cline is that between orientation toward translation as product—that is, words on paper, and toward translation as process, that is, the translator's mental and physical acts. Here, I start from a process base, describing how and why—while translating—I identified certain key translation problems (for example, that stećak has no English equivalent) and weighed up possible strategies (to use an endnote and/or to keep the original Bosnian word).[2] This, however, inevitably leads to an evaluation of the target-text products (such as the line of verse) that resulted.

A third aspect is that of the translator as an actor in a communicative process. As I describe elsewhere, the literary translator has a double task, that of alchemist and that of ambassador.[3] As alchemist, one has to physically make a new text, melting down the metal of the source in order to refashion it in a different but ideally no less precious metal—that is, that of the target language. With such a complex, multi-layered text as *Kameni spavač*, this is not easy; indeed, Bosnians and Herzegovinans pride themselves on the untranslatability of their master poet. As an ambassador, one has to persuade readers in the target culture to read and hear a new voice from an unfamiliar culture. When translating into English a poet deeply rooted in a cultural soil largely unknown to an English-reading public, this is no less a challenge.

Moreover, both ambassadorship and alchemy have an ideological dimension. With ambassadorship, ideology informs the translator's decision to translate, or to refuse a writer's or publisher's request for translation. In my case, the decision to translate and promote Dizdar's work was initially an artistic one (I felt that he was, quite simply, a great poet). But later, during the savage dismemberment of Bosnia in the 1990s, it also became a political decision—an urge to represent to the outside world a culture that I saw being threatened with deliberate extinction. As for alchemy, the fact that no two languages and cultures map exactly onto one another makes perfect reproduction impossible. Within this space of imperfection, translators have to make choices. These choices are shaped not only by linguistic and stylistic concerns, but also by ideological concerns[4]: How do translators choose to portray, in their target text, the source writer and the culture of he or she writes? How is this portrayal colored by their own worldview and the expectations they ascribe to their target readers? Thus, in my translation, choices that were seemingly just linguistic and artistic were also coloured by my own passion for Dizdar's poetry, his culture, and his country.

TRANSLATING THE LOCAL

In *Kameni spavač*, the universal and mythic is reached by way of the local and real. But whereas the universal is what makes his work worth translating, the local makes it difficult to translate—for the translator into English has to recreate Dizdar's world in a language whose culture lacks many of the raw materials to do that job. This, of course, is a challenge central to the philosophy of translation, and of communication in general: How can art intensely based in locality be communicated to those who are alien to that locality?[5] This theme runs through the discussions that follow.

GEOGRAPHY

When describing a locality, it is usual to begin with the physical. The readers of *Kameni spavač*—natives of Yugoslavia and its successor states, or non-natives who have learned the language once known as Serbo-Croat—are familiar with the physical feel of Bosnia and the surrounding region. But relatively few native English readers of *Stone Sleeper* will have visited the region, or will be familiar with its geography, topography, people, and artifacts—at least beyond the television newsreels, which, thankfully, are now too receding into history.

Nevertheless, physical geography itself only rarely presented translation problems. The very familiarity of the landscape means that it is only rarely described or alluded to in *Kameni spavač*, and the world that Dizdar (re)creates is far more a *Tamni vilajet*, a Dark Province of myth, than a physical reality. Only sometimes—for example, when specific towns, rivers, and the like, are named—does physical geography muscle to the fore. Here I used the strategy of explanatory notes only as a last resort, preferring where possible to solve the problem within the text itself. This was not always easy, as shown in the following lines from the poem "Svatovska/Wedding" show (literal version appended):

I za žedne pute	(And for the thirsty roads
Jer pravo od travničke Lašve	Because straight from the Travnik Lašva
Pa preko Rame i Neretve	And across the Rama and Neretva
Do travunjske Lastve	To Travunian Lastva
Lete te laste	Those swallows fly
Na Lastovo	Onto Lastovo
Plavo	The blue

Readers of the original would know that Travnik and Lastva are Bosnian towns; that the Rama, Neretva, and Lašva are Bosnian rivers; that Lastovo is an Adriatic island; and perhaps also that Travunje was a medieval Bosnian province. Moreover, they would realize that Dizdar is highlighting the etymological link between *laste* ("swallows") and *Lašva, Lastva,* and *Lastovo*. In English, by contrast, a mere transcription of names would convey

neither the physical representation nor the etymology to target-text readers. My strategy, therefore, was one of deliberate "explicitation" (making
assumed information in the source into explicitly stated information in
the target[6]), both of the key place-names and of the etymology:

> For Bosnia's thirsty roads
> Because these swallows are swooping
> Across all her rivers from Swiftwater Lašva
> Over the Rama and Neretva
> To Lastva the Swallow
> Above blue Lastovo
> Isle of Swallows

Note here the signalling role of *Bosnia's* (my addition) in the first line, the
dropping (for poetic streamlining purposes) of the modifiers *Travnik* and
Travunian, and the glossing of the last two names (*Lastva the Swallow* and
Lastovo Isle of Swallows). An alternative, explored in an early draft, might
have been to favor the word play and delicate sound structure at the expense of greater geographical precision:

> Because these swallows are swooping
> Swift across her rivers over the Swiftwater
> Over the Rama and Neretva
> As far as Swallowfield
> And the blue
> Isle of Swallows

However, such a radical act of "domestication," that is, of adaptation toward target-language norms[7], would have made my locality more mythic
and less Bosnian. As mentioned earlier, my drive as translator was not
only to translate a text, but also to represent the Bosnian culture. Hence I
chose the former version, which favors using names as signifiers of Bosnian places rather than making them etymologically transparent.

ARTIFACTS

Understanding *Kameni spavač/Stone Sleeper* is crucially dependent upon
knowing the stećci—artifacts so familiar to source-text readers that Dizdar did not need to describe them, but only alluded to them. Target-text
readers, however, need to know not only their physical appearance (without which the poems would make a lot less representational sense), but
also their cultural significance (especially if the translation aims, at least

partially, to be an affirmation of Bosnian culture to the outside world). Hence an English edition needs not only illustrations of the stećí (like the present volume), but also some explicit cultural contextualization—in a whole-text, stand-alone edition, this would probably mean an extensive introduction and notes.

DIALECT

Kameni spavač does not only describe the geographical or material features of Dizdar's place: It is also defined through language itself. Amid the welter of voices in Dizdar's carnival, I—as a non-native reader— often had difficulty distinguishing the local from the historical. But— to my ears, anyway—the language of *Kameni spavač* as a whole is regionally marked only in a broad sense. The Latin script, and the distinction between the non-palatalized *e* and the palatalized *(i)je* (merged in Eastern varieties) show that Dizdar is using a broadly Western variety of what, when he wrote, was known as Serbo-Croat. Within this standard Western matrix, however, he occasionally inserts words such as *hiža* ("house") as deliberate markers of Bosnian regionality— as in the poem "Hiža na Milama" ("House in Milé"), which defines Bosnia as a place of refuge.

Finding an equivalent for the unmarked matrix was not an issue: I simply replaced standard Western Serbo-Croat with standard Eastern (that is, British) English. It was with the source-text items marked as specifically Bosnian that the problems began. Essentially, unless source and target language share the same region, locally marked source-language varieties are untranslatable: There is no Bosnian dialect of English, for instance. It is possible to create such a variety—for example, by including untranslated Bosnian words in the text—but this I chose not to do, as (unlike in a translation from French), they would not be recognizable without footnotes. This left two other options, both of which would inevitably remove the Bosnianness of the language: to delete the markedness altogether (that is, to translate the Bosnian items into standard English) or to use analogous markers of locality from my own language world. I generally chose the former tactic: All but one of my target poems lack the occasional regional sitings present in Dizdar's original. In that one poem ("Slovo o sinu/A word anent a son"), however, I underscored the otherness of Dizdar's locality by asking Brian Holton to re-translate the whole of my draft into his native Scots. Below I show the original plus a literal translation, followed by Holton's Scots version:

Šutjela bih kao kamen	I would [like to be] silent as [a] stone
ali kamen jadna nisam	but I miserable [woman] am not [a] stone
Oprostite zato slovu	Thus forgive a/the word
koje će se skameniti	which will turn to stone
Ljuto hrastu zgromovljenom	Angrily from a/the lightning-struck oak
Uzeše mu zelene grane	they have taken its/his green branches
Skržiše mu vite ruke	They have snapped off its/his slender arms/hands
kojima se gorju dizo	with which it/he rose to the hills
[. . .]	[. . .]

* * *

I wad haud silent like a stane
wae's me I am nae stane
And sae forgie me that I speak
this word that will be stane
They hackit livin branches frae
my levin-blastit aik
They snackit his fair airms that raised
his corp toward the hill
[. . .]

Interestingly, this particular source poem contains no locally marked items. Hence, at first sight, my strategy looks like one of "compensation by place,"[8] that is, where an effect untranslatable at one point in the source text is conveyed elsewhere in the target. The target text's linguistic localization, however, is more radical than that of the source. Not only is the whole target poem (rather than an occasional word) locally marked, but this very fact makes the sense of locality much more salient—especially as Holton's Scots is radically different from standard British English. The strategy, therefore, in which effects scattered throughout the source book are gathered into one target poem might be called "compensation by concentration."

But why Scots—instead of my native Yorkshire dialect, say? And why this particular poem? One reason was artistic: I felt that the theme of the poem echoed that of the old Scots ballad "The Twa Corbies." A second reason was political. I felt that Scots—the language of a potentially breakaway nation with a strong sense of cultural difference from a more powerful neighbor—was the nearest target-language analogy I knew to Bosnian. Whether this strategy succeeds in raising such associations among an English-reading audience is something that I cannot impartially judge. Even if one adds a Scots-English glossary, the poem may simply be inaccessible to non-Scots readers. And even if the poem *is* understood by its readers, the problems bedevilling any use of locally marked language in translations remain. First, all analogies are flawed: here, Scotland vis-à-vis the United Kingdom is like Bosnia vis-à-vis Yugoslavia in some respects, but unlike it in others. Second, the language-place identification (Scots=Scotland) may be so powerful in its effects on target readers that its use in a "foreign" text may seem simply incongruous—"I didn't know they spoke Scots in Bosnia!"

POETIC FORM

Different cultural areas (which are usually larger than nation-states) tend to have preferences for different literary forms. During most of the twentieth century, traditional rhyme- and rhythm-based forms were out of favor in the English-writing world, especially in North America. In the South Slav and Hungarian world, by contrast, their eclipse was much shorter, and many otherwise avant-garde writers—such as Dizdar—still used traditional forms alongside free verse. Moreover, the poetic forms used are rather different from those of the English-writing world. Though accentual stress lines (such as hexameters) have been imported into South Slav poetry, the preferred "traditional" meters are syllabic— that is, based on the number of syllables rather than the number of stress accents in a line.

Poetic meter, therefore, could be seen as another marker of locality. Initially, I translated Dizdar's syllabic poems into free or accentual verse, but with two poems translated later, I deliberately chose to keep a syllabic meter. My overt reason here was to let the target reader feel the music of Dizdar's verse—but, in retrospect, it also fitted in with my wish to recreate a world that was as geographically close to Dizdar's as possible, as in the poem "Zapis o petorici/A text about the five":

Četvorica jednog vode	Four men leading one man bound
Jednog gone četvorica	One men whom the four men hound
Četvorica mrkog lica	Four men's faces dour and dire
Preko vode preko žica	Over water over wire[9]
[. . .]	[. . .]

This is a strategy of "foreignization"—that is, of keeping source-text forms and/or images intact in the target-text, even though they are unfamiliar to target-text readers and/or break the rules of the target genre.[10] It probably succeeded in its first purpose, that is, in conveying the texture of the original. But I suspect that my second purpose—to mark the target text as South Slav—would be appreciated only by those with insider knowledge of South Slav poetics. To the average reader, they probably feel slightly unfamiliar, thus giving a general sense of otherness rather than a specific regionality.

This sense of otherness is probably also strengthened by the strong use of rhyme—a crucial marker of Dizdar's style, which I tried to reproduce wherever possible. It seems, at least in the British Isles, that rhyme has made a comeback in original poetry, but making rhymed translations of rhymed originals is still (deplorably, I feel) the exception rather than the norm. Reproducing a source rhyme scheme in a translated poem, therefore, could be seen as another foreignizing strategy. And foreignization is a two-edged strategy: The "shock of the new" that it delivers may stimulate some target readers but alienate others. This perhaps explains two conflicting reviews of the *Stone Sleeper* translations published (without source texts) by Chris Agee in his 1998 anthology. Agnus Calder writes, "Francis R. Jones's English is wholly convincing"[11] and later quotes lines from "A text about the five." Janet Montefiore, by contrast, writes: "Francis R. Jones's jingling internal rhymes come across as portentous mannerisms."[12] Interestingly, Montefiore precedes her damning verdict of my target poetics with a positive description of their source counterpart, which she had not read: Dizdar's internal rhymes are "echoing" rather than "jingling."

Of course, I am not claiming that my mastery of poetics is equal to Dizdar's. But two implications emerge from this discussion. The first is the assumption (depressingly familiar to most literary translators) that if one does not like the target text, the translator is to blame. Secondly, translators have to live with the fact that there are two distinct target-language genres: English original poetry and English translated poetry. Norms of permissible metric practice may well be narrower in the latter than in the former.[13] One might even speculate whether translated genres are, as a whole, more resistant to innovation than are original target-language genres—although, as we will discuss later, it is probably safer to say that that norms are *more contested* in translated poetry than in original poetry.

HISTORY AND FAITH

So far, we have looked at reconstructing the spatial aspects of Dizdar's locality; let us now turn to the temporal and the spiritual. Alhough non-Bosnian target readers might know a little of Bosnia's geography, they are very un-likely to know anything of its religious and secular history. And once again, providing representational information would give only half the picture: By definition, the way that the source text both assumes and strengthens the grounding of the reader's identity in medieval spirituality cannot be *felt* by a non-Bosnian target reader, even if it is *described* in an introduction or trans-lator's notes. Here, perhaps, we have reached the limits of translatability—which, to my mind, lies not in words but in the relationship between text and reader. At best, one might hope for a different relationship: that the very strangeness of the schismatics' world and story would be compelling to the target reader.

In a narrower sense, Dizdar occasionally refers to people and events in Bosnian history. My approach here was again to communicate meaning as far as possible within the poem, using footnotes only as a last resort. With named historical figures, for example, my first-choice strategy was one of "partial domestication," reviving the pleasantly old-fashioned convention of anglicising foreign names. A straightforward example, from the poem "Razmirje/Strife," is the wonderfully titled *Queen Helen the Coarse* (*Kraljica Jelena Gruba*). Partial domestication could also be strengthened through the context surrounding the name. For example, *U davno u slavno u Bana Stipana Drugog* (literally "During long-ago during glorious during Ban Stipan the Second") became *Once in good King Stephen's golden days*—a line I borrowed from the ballad "The Vicar of Bray." Or by changing *U vrijeme bana i kralja Tvrtka* (literally "In the time of Ban and King Tvrtko") to stress his central importance in Bosnian history: *Once upon a time when Good King Tvrtko ruled this land.*

ARCHAISM

A key way in which Dizdar gives *Kameni spavač* historical texture—or rather, adds historical voices to his polyphony—is through his use of archaized lan-guage. The poem "Pravednik"/"The Rightwise" is a good example:

> A nebo bi plno
> Plno ot olova
> Te ta slova šute
> Oni što brez duše

My translation of these lines runs:

> But only the stillnesse of ledde

Did fille the welkins bowle
Alas the worde was heard
Only by those with no soule

As this example shows, it is relatively simple to mark early modern English through spelling (all the forms in the above quotation are attested by
the *Oxford English Dictionary*) and vocabulary (*welkin, alas*). This, however, is another strategy that has caused mixed reactions in target readers.
Some have been negative: Montefiore labelled such solutions as "sham
medievalisms," and even the otherwise positive were uneasy here.[14]
    It is true that my discourse is not genuine medieval English but a twen-
tieth-century construction; the real thing would, of course, have read
rather differently. In an early draft of one poem ("Gorčin/Gorchin"), I
had tried to give a much more "authentic" middle-English patina:

Ase ležit	Heere lyeth
Vojnik Gorčin	Gorchin soldier
U zemlji svojoj	In owen londe
Na baštini	In straungers
Tuždi	Stede
[. . .]	[. . .]
Mrava ne zgazih	Ne fly nolde I marre
U vojnike	Yet I yede
Odoh	For a soldier
[. . .]	[. . .]

However, feedback from a reader indicated that words like *londe* ("land"),
stede ("town"), *nolde* ("would not"), *yede for* ("went to be"), and *marre*
("hurt") were hard to understand, and even misleading. For example, he
understood *In straungers Stede* as meaning "Instead of a stranger" rather
than the intended "In a stranger's town." So I pulled back, rewriting my
drafts to give a more digestible but obviously more recent Medieval Lite,
as in the lines from "The Rightwise" quoted earlier.
    Yet Dizdar's original poem was also a modern construction, and—to
the best of my knowledge—the accusation of sham medievalism was not
leveled at him. This has three possible implications: (1) Mine is a shoddier
construction than his; (2) It is a construction that I am not licensed to
build; and/or (3) It is more out of place in my cultural landscape than his.
The first possibility I am not qualified to judge. But I do now see "The
Rightwise," an early translation (and one that formed part of the selection
criticized by Montefiore), as one of my least successful medievalized
translations, with its overly heavy reliance on archaic spelling giving a

slightly depressing "Olde Englishe Tea Shoppe" impression. The second possibility, already discussed with respect to poetics, is that translators, unlike "original" poets, are not licensed to break literary or linguistic rules (and if they do, they run the added risk of being accused of mistranslation). Whether or not this is the case here, it is certainly why most verse translators—unless they are target-language poets in their own right and thus already feel licensed to innovate—tend to err on the side of conservatism. In the worst cases, this can mean smoothing out the spikiness that gives the original text its texture; and in the best cases, it may tie the translator to innovating only in the same way and in the same place as the source.[15] The third possibility is that medievalism in English poetry is not merely innovative but also transgressive—in other words, that it breaks a target-culture taboo. Medievalism, as a feature of much nineteenth-century poetry in English, was roundly rejected by the modernists early this century, but (unlike rhyme and rhythm) does not yet seem to have been brought back into the post-modern poet's or poetry translator's toolkit. To the best of my knowledge, however, nineteenth-century poetry in Serbo-Croat did not suffer from medievalism but from folklorism; and hence Dizdar's construction of medieval discourse will have raised fewer hackles among his target readers.

However, not all reactions to the archaism in my Dizdar translations have been negative, and therefore these implications are not the only ones. Agee, writing about *Kameni spavač, Stone Sleeper,* agrees that norms differ between translated and original target-language poetry. But he sees the norms of translated poetry as giving *more* freedom for experimentation and innovation, not less:

> Unencumbered by the need to express himself directly, Jones is, ironically, free to assume a stylistic persona largely unavailable to the contemporary poetic ear in English. For obvious reasons, this older metric and music is not so easily accessed by the contemporary poet writing in his own voice, whose technique is moulded by a different language and a different world; in original work, this "remote sound" would risk courting the inauthenticity of the outmoded, if not outright anachronism. The fact that, in contrast, it succeeds memorably in Jones's handling of Dizdar exemplifies why "the art of collaboration" is just that—a poetic art both inseparable and distinct from that of the original poem. Which is to say that the translation of poetry has an imaginative space not achievable elsewhere; and that this space, from the Renaissance onwards, has been a prime means of refreshing the tradition with stylizations from outside the language and the age.[16]

My personal feeling is that these seemingly opposing views are two sides of the same coin. Literary translation, especially foreignizing translation, *is* probably more likely than original target-language poetry to be seen as transgressive. Yet, though some transgressive acts of translation may be rejected by the target culture, they may equally well be accepted—and without transgression of existing norms, there can be no innovation.

RELIGIOUS DICTION

Just as Dizdar used archaism in *Kameni spavač* to construct a historicized Bosnia, so he used religious diction to define religious faith as the life-blood of his Bosnia. In both cases, my aim paralleled Dizdar's. When searching for target-language analogies, however, I felt I was on safer ground with his religious than with his medieval voices.

The 1611 Authorised Version of the Bible (and, to a lesser extent, the 1559 Book of Common Prayer) are not only crucial texts in the development of the English literary language and common speech, but their discourse has implicitly or explicitly informed English literary writing down the centuries. Moreover, this discourse has not been ousted by modernism, as T. S. Eliot's *Four Quartets* or Arthur Miller's *The Crucible* demonstrate. Hence—although it is slightly anachronistic relative to Dizdar's constructed late-medieval time—I used the 1611 Bible as source and inspiration for the religious voices in *Stone Sleeper*. The religious voice in the following lines, for example, combines direct biblical references (such as the "strait gate") with discourse constructed according to Authorised-Version patterns (for example, "I am that gate and at it enter into Me as I now into thee"). Consider the poem "Vrata"/"*the gate*":

Ovdje smo još uvijek samo steći
  gosti
I trebalo bi već jednom preći u
  krug svjetlosti
Kroz neka uska vrata trebalo bi se
  vratiti
Iz tijela ovog golog u tijelo vječ-
  nosti
Kada se doskitah u ovo veče
  kasno
On mi reče a da ga ne pitah
Ja sam ta porta i kroz nju udji u
  mene jako ja u tebe
On take reče al gdje su usta brave
  gdje prst pravog ključa za
  vrata u stepeništa goruća?

[. . .]

Here just guests we stand out still

Although we should have crossed
  into a ring of light
And passed at last through a strait
  gate in order to return
Out of this naked body into the
  body eterne
When I happened by this evening
  late
Unbidden He said unto me
I am that gate and at it enter into
  Me as I now into thee
So He spoke but where is the mouth
  of the lock where the finger of
  the one true key for the gate to
  the burning stair?

[. . .]

POLYPHONY

We have looked at the translation of various individual elements in Diz-dar's world; but how they fit together is also crucial. As Agee puts it:

> Besides all the usual higher-register challenges of meaning, nuance and tone faced by the translator of poetry, Dizdar poses some special difficul-ties. What I find especially exciting about his poetry, and indeed is unique in my experience of the art, is the way he brings together a series of con-trasts that are folded into a single suppleness of voice: biblical and secular, ancient and modern, dialectical and literary. Thus, the translator is faced not only with rendering each of these dimensions, but with the overall tonal drama they create.[17]

When I look back now on the transmutation of *Kameni spavač* into *Stone Sleeper*, I realize that evoking this sense of polyphony, of Bakhtinian car-nival, was my overriding textual aim—an aim that was again fueled both by artistic loyalty to the text itself and by a more ideological wish to con-vey an extraordinary artifact from a grievously threatened culture.

This, for example, led me to pay close attention to the *juxtaposition* of voices and discourses. Between the last two lines quoted (in the previous section) from "Vrata"/"*the gate,*" for example, I kept the stylistic contrast between the biblical voice giving Christ's words of comfort and the mod-ern voice of the despairing sleeper who is still waiting outside the gate. Sometimes, however, I made the transition sharper than in the original. Raymond Van den Broeck notes that—because translators aim to make communication easier—translation almost inevitably tends to explain, to make the implicit more explicit. Van den Broeck is looking especially at semantics, at how translators tend to explain away source-text ambigui-ties[18]; but on re-reading some of the juxtapositions of voices in my text, I realize that his observation also applies to structures of discourse. Be-tween the first and second verses of "A Text about a Knight," for example, the radical grammar and spelling changes in the English have a very sharp change of voice:

> He loved the grasses loved the birds loved the clouds
> Loved the heavens loved the earth
> Loved each day dancing
> Like a prancing
> Foal
>
> Therefor he never ne soghte him deth

But deth was ay by him
Ay neare to his
Soule
[. . .]

But in the original ("Zapis o vitezu"), the archaism is more subtle. It is largely a matter of using a literary rather than a spoken past tense, except for the archaic *nj vavijek* ("him always": the modern equivalent would be "njega uvijek"):

Volio je trave volio je ptice volio oblake
Volio je nebo volio je zemlju
I dane razigrane
Ko konjice
Lake

I zato i tako smrti nikad ne poiska
Al smrt je uza nj vavijek bila
Prisutna i
Bliska
[. . .]

CONCLUSION

Both the bane and the joy of poetry translators' lives is that poetry translation is a multidimensional crossword in which no clue has a single, obvious solution. As soon as a linguistic and cultural distance opens up between source and target, the translator has to make choices. These are informed by artistic and ideological drives, by one's own readings of the original, by the philosophy of communicating a new text, and/or by personal history and preferences. Thus, when reshaping *Kameni spavač* into *Stone Sleeper,* sometimes—as with place-names or poetics—I chose to transfer source-world features directly into the target world. At other times—as with dialectal, archaic or religious discourse—I chose to look for English-language analogies. Occasionally—as probably happened with "Word anent a son"—the target text went off on a trajectory all its own. More often, as I have shown, the constraints and opportunities of the target language/culture, together with decisions that had little conscious motivation (such as those to boost small historical or modern differences into bigger ones), made the texture of my text subtly rather than grossly different from Dizdar's.

In the end—to return to the metaphor of the translator as Sataniel—a target world, though it is created in the image of the source, ends up following its own rules. But this, I firmly believe, is the only way it can live.

BILINGUAL SELECTIONS FROM *STONE SLEEPER*

ROADS	PUTOVI

You've decreed me not to be cost
    what may
Weeping with grief and joy
You charge me down
You cleanse and destroy
Everything in
Your way
	Ti si nakanio da mene nema i pod
	    svaku cijenu
	Ideš prema meni i u jurišu
	Smijući se i plačući
	Pred sobom
	Sve čistiš
	I ništiš.

You've decided to root me out at
    any price
But nowhere will you find
The real road
To me
	Ti si nakanio da me pod svaku ci-
	    jenu uništiš
	Ali nikako da nadješ
	Istinski put do mene

For You only know roads That are carved and cleared (And these are narrow and barren indeed No matter how weary And long They seem To you So proud and So strong)	Jer Ti poznaješ uklesane i utrte pute I niti jedan drugi (A mali su zapravo i jalovi Bez obzira koliko su Za tebe Oholog i jakog I preteški I Dugi)
You only know the roads That start From eyes And Heart	Ti poznaješ samo one puteve Što prolaze Od srca I Oka
But that's not all	Ali to nije sve

Some roads unfold before us	Ima putova što su se ispružili pred nama
Without a beaten track or almanac	Bez javnog traga kolovoza
A departure time	Bez voznog reda
Or tide	Bez vremena
	I roka
Your path to me poor though I be	Ti misliš da je tvoja putanja do ubogog mene
Seems sure and tried	Veoma sigurna i česna
In your sight	Ona
A path that comes	Što dolazi
From left	S lijeva
Or	Ili
Right	Zdesna
You fool yourself I can be found	Zavaravaš se stalno da do mene treba ići
By setting your course	Smjerovima sličnim
For north	Sa sjevera
Or	Ili
South	Juga
But that's not all	Ali to nije sve
Plague	Kuga oči uvijek
Is wise	Pametno mi traži
It seeks my eyes	Ispod ustalasale na vjetru raži
Beneath the rye which ripples in the wind	Iz korjena zemlje gdje se zgusla tmina
In the roots of earth where the dark has congealed	A iz bezmjernih visina
But from measureless heights	Odozgora
Night's	Pritiskivati
Hag	Grudi
Has pressed	Najjače
On the	Može
Strongest	Móra
Breast	
But that's not all	Ali to nije sve
You don't know the right of way	Ti ne znaš nakon raskrsnice

At the cross-roads	Izmedju svjetlila
Of night	I
And day	Tmice
But that's not all	Ali to nije sve
You don't know that in your life	Jer najmanje znaš da u svom žicu
The one true war	Najteža rvanja su
The hardest strife	I ratovi pravi
Is at your very	U samome
Core	Biću
And so you don't know that	Ti ne znaš dakle da zlo si moje na-
you're the least	jmanje
Of my legion	Izmedju mnogih
Of	Mojih
Great	Velikih
Evils	Zala
You don't know who	Ti ne znaš s kim
You've taken on	Imaš posla
You know nothing about this	Ti ne znaš nista o mojoj mapi
road-map of mine	putova
You don't know that the road	Ti ne znaš da put od tebe do
from you to me	mene
Isn't the same	Nije isto što i put
As the road from me	Od mene
To you	Do tebe
You know nothing about my	Ti ne znaš ništa o mome bogat-
wealth	stvu
Hidden from your mighty eyes	Skrivenom za tvoje moćne oči
(You don't know that fate	(Ti ne znaš da meni je
Has deemed	Mnogo više
And dealt me	Nego što misliš
Much more	Sudbina
Than	Namrijela
You	I
Surmise)	Dala)
You've decided to root me out at	Ti si nakanio da me pod svaku ci-
any price	jenu uništiš

<table>
<tr><td>

But nowhere will you find the real
  road
To me

(I understand you:
You're a man in a single space and
  time
Alive just here and now
You don't know about the bound-
  less
Space of time
In which I exist
Present
From a distant yesterday
To a distant tomorrow
Thinking
Of you

But that's not all)

</td><td>

Ali nikako da nadješ istinsku put

Do mene

(Shvatam te:
Čovjek si u jednom prostoru i
  vremenu
Što živi tek sada i ovdje
I ne zna za bezgranični

Prostor vremena
U kojem se nalazim
Prisutan
Od dalekog jučer
Do dalekog sjutra
Misleći o tebi

Ali to nije sve)

</td></tr>
</table>

## A Word on Heaven	## Slovo o nebu
### A TEXT ABOUT A HUNT	### ZAPIS O LOVU

An underground water wakes from deepest sleep breaks free and streams through a clear and glorious dawn towards a distant river towards a weary sea	Neka se podzemna voda budi u jasnom sjajnom ozoru iz svog dubokog sna i teče nekoj dalekoj rijeci nekom umornom moru
Meekly tripping between the forest's golden green the fawn will not stop until her course bring her to her spring her source	Neko nejako lane posrće kroz zlatnozelenu goru I neće da stane dok ne pristane svom bistrom izvoru
Slipping between the ochre saplings the flustered roe seeks a vanished whisper seeks the fleeting days	Jedna smetena košuta žuri kroz neke žute vriježe tražeći nestali šapat tražeći davne dane što

that pass between the dimlit grass
that flit between the frets
of grassy nets

I see that stag beguiled by the eyes
    of the doe
entranced by her glance till sunset
    come
his limbs grow numb
his tread
go red

A tall horseman masters seething
    spaces of unrest
Handsome Dumb with deep de-
    sire Blind
without a sound he tramps behind
the baying and howling of hounds
panting thirsty straining for the
    blood of future
battlegrounds

I see it all in a second In this day's
    sun
As if with a glance
Of a hand
And

I know that starveling sparkling
    spring will never enter its dis-
    tant delta
its gentle shelter I know that
    source
will never caress its pebble of
    pure
quartz

The restive doe will never hear
    the tiny cry that greets
her trails her tails her through the
    cover
will never hear the bleats
of mother
No more will the stag climb the
    cliff and never again

bježe kroz tavne trave kroz travne
mreže.

Vidim ljeljena onog što pati kad
    prati oči one srne
i slijediće ih omamljen tako sve
    dok
na zahodu sunce ne utrne
sve dok mu koraci
ne ucrne

Jedan konjik velik osvaja vrele
    prostore nespokoja
Lijep Slijep od velje želje Nijem

Bez glasa on gazi za lavežom pasa
Što urla što žedno diše i
kidiše u krv budućeg

razboja

Vidim sve to u jednom trenu U
    suncu ovog dana
Kao na dogledu
dlana
I

Znam da nikada onaj gladni
    harni vrutak neće ući

u daleko ono ušće u svoj krotki
    kutak

da nikada zagrliti neće svoj čisti
bjelutak

Košuta brižna više nikada neće
    čuti onaj mali glas
što pred njom ide što prati je kroz
    vlati
što nikad neće više reći
mati
Na stijenu onu propeti ljeljen
neće se nikada više

will he bell his reply to the green
   cry
of the green
rain

Nor will the tall horseman hunts-
   man splendid in his battledress
amid the cavalcade and all its show
ever loose that battle arrow
from his bended
bow

For in that single instant that split
   second
when rapt in self all were hunters
and utterly
alone

I Grubač the hewer did hunt these
   hunters down threads unseen
them I writ with humble wit
   them I truly drew
in the height
in the white
of this stone

na onaj zelen zov
one zelene kiše
odazvati

Ni konjik tragač velik u sjajnom
   bojnom odijelu
usred sjajne tragačke svite nikad
odapeti neće iz sulice vite
onu ubojnu
strijelu

Jer u tom jednom jedinom trenu
   u tom magnovenju kad
sobom obuzeti bjehu goniči svi
i sasvim
sami

Te strašne lovce ulovih u nev-
   idime konce ja kovač Grubač
i vjerno upisah i smjerno narisah

u ove vele
u bijele
u kāmi

Radimlja

     THE GATE

Here just guests we stand out still

Although we should have crossed
   into a ring of light
And passed at last through a strait
   gate in order to return
Out of this naked body into the
   body eterne

When I happened by this evening
   late
Unbidden He said unto me

Radmilja

     VRATA

Ovdje smo još uvijek samo steći
   gosti
I trebalo bi već jednom preći u
   krug svjetlosti
Kroz neka uska vrata trebalo bi se
   vratiti
Iz tijela ovog golog u tijelo vječ-
   nosti

Kad se doskitah u ovo veče kasno

On mi reče a da ga ne pitah

I am that gate and at it enter into
  Me as I now into thee
So He spoke but where is the
  mouth of the lock where the
  finger of the one true key for
  the gate to the burning stair?
I grope in the grass I scour my
  skull for the one blue key
Seeking a path through spring's
  flowers past death's scythes
  searchig for that golden door

I stoop through ants and plants
  through sooth and untruth I
  seek and find
But when I raise my hand to the
  lock who betrays my desper-
  ate quest?

This dark side of the door an ill
  wind prowls a foul wind howls
I forsake my sister and brother forsake my father and mother between the beasts and the men
To seek my essence my pillar of
  blinding incandescence
How in the world must I find that
  word
And what would be in the finding?

Unbidden He said unto me

Enter ye into Me for I am that
  shining gate But still
I wait I lie I rot I die upon this sill

And the wind the wind the wind

If the gate of the word is just a
  dream a fairy tale
Still I will not leave this door

Here I want to live once more
This supreme
Dream

Ja sam ta porta i kroz nju udji u
  mene jako ja u tebe
On tako reče al gdje su usta brave
  dje prst pravog ključa za vrata
  U stepeništa goruća?

Pa tragam po travi zato i tražim u
  glavi tako ključ taj plavi
Kroz cvijetlja proljetna kroz kose
  smrti tražim ušće u te zlatne
  dveri

Zadjem u mrave u bilje u privide
  u zbilje Tražim i nadjem
Al od ruke moje do ključanice kto
  tu strogu istragu iznevjeri?

Sa ove mračne strane vrata nadire
  vjetar hudi razdire vjetar ludi
Ostavljam sestru i brata ostavljam
  oca i majku izmedju zvijeri i
  ljudi
Da sebe budem našao u svom
  biću na putu svom stubu sjaja
Kako ću kad u tom žiću da
  zgodim se u slovu
Što bi u otkriću?

On reče mi tako kad ga za to i ne
  pitah
Usji u mene jer ja sam ta vrata
  sjajna Pa sada
Bdijem sada gnjijem sada mrijem
  tako na ovom dovratku
A vjetar vjetar vjetar

Ako su vrata iz riječi samo san
  ako su samo gatka bajan
Ja ipak neću više da se s vrata
  vratim
Ja opet hoću tamo da snim
Tu slatku
Gatku

WEDDING	SVATOVSKA
With my death my world has died	Smrću mojom umro je i moj svijet
An age-old darkness	U prazne oči
Occupies	Mrak se
My empty	Pradavni
Eyes	Naseli
With my death my world has died	Smrću mojom umro je i moj svijet
But the world's world	Ali svijet svijeta
Will not be pushed	Neće da se
Aside	Raseli
Memory's white tape	Sada kroz sudbinske tišine
Pierces the armour of darkness	Bijeli trak sjećanja
Between the silences	Probija kroz oklop
Of fate	Tmine
And through that strange pane	Kroz čudno okno tog prozora
A deep new	Rodi se neko novo
Eye is	Duboko
Born	Oko
And on my skyline I see the dawn	Pa vidim na svom obzorju
Rise from	Kako se iz ničeg
Nothing	Podiže opet
Again	Zora
There's a golden noon mature to the core	Eno žuto podne do svog srca zrije
And an evening of toil	Eno veče truda
On toiling	Na trudna ramena
Shoulders	
With my death my world has died	Mojom smrću umro je i moj svijet
But it will not stand still	Ali on neće da stane
Because my hands	Zbog zaustavljenih
Are	Mojih
Stilled	Ruku
And even the stone does not seem	Kamen sam kao da nije
Stony	Od kamena
Under the blue under the high	Pod nebom veoma visokim
And silk-soft sky	Pod nebom plavim

Of Podvisoki	I mekim kao svila
The King's Thing	Opet se stanak
Is	U Podvisokim
Gathering	Sastao
And me with no hands	A ja bez jedinih ruku
And me with no days	A ja bez roka
And me with no eyes	A ja bez oka
And me with no	A ja bez
Wings	Krila
And amidst all the pain	Pa opet mi se nasred tog bola
I dreamed that white	Bijela vila snila
Wood-nymph again	Pa opet se
And all my desires	Želja
Teemed again	Vrela
Again she wound	Opet se ko ljuta guja
Like an angry snake	Pod grlo
Around	Savila
My neck	
With my death my world has died	Mojom smrću umro je i moj svijet
But even at its heart	Ali ni srce smrti
Death is not barren	Nije prazno
Or bare	Ni jalovo
When the green grain mellows the green wheat yellows	Žitka kad požute kad sazru žita
It yearns to be reaped	Zažele da ih žanju
By girls	Žene
For the brave battalions	Za hrabre bojne
For the battles braved	Za hrabre vojne
For their beloved	Za mlade
Braves	Ženike
For Bosnia's thirsty roads	I za žedne pute
Because these swallows are swooping	Jer pravo od travničke Lašve
Across all her rivers from Swift-water Lašva	Pa preko Rame i Neretve
Over the Rama and Neretva	Do travunjske Lastve
To Lastva the Swallow	Lete te laste
Above blue Lastovo	Na Lastovo
Isle of Swallows	Plavo

Only stone-birds these birds here	Samo ptice kamne ove ptice amo
Forever keeping	Sve kroz puzavice
Through the creeping ivy	Čuvaju vječno
Faithfully keeping	Čuvaju
The warmth	Vjerno
Of a mossy	Toplinu rukavice
Glove	Od mahovine
With my death my world has died	Smrću mojom umro je i moj svijet
But the world's flowers	Ali cvijetlja svijeta
Are here and now	Svugdje i sad
On every side	Ima
On wings of smoke	Na krilima dima
On rings	Na kolima
Of sun	Sunca
Between the sunplants	Kroz sunčana bilja
They bud and	I klija i
Bloom	Cvjeta
Somewhere between the banks	Medju obalama negdje
Waters trickle	Otančale vode šume
Praying	Moleći
For rain	Za kišu
Somewhere between the leaves of sleep	Kroz šum kasne mjesečine
Dreamed forests	Opet sad nekog
Sway	U nedohod
In a kolo	Vode
Through a trickle of late moonlight	.
They tempt you to follow	.
To stray from the way	.
Again	.
Prisoners still breathe the thin air	Još sužnji u tankoj nadi dišu
Of hope	Dok hladna rosa
As a cold dew	Na bose im
Falls on their bare	Noge
Feet	Pada
Someone rushes through his city in search of himself	Tražeći trkom sebe u svom gradu

But in the end	Nekto je opet ostao
He's left bereft	Bez svog jedinog
Of his only city	Grada
I'm dead	Mrtav sam
Dead	Mrtav
But with my death	Ali sa smrću mojom
The world	Nije umro
Did not	I
Die	Svijet
Once again the gleam	Opet se u nekim očima
In an eye	Svjetlost
Fades	Zanavjek
For good	Gasi
In another soft eye	U nekim mekim
The dream	Tek počinju
Is just beginning	Da plamte
To blaze	Snovi
And over the high levees	Pa preko visokih brana
Over the nays	Preko zabrana
Over the graves	Preko
And their	Grobnog
Stones	Kamena
Over the bones	Preko kostiju što sve jače
That glow	Svijetle
In the dark	U tami
Like ever brighter lights	
High and low	Gorom i dolom
Elaborate	Kićeni
Wedding rites	Svatovi

A Word on Earth	*Slovo o zemlji*
A TEXT ABOUT THE FIVE	ZAPIS O PETORICI

Four men leading one man bound One man whom the four men hound	Četvorica jednog vode Jednog gone četvorica
Four men's faces dour and dire Over water over wire	Četvorica mrka lica Preko vode preko žica
On they scoff and on they trough Through each thread and through their bread	I od ića i od pića I od ruha i od kruha
Through each hedge and through each Y Until freedom us untie	Kroz živice kroz ižice Od svobode od slobode
Past the homes and past the tombs Through the earth and through the sky	I od hiže i od greba I od zemlje i od neba
Four men leading one man bound One man whom the four men hound	Četvorica jednog vode Jednog vode četvorica
One man counted bound and led One man whom the four men dread	Četvorica jednog broji Četiri se jednog boji.

A TEXT ABOUT A LEAVING	ZAPIS O ODLASKU

In this worlde I lived long My yeres in this worlde were eight and four score	Na svijetu ovom dugo ja žih Bih osamdeset i osam ljeta na simeju svijetu
In house muche rychesse I layed in store Ne gan I ne moment reste ne feasted I ne frende ne geste	U svoj dom mnoga blaga spremih i skrih Ne časih ni časa namjernika ne častih ne pogostih gosta
In this worlde I lived enowe	Na svijetu sijem ja živjeh dosta

Like an emmet in house I gar-
nered muche rychesse

Now I must goe
To mete my ende

Here I lye now pennylesse
Left behynde is my rychesse

I mnoga blaga revno ko mrav u
dom svoj nesoh

Sad u končini
Odlazim

Sa sobom ništa ja ništi ne ponesoh
Pusto iza mene sve blago osta.

COSSARA

When the hunters hunt her
through the thorny brake
With my hands I build a bridge
for her to take

Though they drive her onward
through each muddy stream
She is drawing closer strange
though it may seem

Now beneath the sword they put
her head so pure
In yourself you're tall in me
you're strong and sure

Still you are not dumb although
you are no more
In the sky her star

Shines like a crimson scar

KOSARA

Kad je nekud gone preko oštrog
drača
Gradim most od ruku njime da
korača

Sve dalje je vode preko mutne
vode
Ali čudom stiže meni sve to bliže

Glavu čistu meću pod oštricu
mača
U sebi si viša U meni si jača

Tebe više nema Al ti nisi nijema
Na nebu se javi ko crvena rana

Ozvjezdana

GORCHIN

Here lyeth
Gorchin soldier
In his owen lande
In a straungers
Estate

I was on lyf
Yet deth I hailed
By day and nighte
Ne fly wolde I harme

GORČIN

Ase ležit
Vojnik Gorčin
U zemlji svojoj
Na baštini
Tuždi

Žih
A smrt dozivah
Noć i dan
Mrava ne zgazih

Yet I went	U vojnike
For a soldier	Odoh
I foght	Bil sam
In warres five on five	U pet i pet vojni
Withouten buckler or maile	Bez štita i oklopa
Ay alle at ones	E da ednom
Gorchin	Prestanu
Was ne more	Gorčine
I sterved of straunge sicknesse	Zgiboh od čuden boli
Ne pyke ne perced me	Ne probi me kopje
Ne arrowe ne slewe me	Ne ustreli strijela
Ne sworde	Ne posječe sablja
Ne smote me	
I sterved of sicknesse	Zgiboh od boli
Withouten hele	Nepreboli
I loved	Volju
But my lasse was	A djevu mi ugrabiše
Into bondage taken	U roblje
If thou Cossara meetest	Ako Kosaru sretnete
Upon the paths	Na putevima
Of our Lorde	Gospodnjim
Tell her	Molju
I bid thee	Skažite
That I my troth	Za vjernost
Did kepe	Moju

MESSAGE

PORUKA

You'll come one day at the head of an armoured column from the North	Doći ćeš jednog dana na čelu oklopnika sa sjevera
And reduce my city to rubble	I srušiti do temelja moj grad
Smugly saying	Blažen u sebi
To yourself	Veleći
Now it is razed	*Uništen je on sad*
And razed	*I uništena je*

Its
Faithless
Faith

But then you'll be amazed
To hear me walking through
The city again
Quietly stalking you
Again

And secret and sly as a Western spy

You'll burn my home to the ground
Till all
Fall

And then you'll say these dark
    words

This nest is done for now
This cursed cur
Is slain
With pain

But by a miracle I will still be
    dreaming here on earth

And like a wise watchman from
    the East
Forbidding others to dream and
    think
You'll pour poison
Into the spring
From which

I drink

And you'll laugh you'll roar
That I am
No more

(You know nothing about the
    town in which I dwell
You've no idea about the house in
    which I eat

Nevjerna
Njegova
Vjera.

I čudit ćes se potom kad čujes kako
Ponovno kora©čam
Tih po gradu
Opet te
Želeći.

Pa tajno ćeš kao vješt uhoda sa
    zapada
Moje žilište sažeći
Do samog dna
I pada

I reći ćeš onda svoje tamne riječi

Sada je ovo gnijezdo već gotovo
Crknut će taj pas pseći
Od samih
Jada.

A ja ću začudo još na zemlji
    prisutan sniti

Pa kao mudrac badac sa istoka

Što drugom brani da bdije i snije

Sasut ćeš
Otrov
U moj studenac
Iz koga mi je

Piti

I smijat ćeš se vas opijen
Kako me više neće
Biti

(Ti ništa ne znaš o gradu u kome
    ja živim
Ti nemaš pojma o kući u kojoj ja
    jedem

You know nothing About the icy well From which I drink)	Ti ne znaš ništa O hladnom zdencu Iz kojeg ja Pijem)
A meddler from the South disguised as a peddler You'll hack my vineyard back to the root So that beneath my poor feet There'll be less shade And deeper Chasms	Sa juga lukav prerušen kao trgovac Vinograd ćeš moj do ,žile sasjeći Pod nogama ubogim da Bude manje hlada I ponor Veći
And every home will know famine's Spasms	I više glada ima U staništima
And from afar I'll let it be told This truth of mine Unerring And old	A ja ću ti ovako iz daljine Svoju prastaru I pravu Istinu Izreći
(You know nothing about the sign Of the husbandman Or his vine	(Ti ne znaš ništa o znacima vinograda Niti vinogradara Njegovog
You don't know what such gifts are worth)	Ti ne znaš vrijednost takvog dara)
Yea my stay on this solid earth *Is nasty* *And short*	*Da tavorenje moje na tvrdoj zemlji* *Veoma je kratko* *Ali opako*
By destroying the true shapes it takes *You only confirm it* *Whether it* *Sleeps* *Or* *Whether* *It* *Wakes*	*Ništeći njegove prave pojave* *Utvrdjuješ ti* *Upravo tako* *Njegove* *Jave* *I* *Njegove* *Sne*
In the end you're the hardest guard God's strictest inquisitor	Oružnik si najzad najstrožiji I istražnik božiji

Blooded to the eyes	Krvav do očiju
Desperate	Do očaja
Frenzied	Bijesan
From battles	Od borbe
For dead	Za žive
And living	I mrtve
Chattels	Robe
You'll burn me I know at the end of the show	Zapalit ćeš me znam na kraju priče
You'll burn me I know	Zapalit ćes me znam
At your divine	Na tvojoj presvetoj
Your shining	I svijetloj
Stake	Lomači
Which	Koja
Is	U
Already	Tebi
Rising	Eto
Inside	Već
You	Niče
And on your awesome	A ja se na tvome strasnom
Awful	I strašnome
Scaf-	Stratištu
Fold	Neću
I	Niti
Shall	Po-
Not	Ma-
Shirk	ći
I shall be steadfast as a standing stone	I bit ću vjeruj kao stanac kamen
Till you have done your task	Dok svoj posao svršiš
And your flame	I ne svrši
Has done	Posao
Its	Tvoj
Work	Plamen
Such an end will glorify	Taj kraj rakav slavit će
Your threefold cry	Tvoj trikrati
Amen	*Amen*
Amen	*Amen*
Amen	*Amen*

In my place
Ashes will lie
And for them women will vie

But therefore after me
On the first stone cairn
A message of flowers will still
    remain
In blossoming strands
From good and
Bloody
Hands

When thy goal liketh nigh
Unto its desire—
Know then
That even his
Body
Was
But
A
Moment's
Home

Therefore thou took only his body
    into thy keeping
For that body was only
His prison
And his
Weeping

(How often must I tell you that
    you know
Nothing about me—
Nothing about my arrow and bow
Nothing about my sword and
    shield
That you have no idea how sharp
    is my steel
That you know nothing about my
    poor
Body or
The bright flame
That burns

Na mome mjestu
Ležati će pepeo
Za kojim će se otimati žene
. . . .
Al ostat će zato poslije mene
Na prvoj kamenoj gromači
Z nkih dobrih

I bolnih ruka
Procvala
Cvjetna
Poruka

Kad učini ti se da cilj tvoja je
Svrhi tvojoj najbliža—
Znaj da jest
I tijelo to
Njegovo
Bilo
Samo
Častita
Njegova
Hiža

Ti tijelo to bijahu za njega—

Zatvor njegov
I njegove
Suze

(Ne rekoh li ti već jednom

Da o meni ne znaš ništa
Da ne znaš ništa o mome luku i
    strijeli
Da ništa ne znaš o mome štitu i
    maču
Da nemaš pojma o tim
Ljutim oružjima
Da ne znaš ništa o mom bijed-
    nom tijelu
Niti kakav on žarku plamen
U sebi

Inside

I'm waiting for you
Because I know you
You'll come back one day

(This you've vowed
By chalice and cross and blade of
    sword
Drunk with chants of damnation
    and incense smoke)

So
Come on then
I've long grown used to your rav-
    ages
As if to the throes
Of a disease from far away

As to the icy waters swept savagely
    along
By this night river of darkness
    that grows
Ever more swift
And strong

Ima)

Čekam te
Jer te znam
Doći ćeš opet jednog dana

(Zakleo si se čvrsto na to
Na kaležu na križu na ostrici
    mača
Pijan od pojanja prokletstva i
    dima tamjana)

Pa
Dodji
Navikao sam davno na tvoje po-
    hode
Kao na neke velike bolesti
Što stižu iz daleka

Kao na goleme ledene i strašne
    vode
Što donosi ih sve jača

Ova noćna rijeka
Tmača.

NOTES

NOTES TO INTRODUCTION

1. Zvonko Kovač, "Od komparatistike tekstova do interkulturne povijesti književnosti," *Godišnjak instituta za književnost* (Sarajevo) 20 (1991): 66.
2. Stuart Murray, *Not on Any Map: Essays on Postcoloniality and Cultural Nationalism* (Exeter: University of Exeter Press, 1997), 13.
3. On the history of this term, see chapter two. Its rediscovery in post-Communist times is associated with a heightened self-awareness of Bosnian Muslims as a separate national group belonging to the Bosnian geographical space.
4. Amila Buturović, "Producing and Annihilating the Ethnos of Bosnian Islam," *Cultural Survival Quarterly* 19:2 (Summer 1995): 29–34.
5. Adrian Hastings, *The Construction of Nationhood: Ethnicity, Religion, and Nationalism* (Cambridge: Cambridge University Press, 1997), 130.
6. In fact, the tensions between, for example, Serbs of Serbia and Croatian and Bosnian Serbs increased with the harsh reality of war displacements, as was obvious in the treatment of refugees. In a similar vein, the nationalist Croats of Herzegovina express deep emotional ties to Herceg-Bosna as their motherland, rather than to Croatia.
7. Lisa Malkki, "National Geographic: The Rooting of Peoples and the Territorialization of National Identity Among Scholars and Refugees," *Cultural Anthropology* 7:1 (1992): 24–43.
8. Collections: *Okrutnost kruga* (The Vicious Circle), published in 1961; *Koljena za Madonu* (Knees for Madonna), published in 1963; *Minijature* (Miniatures), published in 1965; *Ostrva* (Islands), published in 1966; *Kameni spavač* (Stone Sleeper), published in 1966; and "Modra rijeka" (Blue River), published in 1971. For a useful synopsis of Dizdar's life see a home page dedicated to him at: http://www.djikic.net/pub/mak/mak.htm.
9. Enes Duraković, *Antologija bošnjačke poezije XX vijeka* (Sarajevo: Alef, 1995), 22. The vicious cycle is a pun on Dizdar's book of poetry, *Okrutnost kruga*, published in 1961.
10. Benedict Anderson, *Imagined Communities* (London: Verso, 1991).

11. It is recorded, for example, that Radovan Karadžic treats Njegoš's master-piece, *The Mountain Wreath*, as a holy scripture, and that Ivo Andrić's sto-ries are reported as true historical incidents and were used by Serb nationalists to justify the expulsion of Muslims from eastern Bosnia in particular. See the interview with Radovan Karadžić, "Govorim stihove kao molitvu" (I recite poetry as a prayer) in *Vesti* (October 20, 1993): 10.
12. Andrew B. Wachtel, *Making a Nation, Breaking a Nation* (Stanford: Stanford University Press, 1998), 4–5.
13. I am referring here to the term explicated by Carl Ortwin Sauer, who as-signs to culture an agential role in fashioning a natural landscape. See his "The Morphology of Landscape," in John Leighy (ed.), *Land and Life: Se-lections from the Writings of Carl Ortwin Sauer* (Berkeley: University of California Press, 1963), 315–350.
14. Risto Trifković, "Pred licem i fenomenom bosanskohercegovačke litera-ture—biti ili ne," in I. Lovrenović, V. Maksimović, and K. Prohić (eds.), *Savremena književnost naroda i narodnosti BiH u književnoj kritici* (Sara-jevo: Svjetlost, 1984), 11.
15. Wachtel, *Making a Nation, Breaking a Nation*, 183–184.
16. Cited in T. Z. Longinović, "Bosnian Cultural Identity in the Works of Ivo Andrić," in W. Vucinich (ed.), *Ivo Andrić Revisited: The Bridge Still Stands* (Berkeley: University of California Press, 1995), 136.
17. Meša Selimović, *Derviš i smrt* (Sarajevo: Svjetlost, 1966), 282–283.
18. Erwin Panofsky, *Tomb Sculpture* (New York: Harry N. Abrams, Inc.,1964), 19.
19. All translations of Dizdar's poetry, unless indicated otherwise, are by Francis R. Jones. Other translations from Bosnian are mine.

NOTES TO CHAPTER ONE

1. "From me to my self / the distance is immense / A string across the hol-low/ How to tie the ends together / Cluster the boundless diffusion of one's life / Shattered memory, dusky haze / Crude substance or a sign?" From Juan Goytisolo, *El sitio de lost sitios* (Madrid: Santillana, S. A., 1995), Appendix. Translation by A. Buturović.
2. Charles Taylor, *Sources of the Self: The Making of the Modern Identity* (Cambridge: Harvard University Press, 1989).
3. Julia Kristeva, *Strangers to Ourselves*, trans. L. S. Roudiez (New York: Co-lumbia University Press, 1991).
4. Mikhail Bakhtin, *Toward the Philosophy of the Act*, trans. and notes V. Li-apunov, ed. V Liapunov and M. Holquist (Austin: University of Texas Press, 1993), 42.
5. Benedict Anderson, *Imagined Communities* (London: Verso, 1991), 7.
6. Mikhail Bakhtin, "Author and Hero in Aesthetic Activity," in V. Liapunov (trans. and notes), *Art and Answerability: Early Philosophical Essays by M. M. Bakhtin* (Austin: University of Texas Press, 1990), 2.

7. Gaston Bachelard, *The Poetics of Space*, trans. M. Jolas (New York: The Orion Press, 1964), 39.

8. For a survey of their differences, see Adrian Hastings, *The Construction of Nationhood: Ethnicity, Religion, and Nationalism* (Cambridge: Cambridge University Press, 1997), 8–14.

9. Tone Bringa, *Being Muslim the Bosnian Way* (Princeton: Princeton University Press, 1995), 20–21; 25–27.

10. Hastings, *The Construction of Nationhood*, 3; Stuart Woolf (ed.), *Nationalism in Europe, 1815 to the Present: A Reader* (London: Routledge, 1996), 25–36.

11. The existence of recognizable, inherent national characteristics among different peoples has been a common belief, and one quite difficult to uproot. See Woolf, *Nationalism in Europe*, 9.

12. Alois Schmaus, "Sa strana zamagljenih," *Misao* 10:209–210 (September 1928): 87–88.

13. Tom Nairn, "The Maladies of Development," in J. Hutchison and A. D. Smith (eds.), *Nationalism* (Oxford: Oxford University Press, 1994), 74.

14. Risto Trifković, *Savremena knjiěvnost u Bosni i Hercegivini* (Sarajevo: Svjetlost, 1986), 194.

15. Woolf, *Nationalism in Europe*, 8.

16. Walker Connor, "A Nation Is a Nation, Is a State, Is an Ethnic Group, Is a . . . ," in J. Hutchison and A. D. Smith (eds.), *Nationalism*, 45.

17. Ernest Gellner, *Nations and Nationalism* (Oxford: Blackwell, 1983), 55.

18. Homi Bhabha, *Nation and Narration* (London: Routledge, 1990).

19. Partha Chattarjee, "Whose Imagined Community?" in G. Balakrishnan (ed.), *Mapping the Nation* (London: Verso, 1996), 217.

20. Woolf, *Nationalism in Europe,*16–25

21. Wachtel, *Making a Nation, Breaking a Nation* (Stanford: Stanford University Press, 1998), 39–40.

22. Herta Kuna, *Hrestomatija starije bosanke književnosti* (Sarajevo: Svjetlost, 1974), 7–8.

23. Cited in Muhamed Hadžijahić, "Neke karakteristike stare bosansko-muslimanske književnosti," in Herta Kuna et al., *Bosanskohercegovačka književna hrestomatija: stara književnost* (Sarajevo: Zavod za izdavanje udžbenika, 1972), 221.

24. Benjamin Braude, "Foundation Myths of the *Millet* System," in B. Braude and B. Lewis (eds.), *Christians and Jews in the Ottoman Empire: The Functioning of a Plural Society* (New York: Holmes & Meier Publishers, 1982), I: 74.

25. Adem Handžić, *Population in Bosnia in the Ottoman Period* (Istanbul: IRCICA, 1994), 12.

26. Ibid., 15–30.

27. Kuna et al., *Bosanskohercegovačka književna hrestomatija: stara književnost*, 3–5.

28. Muhamed Rizvić, "Mihovil Kombol: O književnosti naroda Bosne i Herzegovine," in his *Tokovi i stvaraoci iz književne Bosne* (Tuzla: Univerzal, 1986), 16.

29. Noel Malcolm, *Bosnia: A Short History* (London: Macmillan, 1994), 70–74.
30. Vojislav Maksimović, "Starija književnost bosanskih Jevreja," in Kuna et al., *Bosanska književna hrestomatija: stara književnost,* 315–326.
31. Rizvić, *Tokovi i stvaraoci iz književne Bosne,* 26.
32. Herbert Mol, *Identity and the Sacred* (New York: Free Press, 1976), 9.
33. Čedomir Veljačić, "Istočni utjecaji i interes za Indiju u jugoslavenskoj književnosti i filozofiji," *Rad jugoslavenske akademije* (1986): 530, 590–596. Also, see Derviš Korkut, "Turske ljubavne pjesme u Zborniku Miha Martelenija Dubrovčanina iz 1657 godine," *Prilozi za Orijentalnu Filologiju* 8 (1958): 37–62; and Marija Kleut, "Sevdalinke u srpskim rukopisnim pesmaricama," *Godišnjak Instituta za književnost* (Sarajevo) 16 (1987): 21–28.
34. See Hatidža Krnjević, *Usmene balade Bosne i Hercegovine* (Sarajevo: Svjetlost, 1973), 98–132; also, Branko Letić, "Srpska književna tradicija od XV do XVI veka," *Godišnjak Instituta za književnost* (Sarajevo) 20 (1991): 73–104.
35. "Crkveni oglas naredbe turske vlasti 1794. godine," cited in Kura et al., *Bosanska književna hrestomatija: stara književnost,* 103–105.
36. Donald Quataert, *The Ottoman Empire, 1700–1922* (Cambridge: Cambridge University Press, 2000), 37–53. Quataert mentions other instances of intercommunal solidarity in work- and culture-related activities. Ibid., 178–183.
37. Muhsin Rizvić, "Pisma muslimanskih Krajišnika pisana bosančicom od XVI do sredine XIX stoljeća kao oblik stare epistolarne književnosti," *Godišnjak Instituta za književnost* (Sarajevo) 5 (1976): 217–264.
38. Ibid.; interesting here also are the texts of Muslim heroic poetry of the period—see Djenana Buturović, *Narodne pjesme muslimana u Bosni i Hercegovini* (Sarajevo: Štampa, 1966).
39. Muhsin Rizvić, "Pisma muslimanskih Krajišnika," 260–264.
40. For these and other references, see Jovan Tadić, "Dubrovnik za vreme Diva Gundulića," *Srpski književni glasnik* 4 (February 1939): 281–285; Djenana Buturović, *Bošnjačka usmena epika* (Sarajevo: Alef, 1997), 257–291. "Harambaša" means, roughly, a gang leader (from the Turkish *harami bashi),* which is a curious but common reference to a military notable.
41. Munib Maglajlić, *Antologija bošnjačke usmene lirike* (Sarajevo: Alef, 1997), 5–8.
42. Cited in Munib Malgajlić, *Od zbilje do pjesme* (Banjaluka: Glas, 1983), 24.
43. Ibid., 26.
44. Maria Todorova, "The Ottoman Legacy in the Balkans," in G. G. Ozdoğan and K. Saybasili (eds.), *Balkans: A Mirror of the New International Order* (Istanbul: EREN, 1995), 58.
45. Ibid., 56.
46. For a good summary, see Wachtel, *Making a Nation, Breaking a Nation,* 67–128.
47. Cited in *The Other Balkan Wars: A 1913 Carnegie Endowment Inquiry in Retrospect with a New Introduction and Reflections on the Present Conflict*

by George F. Kennan (Washington, D.C.: Carnegie Endowment for International Peace, 1993).

48. Cited in Ivo Banac, *The National Question in Yugoslavia: Origins, History, Politics* (Ithaca: Cornell University Press, 1994), 371.

49. Pedro Ramet, "Primordial Ethnicity or Modern Nationalism: The Case of Yugoslavia's Muslims," *Nationalities Papers*, 13: 2 (1985): 187.

50. Ibid., and also Irwin Zacharia, "The Islamic Revival and the Muslims of Bosnia-Hercegovina," *East European Quarterly* 17:4 (January 1984).

51. Banac, *National Question*, 375–377.

52. Hastings, *Constructions of Nationhood*, 141–142.

53. Ibid., 124–147; Banac, *National Question*, 31–35.

54. Rogers Brubaker, *Nationalism Reframed: Nationhood and the National Question in the New Europe* (Cambridge: Cambridge University Press, 1996), 17.

55. Ivan Lovrenović, "Stare osnove i nove vertikale," in I. Lovrenović, V. Maksimović, and K. Prohić (eds.), *Savremena književnost naroda i narodnosti u BiH u književnoj kritici*, 17.

56. Miodrag Bogićević's presentation in *Simpozijum o savremenoj književnosti Bosne i Hercegovine* (Sarajevo: Svjetlost, 1971), 93.

57. Sabrina Ramet, *Balkan Babel: Politics, Religion, and Culture in Yugoslavia* (Boulder: Westview Press, 1992), 165–167.

58. Vojislav Maksimović, for example, championed the appellation "Bosnian literature," unlike most other critics who have preferred distinguishing at least three literary trends in accordance with national designations, in his *Nekad i sad* (Sarajevo: Svjetlost, 1973), 31.

59. Risto Trifković, "Jedan pogled na bosansko-hercegovacku književnost, ponovo," *Simpozijum o savremenoj književnosti Bosne i Hercegovine*, 102.

60. As Trifković argues, "Bosnia-Herzegovina has lent itself to a cult of regionalism, of self-ruled kind, which can be traced to the peculiar historical circumstances of Bosnia. Centuries of hardship, an internalized feeling of parochialism, provincialism, even inferiority, provided good conditions for the growth and dissemination of such narrow, close-minded and low literary standards, which did much damage to the overall quality of literary production in Bosnia. Only recently has the critical examination penetrated literary creativity, emphasizing its good sides and underplaying the bad, and overall, albeit indirectly, affecting literary culture in positive ways." In Trifković, *Savremena književnost u Bosni i Hercegivini* (Sarajevo: Svjetlost, 1986), 194.

61. Cited in T. Z. Longinović, "Bosnian Cultural Identity in the Works of Ivo Andrić," in W. Vucinich (ed.), *Ivo Andrić Revisited* (Berkeley: University of California Press), 136.

62. Samuel Huntington, "The Clash of Civilizations?" *Foreign Affairs* 72 (1993): 23–49.

63. Mak Dizdar, *Stari bosanski tekstovi* (Sarajevo: Svjetlost, 1969), 1.

64. In *The Encyclopaedia of Yugoslavia: The Socialist Republic of Bosnia and Hercegovina* (Zagreb: Jugoslovenski leksikografski zavod, 1983), 1–5.

65. J. Nicholas Entrikin, *The Betweenness of Place* (London: Macmillan, 1991), 3.

66. See Martin W. Lewis and Karen E. Wigen, *The Myth of Continents: A Critique of Metageography* (Berkeley: University of California Press, 1997), x.

67. Ibid., xiii.

68. An insightful study on the subject is Dennis Rumley and Julian V. Minghi (eds.), *The Geography of Border Landscapes* (London: Routledge, 1991).

69. Ibid., 51–52.

70. See Roger Ballard, "Islam and the Construction of Europe," in W. Shadid and S. Koningsveld (eds.), *Muslims in the Margin: Political Responses to the Presence of Islam in Western Europe* (Kampon: Kok Pharos, 1996), 15–51.

71. See Stephen G. Nichols, "The New Medievalism: Tradition and Discontinuity in Medieval Culture," in M. S. Brownlee, K. Brownlee, and S. G. Nichols (eds.), *The New Medievalism* (Baltimore: The Johns Hopkins University Press, 1991), 1–26.

72. Maria R. Menocal, *The Arabic Role in Medieval Literary History* (Philadelphia: University of Pennsylvania Press, 1987), 5.

73. Anthony Smith, *The Ethnic Origins of Nations* (Oxford: Blackwell, 1986), 202–204.

74. See Iver B. Neumann, *Russia and the Idea of Europe* (London: Routledge, 1996); and Bernard Lewis, *The Multiple Identities of the Middle East* (London: Weidenfeld & Nicolson, 1998), 134–135.

75. In the final stages of this book's production, a special English edition of the journal *Forum Bosnae* was issued in Sarajevo, entitled *Life at the Crossroads* (November, 2001). Edited by Ivan Lovrenović and Francis Jones, the issue discusses this theme from a variety of perspectives. An especially relevant and insightful essay is by Nirman Moranjak-Bamburać, "The Privileged Crossroads: The Metaphor and Discourse of Space," 233–246.

76. Hastings, *Constructions of Nationhood*, 129–130.

77. Abdul R. JanMohamed, "The Economy of Manichean Allegory," *Critical Inquiry* 12 (1): 59–87.

78. Quoted in Harry Norris, *Islam in the Balkans* (Columbia: University of South Carolina Press, 1993), 254.

79. Anthony Rhodes, *Where the Turk Trod: A Journey to Sarajevo with a Slavonic Mussulman* (London: Weidenfeld and Nicolson, 1956), 10.

80. Irvin Schick, *The Erotic Margin* (London: Verso, 1999), 100.

81. Lovett F. Edwards, *Introducing Yugoslavia* (London: Methuen & Co., 1954), 200.

82. See Hastings, *The Construction of Nationhood*, 139–141.

83. Quoted in Staniša Tutnjević, *Književne krivice i osvete* (Sarajevo: Svjetlost, 1989), 77, fn. 17.

84. Tutnjević discusses the literary image of Bosnia as "a dark province," arguing, quite disputably, that the motif has no extra-literary value, thus exonerating Ivo Andrić and his very vocal supporters from any influence on

the political culture. His advocacy to treat literature as inconsequential for ideological and political processes seems quite problematic, especially from the postwar vantage point.

85. Andrić, *The Development of Spiritual Life in Bosnia under the Turkish Rule* (Durham: Duke University Press, 1990), 16–17.

86. Cited in Norris, *Islam in the Balkans,* 296.

87. For example, as late as 2001, discussions of the legitimacy of a unified Bosnia persist, especially in context of its Islamic culture. See T. Friedman editorial of Jan. 23, 2001, in the *New York Times.* Also, Douglas A. Mac-Gregor, "The Balkan Limits to Power and Principle," in *Orbis* 45: 1 (Winter 2001): 93. I am grateful to Tim Donais for these references.

88. Rebecca West, *Black Lamb and Grey Falcon* (Harmondsworth: Penguin Books, 1982), 301–302.

89. For a detailed and insightful analysis, see chapter four of Schick's *The Erotic Margin,* 75–105.

90. The idea is based in romantic nationalism of "Slavophiles" of the early nineteenth century who cultivated the idea of a native, specifically Russian culture but, after the Crimean War, yielded to more pan-Slavic tendencies. For an important discussion on the movement see Andrzey Walicki, *A History of Russian Thought: From the Enlightenment to Marxism* (Stanford: Stanford University Press, 1979), 92–114.

91. Ibid., 305–306.

92. Wachtel, *Making a Nation, Breaking a Nation,* 19–66; Michael Sells, *The Bridge Betrayed: Religion and Genocide in Bosnia* (Berkeley: University of California Press, 1996).

93. This is discernible in many forums, from the national anthem of the SFR Yugoslavia (*Neka živi duh slavenski*/Long live the Slavic soul) to popular music and literature. One of the pop hits of the 1980s, for example, by the still famous Djordje Balašević, was the song "Slavenska," in which he appeals to "my humble Slavic soul" (*"moja prosta duša slovenska"*). The song was an instant hit.

94. See Banac, *The National Question in Yugoslavia,* 202–214.

95. Wachtel, *Making a Nation, Breaking a Nation,* 151–155.

96. *Sarajevo Survival Guide* (Sarajevo: FAMA, 1993), 94.

97. N. Malcolm, *A Short History of Bosnia,* xix.

98. Rhodes, *Where the Turk Trod,* 10.

99. William Curtis, "The Great Turk and His Lost Provinces," *The National Geographic Magazine* 14:2 (February 1903): 48.

100. Meša Selimović, *Derviš i smrt* (Sarajevo: Sventlost, 1966), 282–3.

101. A comment alluded to by Wachtel who charges Selimović with treating Bosnia as purely Muslim (in *Making a Nation, Breaking a Nation,* 183), as well as by H. R. Cooper, Jr., in the introduction to the English translation of the novel *Death and the Dervish* (Evanston: Northwestern University Press, 1996), p. ix. In my view, as suggested in my introduction, both ignore the gravity of the Muslim question in the national definition of the 1960s

Bosnia. If anything, Selimović centralizes the severity of the dilemma of two conflicting identities—of being identified by space (Bosnian) or by faith (Islamic). Since the seeming incompatibility of the two possibilities is allegorized as the psychological liminality of the main character Nurudin, the focus on the Islamic component is quite compelling. I elaborate on this in "National Question and the Anguish of Salvation: Bosnian Muslim Identity in Meša Selimović's *The Dervish and Death,*" *Edebiyat* 7 (1996): 41–57.

102. Tutnjević, *Književne krivice i osvete,* 58–59.

103. Mak Dizdar, *Antologija starih bosanskih tekstova* (Sarajevo: Alef, 1997), 7 (emphasis mine).

NOTES TO CHAPTER TWO

1. Michel Ragon, *The Space of Death,* trans. A. Sheridan (Charlottesville: University Press of Virginia, 1983), 39.

2. *Yugoslavia,* ed. M. Filipović (Sarajevo: Svjetlost, 1990), 80.

3. Šefik Bešlagić, *Stećci i njihova umjetnost* (Sarajevo: Zavod za izdavanje udžbenika, 1971), 20.

4. Marion Wenzel, *Ukrasni motivi na stećcima* (Sarajevo: n.p., 1965), 15.

5. Bešlagic, *Stećci,* 15–25. More interestingly, in Ottoman discourse mešhetlik seems to have been used in reference to non-Muslim gravesites. I am thankful to Irvin Schick for this remark.

6. Ibid., 25.

7. Arthur Evans, *Through Bosnia and the Herzegovina on Foot* (New York: Arno Press, 1971), 171.

8. Bešlagić, *Stećci i njihova umjetnost,* 90. Also, Šefik Bešlagić, *Stećci—kultura i umjetnost* (Sarajevo: Veselin Masleša, 1982).

9. Wenzel, *Ukrasni motivi,* Introduction.

10. Bešlagić, *Stećci,* 90–93.

11. Alojz Benac and Oto Bihalji-Merin, *Bogomil Sculpture* (Beograd: Jugoslavija, 1962; New York: Harcourt, Brace & World Press, 1963), xx.

12. Wenzel, *Ukrasni motivi,* 13.

13. For a more detailed discussion see Benac and Bihalji-Merin, *Bogomil Sculpture,* xx-xxi.

14. John Fine, *The Bosnian Church: A New Interpretation* (Boulder: East European Quarterly, 1975), 92.

15. Victor Burgin, *The End of Art Theory* (Atlantic Highlands: Humanities Press International, 1986), 154.

16. Wenzel, *Ukrasni motivi,* 13.

17. Ibid., 15.

18. Burgin, *The End of Art Theory,* 153–154.

19. Fine, *The Bosnian Church,* 42–46.

20. Sima Ćirković, *Istorija srednjovekovne bosanke države* (Beograd: n.p.,1964), 8–15.

21. Cited in Robert Donia, *Islam under the Double Eagle: The Muslims of Bosnia and Hercegovina, 1878–1914* (Boulder: East European Monographs, 1981), 14.

22. Muhamed Hadžijahić, *Od tradicije do identiteta: Geneza nacionalnog pitanja bosanskih muslimana* (Sarajevo: Svjetlost, 1974).

23. Andreas Huyssen, *Twilight Memories* (London: Routledge, 1995), 15.

24. See Ivo Banac, *National Question in Yugoslavia* (Ithaca: Cornell University Press, 1994), 350–362.

25. For a detailed discussion see Dominik Mandić, *Bogomilska crkva bosanskih krstjana* (Chicago: The Croatian Historical Institute, 1962); also, Milan Loos, *Dualist Heresy in the Middle Ages* (Prague: Academia, 1974), 162–166; 292–328.

26. Benac and Bihalji-Merin, *Bogomil Sculpture*, xix.

27. Evans, *Through Bosnia and Herzegovina*, ix

28. Irvin Schick, *The Erotic Margin: Sexuality and Spatiality in Alterist Discourse* (London: Verso, 1999),12.

29. Evans, *Through Bosnia and the Herzegovina*, x.

30. William Curtis, "The Great Turk and His Lost Provinces," *National Geographic* 14 (February 1903): 46–47.

31. Evans, *Through Bosnia and Herzegovina*, lv.

32. Michel de Certeau, *Heterologies: Discourse on the Other*, trans. B. Massumi (Minneapolis: University of Minnesota Press, 1985), 180.

33. A. R. JanMohamed, "The Economy of Manichean Allegory," *Critical Inquiry* 12 (1): 59–87.

34. Evans, *Through Bosnia and the Herzegovina*, xciv-civ.

35. Ibid., lvii.

36. Benac and Bihalji-Merin, *Bogomil Sculpture*, xxxiv (emphasis mine).

37. Ibid., xii. Also, Ivo Andrić, *The Development of Spiritual Life in Bosnia under the Influence of Turkish Rule* (Durham: Duke University Press, 1990).

38. On Christoslavism, the ideology that merges Slavic race with Christian religion, see Michael Sells, *The Bridge Betrayed: Religion and Genocide in Bosnia* (Berkeley: The University of California Press, 1996), 45–52.

39. Benac and Bihalji-Merin, *Bogomil Sculpture*, xxxvi.

40. Pierre Nora, *Realms of Memory*, trans. A. Goldhammer (New York: Columbia University Press, 1996), 1–20.

41. Ibid., 3.

42. Jay Winter, *Sites of Memory, Sites of Mourning* (Cambridge: Cambridge University Press, 1995), 5.

43. For a detailed discussion on this issue see András Riedlmayer, "Convivencia under Fire: Genocide and Book-Burning in Bosnia," in J. Rose (ed.), *The Holocaust and the Book: Preservation and Loss* (Amherst: University of Massachusetts Press, 2001), 266–291.

44. Nora, *Realms of Memory*, 7.

45. Roland Barthes, *Mythologies*, trans. A. Lavers (New York: Hill and Wang, 1972), 143.

46. For the abuse of stećak, see Bešlagić, *Stećci*, 132–133.
47. Steven Runciman, *The Medieval Manichee* (Cambridge: Cambridge University Press, 1960).
48. Vaso Glušac, "Problem Bogomilstva," *GID* (Beograd) 5 (1953): 105–138.
49. Fine, *The Bosnian Church*, 5–6.
50. The champions of the Bogomil theory were scholars and writers of both foreign and local Bosnian background, and Arthur Evans has already been mentioned as one of its early proponents. Among other influential scholars and writers who encouraged further investigation in that direction were John de Asboth and Alexander Solovyev. Locally, they were Ćiro Truhelka, Miroslav Krleža, Vladimir Dedijer, Oto Bihalji-Merin, and others.
51. Cited in Fine, *The Bosnian Church*, 124.
52. Ibid., 58.
53. For more details on dualist cosmology see Runciman, *The Medieval Manichee*, 5–25. Also, Aleksandar Solovjev, "Simbolika srednjovekovnih grobnih spomenika u Bosni i Herzegovini," *Godišnjak Istorijskog društva Bosne i Hercegovine* 8 (1956): 5–67.
54. Benac and Bihalji-Merin, *Bogomil Sculpture*, xxxi.
55. This is the (in)famous Albigensian crusade. See Runciman, *The Medieval Manichee*, 148.
56. Adem Handžić, *Population of Bosnia in the Ottoman Period* (Istanbul: IR-CICA, 1994), 23.
57. Dominik Mandić, *Bogumilska crkva bosanskih krstjana* (Chicago: The Croatian Historical Institute, 1962), 420–423.
58. Fine, *The Bosnian Church*, 41–111.
59. Ibid., 50.
60. Ibid., 62.
61. Benedict Anderson, *Imagined Communities* (London: Verso, 1991), 6.
62. Cited in Benac and Bihalji-Merin, *Bogomil Sculpture*, xiii.
63. David Price, *History Made, History Imagined* (Urbana: University of Illinois Press, 1999), 3.
64. Cited in Enes Duraković, *Govor i šutnja tajanstva* (Sarajevo: Svjetlost, 1979), 120.

NOTES TO CHAPTER THREE

1. Jahan Ramazani, *Poetry of Mourning: The Modern Elegy from Hardy to Heaney* (Chicago: University of Chicago Press, 1994), 3.
2. Sabrina (Pedro) Ramet speaks of a sense of common cultural interests as characteristic of any ethnic group in "Primordial Ethnicity or Modern Nationalism," *Nationalities Papers*, 13:2 (1985): 168; in a similar vein, Adrian Hastings defines ethnicity as "a group of people with a shared cultural identity and spoken language" in his *The Construction of Nationhood* (Cambridge: Cambridge University Press, 1997), 3.

3. Midhat Begić, "Epitafi kao osnova poeziji: o *Kamenom spavaču* Maka Dizdara," in E. Duraković (ed.), *Bošnjačka književnost u književnoj kritici* (Sarajevo: Alef, 1998), 3:351.

4. For example, Kasim Prohić, *Apokrifnost poetskog govora* (Sarajevo: Veselin Masleša, 1974); Enes Duraković, *Govor i šutnja tajanstva;* Jasmina Musabegović, *Tajna i smisao književnog djela* (Sarajevo: Veselin Masleša, 1977).

5. Cited in Paul Morris (ed.), *The Bakhtin Reader* (London: Edward Arnold, 1994), 19.

6. Ibid., 98–122.

7. Homi Bhabha, "DissemiNation: Time, Narrative, and the Margins of the Modern Nation," in Homi Bhabha, *Nation and Narration* (New York and London: Routledge, 1990), 297.

8. Cited in Safet Plakalo's overview of Dizdar's life: www.djikic.net/pub/mak/mak.htm.

9. Midhat Begić, "Epitafi kao osnova poeziji," 356.

10. Cited in Duraković, *Govor i šutnja tajanstva,* 76–77. Translation by A. Buturović.

11. Roland Barthes, "Le mythe, aujourd'hui," *Mythologies,* trans. A. Lavers (Paris: Editions du Seuil, 1957), 241.

12. Ibid., 242.

13. Cited in Duraković, *Govor i šutnja tajanstva,* 108. Translation by Francis Jones.

14. Michael Fischer, "Ethnicity and the Post-Modern Arts of Memory," in J. Clifford and G. Marcus, *Writing Culture: The Poetics and Politics of Ethnography* (Berkeley and Los Angeles: University of California Press, 1986), 196–197.

15. Ibid., 206.

16. S. Fish, *Is There a Text in This Class? The Authority of Interpretive Communities* (Cambridge, MA: Harvard University Press, 1980).

17. Michael Taussig, *Mimesis and Alterity* (New York: Routledge, 1993), 19–20.

18. Jonathan Culler, *Structuralist Poetics: Structuralism, Linguistics and the Study of Literature* (London: Routledge and Kegan Paul, 1975), 135–155.

19. A detailed overview can be found in Duraković, *Govor i šutnja tajanstva,* 94–97.

20. The bilingual edition from which the translations appearing here originate is based on the third edition of *Stone Sleeper.*

21. Duraković, *Govor i šutnja tajanstva,* 96.

22. Amina Idrizbegović, "Poetska snaga Dizdarovog *Kamenog spavača,*" Introduction to *Mak Dizdar: Kameni spavač* (Sarajevo: Svjetlost, 1996).

23. Elizabeth Helsinger, *Rural Scenes and National Representation* (Princeton: Princeton University Press, 1997), 17.

24. Translation by A. Buturović.

25. Karen Mills-Courts, *Poetry as Epitaph: Representation and Poetic Language* (Baton Rouge: Louisiana State University Press, 1990), 18.

26. Translation by A. Buturović.
27. Martin Buber, *I and Thou*, trans. R. G. Smith (Edinburgh: T & T Clark, 1937).
28. See Alan Renoir, "Oral-Formulaic Rhetoric: An Approach to Image and Message in Medieval Poetry," in L. A. Finke and M. A. Shichtman (eds.), *Medieval Texts and Contemporary Readers* (Ithaca: Cornell University Press, 1987), 234–253.
29. Mak Dizdar, *Antologija starih bosankih tekstova* (Sarajevo: Alef, 1997), 7.
30. Hastings, *The Construction of Nationhood*, 137–138.
31. Dizdar, *Antologija starih bosankih tekstova*, 8–9.
32. Ernest B. Gilman, "Words and Image in Quarles' *Emblemes*," in W. J. T. Mitchell (ed.), *The Language of Images* (Chicago: University of Chicago Press, 1980), 61.
33. Ibid., 63.
34. Alojz Benac and Oto Bihalji-Merin, *Bogomil Sculpture* (Beograd: Jugoslavija, 1962; New York: Harcourt, Brace & World Press, 1963), xxiv.
35. Ibid., xxxi.
36. Charles S. Pierce, *Collected Papers* (Cambridge, MA: Harvard University Press, 1931–1958).
37. Benac and Bihalji-Merin, *Bogomil Sculpture*, xxxi.
38. W. J. T. Mitchell, *Iconology: Image, Text, Ideology* (Chicago: University of Chicago Press, 1986), 17.
39. Quoted in Benac and Bihalji-Merin, *Bogomil Sculpture*, xxxi.
40. Dizdar, *Antologija starih bosankih tekstova*, 16–17.
41. Erwin Panofsky, *Tomb Sculpture* (New York: Harry N. Abrams, Inc., 1964), 35–36.
42. Dizdar, *Antologija starih bosankih tekstova*, 17, 354.
43. Homi Bhabha, "On Mimicry and Man: The Ambivalence of Colonial Discourse," in *The Location of Culture* (London: Routledge, 1994), 86.
44. Dizdar, *Antologija starih bosankih tekstova*, 45.

NOTES TO CHAPTER FOUR

1. Guntram H. Herb and David H. Kaplan, *Nested Identities: Nationalism, Territory, and Scale* (Lanham: Rowman & Littlefield Publisher, Inc., 1999), 2.
2. Cited in Ibid., 22.
3. For a detailed discussion see Christopher Park, *Sacred Worlds: An Introduction to Geography and Religion* (London: Routledge, 1994); also, Bruce Gordon and Peter Marshall (eds.), *The Place of the Dead: Death and Remembrance in Late Medieval and Early Modern Europe* (Cambridge: Cambridge University Press, 2000), 1–16.
4. Jamie Scott and Paul Simpson-Housley (eds.), *Mapping the Sacred in Postcolonial Literatures* (Atlanta: Rodopi VP, 2001), xv-xvii.

5. Mircea Eliade, *The Sacred and the Profane,* trans. W. R. Trask (New York: Harcourt Brace Jovanovich, 1961), 11.

6. Ibid., 24.

7. Ibid., 10–11, 64–66.

8. Scott and Simpson-Housley, *Mapping the Sacred in Postcolonial Literatures,* xv-xvi.

9. Eliade, *The Sacred and the Profane,* 30.

10. Ibid., 29.

11. Ibid.

12. Scott and Simpson-Housley, *Mapping the Sacred in Postcolonial Literatures,* xvi.

13. Eliade, *The Sacred and the Profane,* 11.

14. Ibid., 65.

15. Ibid., 64.

16. Erving Goffman, *Frame Analysis: An Essay on the Organization of Space* (New York: Harper & Row, 1974), 21.

17. Ibid.

18. Anne Janowitz, *England's Ruins: Poetic Purpose and the National Landscape* (Oxford: Basil Blackwell, 1990), 10.

19. Wyman H. Herendeen, *From Landscape to Literature: The River and the Myth of Geography* (Pittsburgh: Duquesne University Press, 1986), 5.

20. Nigel Pennick, *Celtic Sacred Landscapes* (New York: Thames and Hudson, 1996), 14.

21. Victor Turner and Edith Turner, *Image and Pilgrimage in Christian Culture: Anthropological Perspectives* (New York: Columbia University Press, 1978), 197–207.

22. Rusmir Mahmutćehajić, in Mak Dizdar, *Kameni spavač: Stone Sleeper,* trans. F. Jones (Sarajevo: DID, 1999), 208–209.

23. Stanley Fish, *Is There a Text in This Class? The Authority of Interpretive Communities* (Cambridge, MA: Harvard University Press, 1980), 174.

24. David Lowenthal, "Past Time, Present Place: Landscape and Memory," *The Geographical Review,* 65:1 (1975): 5–6.

25. See Kenneth Kramer, *The Sacred Art of Dying* (New York and Mahwah: Paulist Press, 1988); also, S. G. F. Brandon, *The Judgment of the Dead: The Idea of Life after Death in the Major Religions* (New York: Charles Scribner's Sons, 1967).

26. Michael Fischer, "Ethnicity and the Post-Modern Art of Memory," in J. Clifford and G. Marcus (eds.), *Writing Culture: The Poetics and Politics of Ethnography* (Berkeley: University of California Press, 1986), 206, 218.

27. Ibid., 231–232.

28. Yi-Fu Tuan, "Rootedness Versus Sense of Place," *Landscape* 25 (1980): 3–8.

29. John A. Agnew, *Place and Politics: The Geographic Mediation of State and Society* (Boston: Allen and Unwin, 1987).

30. Herb, "National Identity and Territory," in Herb and Kaplan (eds.), *Nested Identities: Nationalism Territory, and Scale,* 17.

31. Anderson, *Imagined Communities* (London: Verso, 1991), 9–10.

32. Ibid., 36.

33. Gopal Balakrishnan, "The National Imagination," in Gopal Balakrishnan (ed.), *Mapping the Nation* (London: Verso, 1996), 206.

34. J. B. Jackson, "The Vanishing Epitaph: From Monument to Place," *Landscape* 17 (1967–1968): 22–26.

35. Jay Winter, *Sites of Memory, Sites of Mourning* (Cambridge: Cambridge University Press, 1995), 15–16.

36. On the Mesoamerican structure of divine cosmos, for example, see David Carrasco, "Religions of Mesoamerica: Cosmovision and Ceremonial Centers," in H. Byron Earhart (ed.), *Religious Traditions of the World* (New York: HarperCollins Publishers, 1993), 107–254.

37. Balakrishnan, "The National Imagination," 206–207.

38. For argument's sake, I have re-translated this into English from the otherwise splendid Scots version that appears in Francis Jones's edition:

I wad haud silent like a stane
wae's me I am nae stane
And sae forgive me that I speak
this word that will be stane.

39. Michel Ragon, *The Space of Death*, trans. A. Sheridan (Charlottesville: University Press of Virginia, 1983), 39.

40. Michel Foucault, "Nietzsche, Genealogy, History," *Language, Counter-Memory, Practice*, ed. D. F. Bouchard, trans. D. F. Bouchard and S. Simon (Ithaca: Cornell University Press, 1977), 143.

41. Ibid., 142.

42. Ibid., 150.

43. Ibid., 164.

44. Mak Dizdar, "Author's Notes," *Stone Sleeper*, 201.

45. Herb, "National Identity and Territory," 19.

46. Stuart Woolf, *Nationalism in Europe: 1815 to the Present: A Reader* (London and New York: Routledge, 1996),10–12.

47. Anderson, *Imagined Communities*, 196.

NOTES TO THE APPENDIX

1. Francis Jones, "Return," Rabia Ali and Lawrence Lifschultz (eds.), *Why Bosnia? Writings on the Balkan War* (Stony Creek: Pamphleteer's Press, 1993); also Francis Jones, "Borderland: Language and Loyalty in Old Yugoslavia," In Robert Hudson and Fred Réno (eds.), *The Politics of Identity: A Comparative Study of Europe and the Caribbean* (London: Macmillan, 2000).

2. For an overview of translators' strategies see Peter Fawcett, *Translation and Language* (Manchester: St. Jerome, 1997).

3. Francis Jones, "The Poet and the Ambassador: Communicating Mak Dizdar's '*Stone Sleeper*,'" *Translation and Literature* 9 (2000): 65–87.
4. Lawrence Venuti, *The Translator's Invisibility* (London: Routledge, 1995).
5. This essay—like virtually all discussions of translated texts—assumes that the target readers are native readers of the target language. One should not forget, however, that many readers of Dizdar in English are likely to be Bosnians, for whom *Stone Sleeper's* reconstructed space-time is far from alien, and many of whom see the translation of their master poet's key work into a world language as powerfully validating their own identity.
6. Kinga Klaudy, "Explicitation," in Mona Baker (ed.), *The Routledge Encyclopaedia of Translation Studies* (London: Routledge, 1998).
7. Sture Allén (ed.), *Translation of Poetry and Poetic Prose. Proceedings of Nobel Symposium 110* (Stockholm: Swedish Academy / New York: World Publishing, 1999), 29–79.
8. Keith Harvey, "Compensation," in Baker (ed.), *The Routledge Encyclopaedia of Translation Studies.*
9. In English, masculine lines (stressed on the last syllable) tend to be easier to write than feminine lines (stressed on the penultimate syllable): Hence the source's eight-syllable line has become a seven-syllable line in the target.
10. Allén (ed.), *Translation of Poetry and Poetic Prose;* Venuti, *The Translator's Invisibility.*
11. Angus Calder, " Poetry and War, " *Eurozine* (2000) http://www.eurozine.com/online/articles/20000309-ep-calder.html.
12. Janet Montefiore, "Uncertain Delight. Review of Agee (1998)," *Times Literary Supplement,* December 4 1998, 24.
13. Thus Agee writes that "[this] *chef d'oeuvre* will not be everyone's cup of tea. It cuts too originally against the general run of literary translation in English, with its overwhelming preference for free-verse rhythms and eschewal of high musicality," in Chris Agee, "Stone and Poppy," *Forum Bosnae* (Winter 2001): 7.
14. Montefiore, "Uncertain Delight," 24; Calder, "Poetry and War."
15. For a discussion on innovation in poetry translation see Allén, *Translation of Poetry and Poetic Prose,* 29–79.
16. Chris Agee, "Stone and Poppy," 14.
17. Ibid., 7.
18. Raymond Van den Broeck, "Translational Interpretation: A Complex Strategic Game," in Ann Beylard-Ozeroff, Jana Králová and Barbara Moser-Mercer (eds.), *Translators' Strategies and Creativity* (Amsterdam/Philadelphia: Benjamins, 1998).

BIBLIOGRAPHY

Agee, Chris (ed.) *Scar on the Stone: Contemporary Poetry from Bosnia.* Newcastle upon Tyne: Bloodaxe Books, 1998.

Agee, Chris. "Stone and Poppy." *Forum Bosnae.* Winter 2001.

Agnew, John A. and James Duncan (eds.) *The Power of Place: Bringing Together Geographical and Sociological Imaginations.* Winchester: Unwin Hyman, 1989.

Ali, Rabia, and Lawrence Lifschultz (eds.) *Why Bosnia?* Stony Creek: The Pamphleteer's Press, 1994.

Allén, Sture (ed.) *Translation of Poetry and Poetic Prose. Proceedings of Nobel Symposium 110.* Stockholm: Swedish Academy / New York: World Publishing, 1999.

Anderson, Benedict. *Imagined Communities.* London: Verso, 1991.

Andrić, Ivo. The *Development of Spiritual Life in Bosnia under the Influence of Turkish Rule.* Durham: Duke University Press, 1990.

Bachelard, Gaston. *The Poetics of Space.* Trans. M. Jolas. New York: The Orion Press, 1964.

Baker, Mona (ed.) *The Routledge Encyclopaedia of Translation Studies.* London: Routledge, 1998.

Bakhtin, Mikhail. "Author and Hero in Aesthetic Activity." *Art and Answerability: Early Philosophical Essays by M. M. Bakhtin.* Trans. and ed. V. Liapunov. Austin: University of Texas Press, 1990.

Bakhtin, Mikhail. *Towards the Philosophy of the Act.* Trans. V. Liapunov. Ed. V. Liapunov and M. Holquist. Austin: University of Texas Press, 1993.

Balakrishnan, Gopal. "The National Imagination." *Mapping the Nation.* Ed. G. Balakrishnan. London: Verso, 1996.

Ballard, Roger. "Islam and the Construction of Europe." *Muslims in the Margin: Political Responses to the Presence of Islam in Western Europe.* Ed. W. Shadid and S. Koningsveld. Kampen: Kok Pharos, 1996.

Banac, Ivo. *The National Question in Yugoslavia: Origins, History, Politics.* Ithaca: Cornell University Press, 1994.

Barthes, Roland. *Mythologies.* Trans. A. Lavers. New York: Hill and Wang, 1972.

Begić, Midhat. "Epitafi kao osnova poeziji: o *Kamenom spavaču* Maka Dizdara." *Bosnjačka književnost u književnoj kritici: novija književnost.* Ed. E. Duraković. Sarajevo: Alef, 1998.

Benac, Alojz and Oto Bihalji-Merin. *Bogomil Sculpture.* Beograd: Jugoslavija, 1962; New York: Harcourt, Brace & World Press, 1963.

Bešlagić, Šefik. *Stećci i njihova umjetnost*. Sarajevo: Zavod za izdavanje udžbenika, 1971.

Bešlagić, Šefik, *Stećci—kultura i umjetnost*. Sarajevo: Veselin Masleša, 1982.

Bhabha, Homi. "Of Mimicry and Men: The Ambivalence of Colonial Discourse." *The Location of Culture*. London: Routledge, 1994.

Bhabha, Homi. *Nation and Narration*. New York: Routledge, 1990.

Bogićević, Miodrag. "Presentation." In *Simpozijum o savremenoj književnosti Bosne i Hercegovine*. Sarajevo: Svjetlost, 1971.

Bollig, Michael. "Contested Places: Graves and Gravesites in Himba Culture." *Anthropos* 92 (1997): 35–50.

Brandon, S. G. F. *The Judgment of the Dead: The Idea of Life after Death in the Major Religions*. New York: Charles Scribner's Sons, 1967.

Braude, Benjamin. "Foundation Myths of the *Millet* System." *Christians and Jews in the Ottoman Empire: The Functioning of a Plural Society*. Ed. B. Braude and B. Lewis. New York: Holmes & Meier Publishers, 1982.

Bringa, Tone. *Being Muslim the Bosnian Way*. Princeton: Princeton University Press, 1995.

Brubaker, Rogers. *Nationalism Reframed: Nationhood and the National Question in the New Europe*. Cambridge: Cambridge University Press, 1996.

Buber, Martin. *I and Thou*. Trans. R. G. Smith. Edinburgh: T & T Clark, 1937.

Burgin, Victor. *The End of Art Theory*. Atlantic Highlands: Humanities Press International, 1986.

Buturović, Amila. "Medieval Cemeteries as Sites of Memory: The Poetry of Mak Dizdar." *Islam in Bosnia*. Ed. Maya Shatzmiller. Montreal: McGill-Queen's University Press, forthcoming.

Buturović, Amila. "National Question and the Anguish of Salvation: Bosnian Muslim Identity in Meša Selimović's *The Dervish and Death*." *Edebiyat* 7 (1996): 41–57.

Buturović, Amila. "Producing and Annihilating the Ethnos of Bosnian Islam." *Cultural Survival Quarterly* 19:2 (Summer 1995): 29–34.

Buturović, Amila. "Reasserting Authenticity: Bosnian Identity, Religion, and Landscape in the Poetry of Mak Dizdar." *Mapping the Sacred in Postcolonial Literatures*. Ed. J. Scott and P. Simpson-Housley. Atlanta: Rodopi VP, 2001.

Buturović, Djenana. *Bošnjačka usmena epika*. Sarajevo: Alef, 1997.

Buturović, Djenana. *Narodne pjesme muslimana u Bosni i Hercegovini*. Sarajevo: Štampa, 1966.

Calder, Angus. " Poetry and War." *Eurozine* (2000) <http://www.eurozine.com/online/articles/20000309-ep-calder.html>.

Carrasco, David. "Religions of Mesoamerica: Cosmovision and Ceremonial Centers." *Religious Traditions of the World*. Ed. H. Byron Earhart. New York: HarperCollins Publishers, 1993.

Chatterjee, Partha. "Whose Imagined Community?" *Mapping the Nation*. Ed. G. Balakrishnan. London: Verso, 1996.

Ćirković, Sima. *Istorija srednjovekovne bosanke države*. Beograd: n.p.,1964.

Connor, Walker. "A Nation Is a Nation, Is a State, Is an Ethnic Group, Is a. . . ." *Nationalism*. Ed. J. Hutchison and A. D. Smith. Oxford: Oxford University Press, 1994.

Culler, Jonathan. *Structuralist Poetics: Structuralism, Linguistics and the Study of Literature*. London: Routledge and Kegan Paul, 1975.

Curtis, William. "The Great Turk and His Lost Provinces." *The National Geographic Magazine* 14:2 (February 1903): 45–51.

De Certeau, Michel. *Heterologies: Discourse on the Other*. Trans. B. Massumi Minneapolis: University of Minnesota Press, 1985.

Dizdar, Mak. *Antologija starih bosanskih tekstova* [An Anthology of Old Bosnian Texts]. Sarajevo: Alef, 1997.

Dizdar, Mak. *Kameni Spavač: Stone Sleeper*. Trans. F. R. Jones. Afterword R. Mahmutćehajić. Sarajevo: DiD, Kuća bosanska, 1999.

Dizdar, Mak. *Kameni spavač* [Stone Sleeper]. Sarajevo: Veselin Masleša, 1996.

Dizdar, Mak. *Kameni spavač* [Stone Sleeper]. Sarajevo: Veselin Masleša, 1966.

Dizdar, Mak. *Koljena za madonu*. [Knees for a Madonna] Sarajevo: Svjelost, 1963.

Dizdar, Mak. *Stari bosanski tekstovi* [Old Bosnian Texts]. Sarajevo: Veselin Masleša, 1967.

Donia, Robert. *Islam under the Double Eagle: The Muslims of Bosnia and Hercegovina, 1878–1914*. Boulder: East European Monographs, 1981.

Duraković, Enes (ed.) *Antologija bošnjačke poezije XX vijeka*. Sarajevo: Alef, 1995.

Duraković, Enes (ed.) *Bošnjačka književnost u književnoj kritici: novija književnost*. Sarajevo: Alef, 1998.

Duraković, Enes. *Govor i šutnja tajanstva: pjesničko djelo Maka Dizdara*. Sarajevo: Svjetlost, 1979.

Edwards, Lovett F. *Introducing Yugoslavia*. London: Methuen & Co. Ltd., 1954.

Eliade, Mircea. *The Sacred and the Profane*. Trans. W. R. Trask. New York: Harcourt Brace Jovanovich, 1961.

The Encyclopaedia of Yugoslavia: The Socialist Republic of Bosnia and Hercegovina. Zagreb: Jugoslovenski leksikografski zavod, 1983.

Entrikin, J. Nicholas. *The Betweenness of Place*. London: Macmillan, 1991.

Evans, Arthur. *Through Bosnia and the Herzegovina on Foot*. New York: Arno Press, 1971.

Fawcett, Peter. *Translation and Language*. Manchester: St. Jerome, 1997.

Fine, John. *The Bosnian Church: A New Interpretation: A Study of the Bosnian Church and Its Place in State and Society from the 13th to the 15th Centuries*. Boulder, CO: East European Quarterly; New York: Columbia University Press, 1975.

Fine, John. *The Late Medieval Balkans: A Critical Survey from the Late Twelfth Century to the Ottoman Conquest*. Ann Arbor: University of Michigan Press, 1987.

Fine, John. "The Medieval and Ottoman Roots of Modern Bosnia." *The Muslims of Bosnia-Herzegovina*. Ed. M. Pinson. Cambridge: Harvard University Press, 1994.

Finke, Laurie, and Martin A. Shichtman (eds.). *Medieval Texts and Contemporary Readers*. Ithaca: Cornell University Press, 1987.

Fischer, Michael. "Ethnicity and the Post-Modern Arts of Memory." *Writing Culture: The Poetics and Politics of Ethnography.* Ed. J. Clifford and G. Marcus. Berkeley: University of California Press, 1986.

Fish, Stanley. *Is There a Text in This Class? The Authority of Interpretive Communities.* Cambridge: Harvard University Press, 1980.

Foucault, Michel. "Nietzsche, Genealogy, History." *Language, Counter-Memory, Practice.* Ed. Donald F. Bouchard. Trans. Donald F. Bouchard and Sherry Simon. Ithaca: Cornell University Press, 1977.

Gellner, Ernest. *Nations and Nationalism.* Oxford: Blackwell, 1983.

Gilman, Ernest B. "Words and Image in Quarles' *Emblemes.*" *The Language of Images.* Ed. W. J. T. Mitchell. Chicago: University of Chicago Press, 1980.

Glušac, Vaso. "Problem Bogomilstva." *GID* (Beograd) 5 (1953): 105–138.

Glušac, Vaso. "Srednjovekona 'bosanska crkva.'" *Prilozi za književnost, jezik, istoriju i folklor* 4 (1924): 1–54.

Goffman, Erving. *Frame Analysis: An Essay on the Organization of Space.* New York: Harper & Row, 1974.

Gordon, Bruce, and Peter Marshall (eds.) *The Place of the Dead: Death and Remembrance in Late Medieval and Early Modern Europe.* Cambridge: Cambridge University Press, 2000.

Goytisolo, Juan. *El sitio de lost sitios.* Madrid: Santillana, S. A., 1995.

Hadžijahić, Muhamed. "Neke karakteristike stare bosansko-muslimanske književnosti." *Bosanska književna hrestomatija: stara književnost.* Ed. Kuna Herta et al. Sarajevo: Zavod za izdavanje udžbenika, 1972.

Hadžijahić, Muhamed. *Od tradicije do identiteta: geneza nacionalnog pitanja bosanskih muslimana.* Sarajevo: Svjetlost, 1974.

Handžić, Adem. *Population in Bosnia in the Ottoman Period.* Istanbul: IRCICA, 1994.

Harvey, Keith. "Compensation." *The Routledge Encyclopaedia of Translation Studies.* Ed. Mona Baker. London: Routledge, 1998.

Hastings, Adrian. *The Construction of Nationhood: Ethnicity, Religion, and Nationalism.* Cambridge: Cambridge University Press, 1997.

Helsinger, Elizabeth. *Rural Scenes and National Representation.* Princeton: Princeton University Press, 1997.

Herb, Guntram, and David Kaplan (eds.) *Nested Identities: Nationalism, Territory, and Scale.* Lanham: Rowman & Littlefield Publisher, Inc., 1999.

Herendeen, Wyman H. *From Landscape to Literature: The River and the Myth of Geography.* Pittsburgh: Duquesne University Press, 1986.

Huntington, Samuel. "The Clash of Civilizations?" *Foreign Affairs* 72 (1993): 23–49.

Huyssen, Andreas. *Twilight Memories.* London: Routledge, 1995.

Idrizbegović, Amina. "Poetska snaga Dizdarovog *Kamenog spavača.*" *Mak Dizdar: Kameni spavač.* Sarajevo: Svjetlost, 1996.

Jackson, J. B. "The Vanishing Epitaph: From Monument to Place." *Landscape* 17 (1967–1968): 22–26.

JanMohamed, Abdul R. "The Economy of Manichean Allegory: The Function of Racial Difference in Colonialist Literature." *Critical Inquiry* 12:1 (1985), 59–87.

Janowitz, Anne. *England's Ruins: Poetic Purpose and the National Landscape*. Oxford: Basil Blackwell, 1990.

Jones, Francis R. "Borderland: Language and Loyalty in Old Yugoslavia." *The Politics of Identity: A Comparative Study of Europe and the Caribbean*. Ed. Robert Hudson and Fred Réno. London: Macmillan, 2000.

Jones, Francis R. "The Poet and the Ambassador: Communicating Mak Dizdar's 'Stone Sleeper.'" *Translation and Literature* 9 (2000): 65–87.

Jones, Francis R. "Return." *Why Bosnia? Writings on the Balkan War*. Ed. Rabia Ali and Lawrence Lifschultz. Stony Creek: Pamphleteer's Press, 1993.

Klaudy, Kinga. "Explicitation." *The Routledge Encyclopaedia of Translation Studies*. Ed. Mona Baker. London: Routledge, 1998.

Kleut, Marija. "Sevdalinke u srpskim rukopisnim pesmaricama." *Godišnjak Instituta za književnost* (Sarajevo) 16 (1987): 21–28.

Kong, Lily. "Cemeteries and Columbaria, Memorials and Mausoleums: Narrative and Interpretation in the Study of Deathscapes in Geography." *The Institute of Australian Geographers Inc*. 37:1 (1999): 1–10.

Korkut, Derviš. "Turske ljubavne pjesme u Zborniku Miha Martelenija Dubrovčanina iz 1657 godine." *Prilozi za Orijentalnu Filologiju* 8 (1958): 37–62.

Kovač, Zvonko. "Od komparatistike tekstova do interkulturne povijesti književnosti." *Godišnjak Instituta za književnost* (Sarajevo) 20 (1991).

Kramer, Kenneth. *The Sacred Art of Dying*. New York: Paulist Press, 1988.

Kristeva, Julia. *Strangers to Ourselves*. Trans. L. S. Roudiez. New York: Columbia University Press, 1991.

Krnjević, Hatidža. *Usmene balade Bosne i Hercegovine*. Sarajevo: Svjetlost, 1973.

Kuna Herta et al. *Bosanskohercegovačka književna hrestomatija: stara književnost*. Sarajevo: Zavod za izdavanje udžbenika, 1972.

Kuna, Herta. *Hrestomatija starije bosanke književnosti*. Sarajevo: Svjetlost, 1974.

Letić, Branko. "Srpska književna tradicija od XV do XVI veka." *Godišnjak Instituta za književnost* (Sarajevo) 20 (1991): 73–104.

Lewis, Bernard. *The Multiple Identities of the Middle East*. London: Weidenfeld & Nicolson, 1998.

Lewis, Martin W. and Karen E. Wigen, *The Myth of Continents: A Critique of Metageography*. Berkeley: University of California Press, 1997.

Loos, Milan. *Dualist Heresy in the Middle Ages*. Prague: Academia Publishing, 1974.

Lovrenović, Ivan. "Stare osnove i nove vertikale." *Savremena književnost naroda i narodnosti u BiH u književnoj kritici*. Ed. I. Lovrenović, V. Maksimović, and K. Prohić. Sarajevo: Svjetlost, 1984.

Lowenthal, David. "Past Time, Present Place: Landscape and Memory." *Geographical Review* 65:1 (1975).

MacGregor, Douglas A. "The Balkan Limits to Power and Principle." *Orbis* 45:1 (Winter 2001).

Maglajlić, Munib. *Antologija bošnjačke usmene lirike*. Sarajevo: Alef, 1997.

Maglajlić, Munib. *Od zbilje do pjesme*. Banjaluka: Glas, 1983.

Maksimović, Vojislav. "Starija književnost bosanskih Jevreja." *Bosanska književna hrestomatija: stara književnost.* Ed. H. Kuna et al. Sarajevo: Zavod za izdavanje udžbenika, 1972.

Maksimović, Vojislav. *Nekad i sad.* Sarajevo: Svjetlost, 1973.

Malcolm, Noel *Bosnia: A Short History.* London: Macmillan, 1994.

Malkki, Lisa. "National Geographic: The Rooting of Peoples and the Territorialization of National Identity Among Scholars and Refugees. " *Cultural Anthropology* 7:1 (1992): 24–43.

Mandić, Dominik. *Bogomilska crkva bosanskih krstjana.* Chicago: The Croatian Historical Institute, 1962.

Mayo, James M. "War Memorials as Political Memory." *Geographical Review* 78 (1988): 62–75.

Menocal, Maria R. *The Arabic Role in Medieval Literary History.* Philadelphia: University of Pennsylvania Press, 1987.

Mills-Courts, Karen. *Poetry as Epitaph: Representation and Poetic Language.* Baton Rouge: Louisiana State University Press, 1990.

Mitchell, W. J. T. *Iconology: Image, Text, Ideology.* Chicago: University of Chicago Press, 1986.

Mitchell, W. J. T. "Spatial Form in Literature: Toward a General Theory." *The Language of Images.* Ed. W. J. T. Mitchell. Chicago: University of Chicago Press, 1980.

Mol, Herbert. *Identity and the Sacred.* New York: Free Press, 1976.

Montefiore, Janet. "Uncertain Delight. Review of Agee (1998)." *Times Literary Supplement,* December 4, 1998: 24

Moranjak-Bamburać, Nirman. "The Privileged Crossroads: The Metaphor and Discourse of Space." *Forum Bosnae* 1 (November, 2001): 233–246.

Morris, Paul (ed.). *The Bakhtin Reader.* London: Edward Arnold, 1994.

Murray, Stuart. *Not on Any Map: Essays on Postcoloniality and Cultural Nationalism.* Exeter: University of Exeter Press, 1997.

Musabegović, Jasmina. *Tajna i smisao književnog djela.* Sarajevo: Veselin Masleša, 1977.

Nairn, Tom. "The Maladies of Development." *Nationalism.* Ed. J. Hutchison and A. D. Smith. Oxford: Oxford University Press, 1994.

Neumann, Iver B. *Russia and the Idea of Europe.* London: Routledge, 1996.

Nichols, Stephen G. "The New Medievalism: Tradition and Discontinuity in Medieval Culture." *The New Medievalism.* Ed. M. S. Brownlee, K. Brownlee, and S. G. Nichols. Baltimore: The Johns Hopkins University Press, 1991.

Nora, Pierre. *Realms of Memory.* Trans. A. Goldhammer. New York: Columbia University Press, 1996.

Norris, Harry. *Islam in the Balkans.* Columbia: University of South Carolina Press, 1993.

The Other Balkan Wars: A 1913 Carnegie Endowment Inquiry in Retrospect with a New Introduction and Reflection on the Present Conflict by George F. Kennan. Washington, D.C.: Carnegie Endowment for International Peace, 1993.

Panofsky, Erwin. *Tomb Sculpture.* New York: Harry N. Abrams, Inc., 1964.

Park, Christopher. *Sacred Worlds: An Introduction to Geography and Religion*. London: Routledge, 1994.

Pennick, Nigel. *Celtic Sacred Landscapes*. New York: Thames and Hudson, 1996.

Pierce, Charles S. *Collected Papers*. Cambridge: Harvard University Press, 1931–1958.

Price, David. *History Made, History Imagined*. Urbana: University of Illinois Press, 1999.

Prohić, Kasim. *Apokrifnost poetskog izraza: poezija Maka Dizdara*. Sarajevo: Veselin Masleša, 1974.

Quataert, Donald. *The Ottoman Empire, 1700–1922*. Cambridge: Cambridge University Press, 2000.

Ragon, Michel. *The Space of Death*. Trans. A. Sheridan. Charlottesville: University Press of Virginia, 1983.

Ramazani, Jahan. *Poetry of Mourning: The Modern Elegy from Hardy to Heaney*. Chicago: University of Chicago Press, 1994.

Ramet, Pedro. "Primordial Ethnicity or Modern Nationalism: The Case of Yugoslavia's Muslims." *Nationalities Papers* 13: 2 (1985): 165–187.

Ramet, Pedro. "Religion and Nationalism in Yugoslavia." *Religion and Nationalism in Soviet and East European Politics*. Ed. P. Ramet. Durham: Duke University Press, 1989.

Ramet, Sabrina. *Balkan Babel: Politics, Religion, and Culture in Yugoslavia*. Boulder: Westview Press, 1992.

Renoir, Alain. "Oral-Formulaic Rhetoric: An Approach to Image and Message in Medieval Poetry." *Medieval Texts and Contemporary Readers*. Ed. Laurie A. Finke and Martin Shichtman. Ithaca: Cornell University Press, 1987.

Rhodes, Anthony. *Where the Turk Trod*. London: Wiedenfeld and Nicolson, 1956.

Riedlmayer, András. "Convivencia under Fire: Genocide and Book-Burning in Bosnia." *The Holocaust and the Book: Preservation and Loss*. Ed. J. Rose. Amherst: University of Massachusetts Press, 2001.

Rizvić, Muhsin. "Mihovil Kombol: O književnosti naroda Bosne i Herzegovine." *Tokovi i stvaraoci iz književne Bosne*. Tuzla: Univerzal, 1986.

Rizvić, Muhsin. "Pisma muslimanskih Krajišnika pisana bosančicom od XVI do sredine XIX stoljeća kao oblik stare epistolarne književnosti." *Godišnjak Instituta za književnost* (Sarajevo) 5 (1976): 217–264.

Rumley, Dennis and Julian V. Minghi (eds.) *The Geography of Border Landscapes*. London: Routledge, 1991.

Runciman, Steven. *The Medieval Manichee: A Study of the Christian Dualist Heresy*. Cambridge: Cambridge University Press, 1960.

Said, Edward. *Orientalism*. Harmondsworth: Penguin, 1978.

Sanjek, Frank. *Les Chretiens Bosniaque et le mouvement Cathare: XIIe - Xve siècles*. Louvain: Nauwelaerts, 1976.

Sarajevo Survival Guide. Sarajevo: FAMA, 1993.

Sauer, Carl Ortwin. "The Morphology of Landscape." *Land and Life: Selections from the Writings of Carl Ortwin Sauer*. Ed. John Leighy. Berkeley: University of California Press, 1963.

222   STONE SPEAKER

Schick, Irvin. *The Erotic Margin: Sexuality and Spatiality in Alterist Discourse.* London: Verso, 1999.

Schmaus, Alois. "Sa strana zamagljenih." *Misao* 10:209–210 (September 1928): 87–88.

Scott, Jamie and Paul Simpson-Housley (eds.). *Mapping the Sacred in Postcolonial Literatures.* Atlanta: Rodopi VP, 2001.

Selimović, Meša. *Derviš i smrt.* Sarajevo: Svjetlost, 1966.

Selimović, Mesa. *Death and the Dervish.* Trans. B. Rakić and S. M. Dickey. Evanston: Northwestern University Press, 1996.

Sells, Michael. *The Bridge Betrayed: Religion and Genocide in Bosnia.* Berkeley: University of California Press, 1996.

Sharenkoff, Victor. *A Study of Manichaeism in Bulgaria with Special Reference to the Bogomils.* New York: Carranza & Co., 1927.

Šindić, Miljko. *Poetika Maka Dizdara.* Sarajevo: Svjetlost, 1971.

Smith, Anthony. *The Ethnic Origins of Nations.* Oxford: Blackwell, 1986.

Soja, Edward. *Postmodern Geographies.* London: Verso, 1989.

Solovyev, Aleksandar. "Simbolika srednjovekovnih grobnih spomenika u Bosni i Herzegovini." *Godišnjak Istorijskog društva Bosne i Hercegovine* 8 (1956): 5–67.

Tadić, Jovan. "Dubrovnik za vreme Diva Gundulića." *Srpski književni glasnik* 4 (February 1939): 281–285.

Taussig, Michael. *Mimesis and Alterity.* London: Routledge, 1993.

Taylor, Charles. *Sources of the Self: The Making of the Modern Identity.* Cambridge: Harvard University Press, 1989.

Todorova, Maria. "The Ottoman Legacy in the Balkans." *Balkans: A Mirror of the New International Order.* Ed. G. G. Ozdogan and K. Saybasili. Istanbul: EREN, 1995.

Trifković, Risto. "Jedan pogled na bosansko-hercegovačku književnost, ponovo." *Simpozijum o savremenoj književnosti Bosne i Hercegovine.* Sarajevo; Svjetlost, 1971.

Trifković, Risto. "Pred licem i fenomenom bosanskohercegovačke literature - biti ili ne." *Savremena književnost naroda i narodnosti BiH u književnoj kritici.* Ed. I. Lovrenović, V. Maksimović and K. Prohić. Sarajevo: Svjetlost, 1984.

Trifković, Risto. *Savremena književnost u Bosni i Hercegovini.* Sarajevo: Svjetlost, 1986.

Turner Victor and Edith Turner. *Image and Pilgrimage in Christian Culture: Anthropological Perspectives.* New York: Columbia University Press, 1978.

Tutnjević, Staniša. *Književne krivice i osvete.* Sarajevo: Svjetlost, 1989.

Van den Broeck, Raymond. "Translational Interpretation: A Complex Strategic Game." *Translators' Strategies and Creativity.* Ed. Ann Beylard-Ozeroff, Jana Králová and Barbara Moser-Mercer. Amsterdam/Philadelphia: Benjamins, 1998, 1–13.

Veljačić, Čedomir. "Istočni utjecaji i interes za Indiju u jugoslavenskoj književnosti i filozofiji." *Rad Jugoslavenkse akademije* (1986): 590–596.

Venuti, Lawrence. *The Translator's Invisibility.* London: Routledge, 1995.

Vucinich, Wayne S. (ed.) *Ivo Andrić Revisited: The Bridge Still Stands.* Berkeley: University of California Press, 1995.

Wachtel, Andrew B. *Making a Nation, Breaking a Nation.* Stanford: Stanford University Press, 1998.

Walicki, Andrzey. *A History of Russian Thought: From the Enlightenment to Marxism.* Stanford: Stanford University Press, 1979.

Wenzel, Marion. *Ukrasni motivi na stećcima.* Sarajevo: n.p., 1965.

West, Rebecca. *Black Lamb and Grey Falcon.* Harmondsworth: Penguin Books, 1982.

Winter, Jay. *Sites of Memory, Sites of Mourning.* Cambridge: Cambridge University Press, 1995.

Woolf, Stuart (ed.) *Nationalism in Europe, 1815 to the Present: A Reader.* London: Routledge, 1996.

Yi-Fu Tuan. "Rootedness versus Sense of Place." *Landscape* 25 (1980): 3–8.

Yugoslavia. Ed. Mirza Filipović. Sarajevo: Svjetlost, 1990.

Zacharia, Irwin. "The Islamic Revival and the Muslims of Bosnia-Hercegovina." *East European Quarterly* 17:4 (January 1984).

Zemon-Davis, Natalie and Randolph Starn. Introduction to *Representations* 26 (1989): 1–6.

<www.djikic.net/pub/mak/mak.htm>.

INDEX

Brubaker, Rogers, 32
Buber, Martin, 111
Bulgaria, 71, 72

Calder, Agnus, 173
Cardinal Torquemada, 72
Cathars, 75
De Certeau, Michel, 65
Chatterjee, Partha, 20
Christ, 74, 119, 156, 178
Christo-Slavism, 8, 67
Ćirković, Sima, 59
colonialism, 11, 20, 39, 40, 42, 46, 52,
    60, 64–6, 81, 90–1, 99, 101
commemoration, 57, 86, 136
Communist Party, 29, 34
communitas, 16, 83, 91, 145
Connor, Walker, 19–20
consanguinity, 19, 25, 86, 155, 164
continuity, 30, 33, 65, 68, 82, 90, 109,
    111, 113, 124, 129, 155
conversion, 22, 75–6, 78
crusades, 64, 72, 78, 97
Culler, Jonathan, 94
culture
    genealogy of, 91, 13, 127, 150, 161
    pluralism in, 39, 143
    roots of, 7, 60, 61, 72, 90, 93, 144,
        151, 160, 162–3
Curtis, William, 46
Cyrillic script, 112

Dayton agreement, 1
defiance
    as ethos, 44, 48–9, 120, 157
    as trope, 45, 87–8, 97, 141, 157
dialogic, 44, 45, 66, 84, 86, 89, 123
dichotomous identity 11, 19, 34
Dijak Semorad, 56
Disclosure, 17, 81, 89–90, 94, 123, 138,
    162
Divković, Matija, 23
diwan literature, 22
Dizdar, Mak
    life of, 4–6

works of, 4–5
djed, 157
domestication, 169
double vocality, 125
dualism, 6, 11, 71, 74–5, 99, *see also*
    Bogomils
Duraković, Enes, 5, 94, 95

East and West, 38, 39, 43
Elegy, 82
Eliade, Mircea, 130–2
emblems, 115
Entrikin, J. Nicholas, 37
epic, 25, 54, 83, 114
epitaph
    on tombs, 5, 56, 59, 109, 121–2,
        124, 156, 159–60
    in poetry, 12, 84, 91, 109, 123,
        124–5
ethnic anxiety, 93, 145
ethnic cleansing, 28, 69
ethnography, 43, 82, 87, 93
ethnoreligious relations, 18, 29, 84
Evans, Arthur, 54, 64–5

Fine, John, 71, 75–7
Fischer, Michael, 90, 145
Fish, Stanley, 92, 143
folk
    lore, 4, 20, 22, 24, 46, 53, 71, 85, 90,
        93, 111, 114, 116, 118, 134
    poetry, 69, 83, 86, 102, 110, 114
    spirit, 19, 71, 82, 86, 91, 107, 112,
        135
folklorism, 176
foreignization, 173
Foucault, Michel, 162
fratricide, 160

genealogy, 12, 91, 127, 150, 156, 161–3
genocide, 1
Germanus, 41
Glagolitic script, 112–13
Goffman, Erving, 133
Gorčin, 94, 122, 175